# Stories I Only Tell My Friends

# Stories I Only Tell My Friends

AN AUTOBIOGRAPHY

# ROB LOWE

HENRY HOLT AND COMPANY • NEW YORK

Henry Holt and Company, LLC
*Publishers since 1866*
175 Fifth Avenue
New York, New York 10010
www.henryholt.com

Henry Holt ® and 🎜® are registered trademarks of Henry Holt and Company, LLC.

Library of Congress Cataloging-in-Publication Data

Lowe, Rob.
    Stories I only tell my friends : an autobiography / Rob Lowe. — 1st ed.
        p.        cm.
    ISBN 978-0-8050-9329-2 (hardcover)
    1. Lowe, Rob.    2. Actors—United States—Biography.    I. Title.
    PN2287.L664A3 2011
    791.4302'8092—dc22
    [B]                                                    2011001622

Henry Holt books are available for special promotions and premiums.
For details contact: Director, Special Markets.

First Edition 2011

Designed by Meryl Sussman Levavi

Unless otherwise noted, all photographs are courtesy of author's personal collection.
Photograph on page 309 of Rob Lowe by Jim Wright / Icon International.

Printed in the United States of America

10 9 8 7 6

*For my family:*
*Sheryl, Matthew, and Johnowen.*
*In memory of my mother, Barbara.*

# Stories I Only Tell My Friends

CHAPTER 1

I had always had an affinity for him, an admiration for his easy grace, his natural charisma, despite the fact that for the better part of a decade my then girlfriend kept a picture of him running shirtless through Central Park on her refrigerator door. Maybe my lack of jealousy toward this particular pin-up was tamped down by empathy for his loss of his father and an appreciation for how complicated it is to be the subject of curiosity and objectification from a very young age. That said, when my girlfriend and others would constantly swoon over him, when I would see him continually splashed across the newspapers, resplendent like an American prince, I wasn't above the occasional male thought of: Screw that guy.

As a person navigating the waters of public scrutiny, you are often unable to hold on to personal heroes or villains. Inevitably you will meet your hero, and he may turn out to be less than impressive, while your villain turns out to be the coolest cat you've ever met. You never can tell, so you eventually learn to live without a rooting interest in the parade of stars, musicians, sports champions, and politicians. And you lose the ability to participate in the *real* American pastime: beating up on people you don't like and glorifying people you do.

I had not yet learned that truism when he and I first met. I was at a point where I was deeply unhappy with my personal life, increasingly frustrated about where my career seemed to be going—although from the outside it would probably appear to anyone observing that I was among the most blessed twenty-four-year-olds on the planet. In an effort to find substance, meaning, and excitement, I had become deeply involved in the world of politics.

It was at one of these political events, the kind where movie stars mix with political stars, each trading in the other's reflective glory, both looking to have the other fill something missing inside them, that we were introduced. "Rob Lowe, I'd like you to meet John Kennedy Jr.," someone said. "Hey, man, good to meet you," I said. He smiled. We shook hands and I was relieved that my by then ex-girlfriend wasn't there to notice that he was slightly taller than I was, or to comment on who had better-looking hair. We made some small talk, and I remember thinking, *How does he do it? How does he carry the scrutiny? How does he attempt a normal life? Is it even possible? Is it even worth trying?*

He was charming and gracious and didn't seem to be unnerved by the multitudes of eyeballs stealing glances as we spoke. Eventually, as we were both single guys in our twenties, the talk turned to girls. "Maybe we should get outta here, go find where the action is," he said. I looked at him. "Dude. You're fucking JFK Jr.! All right?! You don't need to go anywhere!" He looked at me and laughed, and as he did I saw a glimpse of his father and was reminded of his family's legacy of sacrifice and tragedy, and was glad that he was carrying the mantle so well and with so much promise for the future.

Eventually we went our separate ways, never teaming up to hunt down any fun that night (although I later wrestled open a wet bar at 2:00 a.m. with a vice presidential short-list candidate). Over the years I watched him navigate the currents of fame, dating, and career ups and downs, curious to see how his life would play out. Sometimes he and I would both appear on those shameful lists of "Hunks." (Could there be a more degrading or, frankly, gross word than "hunk"? Hunk of what? Hunk of wood? Hunk of cheese? Yikes!) There may have even been a girl or two whom we both coveted, but that was the extent of my contact with him.

In the late '90s my wife, Sheryl, and I were on a romantic ski vacation in Sun Valley, Idaho. We still felt like newlyweds, in spite of having two beautiful baby boys from whom we'd escaped for a rare evening out. Sun Valley is one of my favorite spots. It's old school (as the site of North America's first chair lift) and glamorous (the home of Hemingway and early Hollywood royalty), and boasts one of the greatest ski mountains in the country. I had been going there since the mid-'80s and always liked the mix of people you might encounter at any given time. One evening at a big holiday party, I felt a tap on the shoulder. It was John Jr. "How've you been, man?" he asked with a smile. I introduced him to Sheryl. He congratulated us on our marriage. After a while Sheryl went off on her own, leaving the two of us alone in the corner watching the party move on around us. Even in this more rarefied crowd, you could feel the occasional glare of curious observation. A ski instructor passed by, a movie star; a local ski bunny brushed by John and flipped her hair. "How did you do it?" he asked, so low against the buzz of the party that I couldn't quite hear.

"I'm sorry?"

"How did you do it?" he repeated. "I mean how did you settle down? You of all people."

I looked at him and he was smiling, almost laughing, as if covering something else, some other emotion, something I couldn't quite discern. At first I thought he might be gently poking fun at me; up until my marriage, my life had been publicly marked by a fair number of romances, some covered with great interest in the papers. But I saw that his question was real, and that he seemed to be grappling with a sort of puzzle he could not solve. I realized he was looking across the room to a willowy blonde. She had fantastic blue eyes, and the kind of beauty and magnetism that was usually reserved for film stars. She was standing next to my wife, Sheryl, also a blue-eyed blonde with a beauty and presence that made her seem as if a spotlight and wind machine were constantly trained on her.

I put two and two together. "Looks like you have a great girl. That's half the battle right there. She's obviously amazing and if she's your best friend, marry her. You can do it. Don't let anyone tell you that you can't, that you're not ready, or not capable. Come on in, man, the water's warm. I'm here to tell you it is; if she's your friend in addition to all of the other stuff, pull the trigger, don't let her get away. You never know what life will bring."

I think he was a little taken aback at the passion of my response. I'm not at all sure what he had expected me to say. But he asked, so what the hell. John nodded and we went on to other topics. The next day, we met to ski on the mountain he snowboarded, ripping down the face, fast and free. But the weather was turning and a white-out was upon us. In the snow and the speed and the wind, we were separated. I looked up over a ridge and he was gone, lost in the clouds.

John did marry his blonde, his Carolyn. I was glad for him

and thought about sending him a note, but somehow I didn't (of all my character flaws—and there are a number of them—procrastination is one of the most distinctive). Instead I wished him luck, children, and longevity of love with one of my nonalcoholic beers as I watched the coverage on *Entertainment Tonight*. As a political junkie and unashamed admirer of our country, I was a huge fan of his brainchild, *George* magazine. When someone finally stopped asking celebrities appearing on its cover to pose in those George Washington wigs I thought: Okay, they're rollin' now!

The end of the century approached. The '90s were a time of building for me. Building a life that was sober, drained of harmful, wasteful excess and manufacturing in its place a family of my own. This was my priority through the decade and that work continues to pay off today with the love of my sons, Matthew and Johnowen, and the constant gift of the love of my wife, Sheryl. Whereas the '80s had been about building a career, the '90s ended with my having built a life.

At the end of the decade, my career was very much in flux, just as it had been at the end of the previous one. I had had some successes in the '90s, always made money, but the truth was I was like a man pushing a boulder up a hill. A huge, heavy, difficult boulder made up of some career mistakes, projects that didn't meet expectations, and twenty years of being a known quantity. And not only not being the new sensation, but worse, being someone people in Hollywood took for granted, someone with no surprises left in him. For example, the ability to appear on the cover of magazines is critical for any major actor. It's just a fact of the business end of show business. And I hadn't been on the cover of a magazine in almost ten years. To have the kind of career one aspires to, comprising good, major work over the course of a lifetime, it was critical that I find two things: the breakout, watershed project to remind people what I could accomplish as an actor, and that first magazine cover and profile to publicize it. It was June of 1999 and John Kennedy Jr. was about to help me get both.

My longtime publicist Alan Nierob was on the line. "Apparently JFK Jr. stood up in today's staff meeting and said he had just seen a pilot for a new TV series that was the embodiment of everything he founded *George* magazine to be. He was emotional about it, very moved by the show and inspired to help people hear about it. He thinks *The West Wing* can be one of those once-in-a-lifetime shows that can change people's lives. Your character of Sam Seaborn was his favorite and he wants to put you on *George*'s September cover."

Although the advance copy of *The West Wing* had been receiving freakishly unanimous raves, I was ecstatic and humbled by this particular endorsement. It's impossible to imagine living JFK Jr.'s life and then watching a show whose central theme was the heart and soul of the American presidency. His whole world has been shaped by the office, the service to it, and the tragic sacrifice in its name. *The West Wing* was going to be about "the best and the brightest." His father's administration all but coined the phrase.

"Um, Alan, does John realize that there is no guarantee that the show will last through the fall?" I knew that *George* was in serious financial trouble and could ill-afford to feature a show with the high likelihood of attaining the ultimate creative Pyrrhic victory: worshipped by critics, ignored by the public. If the show was quickly canceled (and quite a few thought it would be) it would be a financial disaster for John and, possibly, could be the end of the magazine. "Rob," Alan said, "John is putting you on the cover. He couldn't care less."

The politics of the workplace can be complicated, Machiavellian, self-serving, and just downright stupid no matter where you work. My grandpa ran a restaurant in Ohio for fifty years. I'm sure every now and then he would get nervous when his most popular carhop got uppity and started wanting better hours. My father practices law to this day and deals with those who smile to his face, then wish he would step on a limpet mine in the middle of Ludlow Street. That's the way it is in the world. It's just worse in Hollywood.

Someone, somewhere, got it into their heads that it would be a bad thing for the launch of our new show if I was on the cover of *George*. It was made very clear to me that I had no right to be on this cover and that John should rescind the offer. When pushed for a reason as to why it would be a bad thing for a show no one had ever heard of to get this kind of recognition, the response was: "Everyone should be on the cover. Not you." I understood that there was no single "star" of the show, but still thought it was a great opportunity for all concerned. The higher-ups remained adamant and they asked John to take me off the cover. He refused.

As I puzzled over (and was hurt by) this disconnect between me and my new bosses on *The West Wing*, John was in New York planning the cover shoot. He chose Platon, one of the great photographers, and lined up the journalist for the profile. After it was clear that John made his own choices on his covers, and could not be pushed around, the folks at *The West Wing* backed down and allowed an on-set visit and an additional article about the show, cast, and writers to be written. John wanted to throw a party for me in New York to coincide with the magazine's release and the premiere of the show. I made plans to attend and to thank him for supporting me at a time when no one else had. I picked up the phone and called his offices, and got an assistant. "He just came out of the last meeting on your cover issue and is running late for the airport. Can he call you Monday?"

"No problem," I said, "we'll talk then."

I hung up and started preparing for Monday's table reading

of the first episode of *The West Wing*. John hopped into his car. He was rushing to meet Carolyn and her sister Lauren, eager to get to the airport to fly them to his cousin Rory's wedding. It was a hazy summer evening, the kind we remember from childhood. He was probably excited. He was going back to his family. He was going home.

It's been my experience that when a phone call wakes you, it's never good news. I had taken a small cottage in Burbank, a few blocks from the studio for late nights and I was asleep when I got the call. It was Sheryl and I could tell she was upset. She wanted me to turn on the news.

At first it seemed like it couldn't possibly be happening. Clearly these reporters had it wrong. John, his beloved wife, and her sister would surely be found in an embarrassing mix-up or miscommunication. They could not be gone. No one is that cruel. No God can ask that of a family. No one would so much as imagine the possibility of the horrific and arbitrary sudden nature of fate. Search teams scrambled and, like most Americans, I said a prayer of hope.

Monday came. The search for John, Carolyn, and Lauren continued. At the studio the cast and producers gathered for the very first table reading of *The West Wing*. I stood and told the group how much John admired the show and asked that we pray for him and work with his inspiration. It was very quiet. People were numb.

Later there was talk of canceling the cover shoot, now just days away. I was devastated and in no mood for it. But John's editors insisted, pointing out that John's last editorial decision was to make this happen. It was what he wanted. By Tuesday the worst had been confirmed. The plane had been found. There were no survivors. John, Carolyn, and Lauren were gone. I heard the news on my way to the photo session.

Being on the Oval Office set is very moving. It is an exact

replica of the Clinton version, down to the artwork on the walls and the fabrics on the couches. (It was designed by the amazing movie production designer Jon Hutman, who does all of Robert Redford's movies and whom I've known since he was Jodie Foster's roommate at Yale.) It is so realistic that when I later found myself in the actual Oval Office, I felt as if it was just "another day at the office." I was, however, fascinated with the one thing the real Oval Office has that ours did not, and that was a ceiling. I stood looking up at it, staring like an idiot while everyone else oohed and aahed at all the amazing historical pieces that fill the room. However, it's not authenticity that takes your breath away when you step onto that soundstage at Warner Bros. Studios. It is the solemnity of history, of destiny, and of fate; you are certain that you are actually in the room where power, patriotism, faith, the ability to change the world, and the specter of both success and tragedy flow like tangible, unbridled currents. You feel the presence of the men who navigated them as they created our collective American history, and you fully realize that they were not disembodied images on the nightly news or unknowable titans or partisan figureheads to be applauded or ridiculed. It feels as if you are standing where they stood, you can open their desk drawers, sit in their seat, and dial their phone. They are somehow more real to you now, they are not the sum of their successes or failures, they are human beings.

Presidents get to redesign the Oval Office to their own tastes and they have the National Gallery, Smithsonian, and National Archives warehouses of priceless pieces to choose from. John Jr.'s mother knew her way around a swatch or two, so she made sure her husband's Oval Office was simple and chic (but with enough plausible deniability if called out for it) and with the proper nod to history. For the president's desk she chose the "Resolute" desk, fashioned from the timbers of the HMS *Resolute*, found abandoned by an American vessel and returned to England, where

Queen Victoria later had the timbers made into a desk and sent to President Rutherford Hayes as a goodwill gesture. FDR also loved the desk, but insisted that a modesty panel be installed to swing closed at the front in order to prevent people from seeing his leg braces as he sat. Years later, as JFK attended to the nation's business, tiny John Jr. would be famously photographed impishly peeking out from being the desk's panel.

I am leaning against a replica of that desk now, the flash of the photographer's strobe jolting me, illuminating the darkened soundstage, cutting the tension and sadness of the *George* cover shoot. A number of staff have flown in from New York. John was more than a boss to them, obviously, and they are devastated. They share stories of John's life. Some cry, but all soldier on through this melancholy and bizarre photo shoot on the Oval Office set.

Platon wants me to embody strength, dignity, and power. He is asking me to focus in on his lens, to bring the sparkle that sells magazines. But my thoughts are elsewhere. I'm thinking of how unexpected yet oddly preordained life can be. Events are upon you in an instant, unforeseen and without warning, and oftentimes marked by disappointment and tragedy but equally often leading to a better understanding of the bittersweet truth of life. A father is taken from his son, a promise is unfulfilled, and then the son is reunited with him, also in an instant and under the cover of sadness. A theme continues in that unique, awful beauty that marks our human experience.

The flash explodes in my face again. I put on a smile (none of these shots will ever be used) and remind myself that John's journey is over and, with some thanks to him, a new journey for me is ahead. I never knew him well. Many Americans also felt a connection to him without knowing him at all. In some ways, he was America's son. But I will always be moved by John Kennedy Jr.'s steadiness in the harsh, unrelenting spotlight, his quest for personal identity and substance, for going his own way and building a life of his choosing. I will always remember his support and kindness to me and be grateful to him for being among the first to recognize that with my next project, *The West Wing*, I just might be a part of something great.

CHAPTER 2

My mother awakens me. She is worked up, highly strung. She is pulling me out of bed from a deep sleep. I'm scared. It feels like it's the middle of the night, although in a weird example of the capabilities of our modern age, a quick Google search today tells me it was probably just about 10:15 p.m.

"Robbie! Wake up! It's important!" she urges. She has tears in her eyes. Quickly I'm placed into my footie pajamas and she hustles me downstairs. My baby brother is asleep; if my dad is home, he is not awake. It's just the two of us. Coming down the stairs, I see the glow of the television, her favorite blanket on the couch. She must have been watching TV right before she rushed upstairs to wake me. I'm groggy and confused as she sits me next to her in front of the eerie gray-blue light of our Zenith black-and-white television. She takes my hand and I notice it is shaking.

I try to make out images on the television screen, but they are fuzzy and garbled. Mom is hugging me now, as I finally begin to make out some clarity in the picture. "We copy you down, Eagle," a man is saying. A slight gasp from my mother, as on the television a fellow Ohioan is saying, "Engine arm is off. Houston, Tranquility Base here. The Eagle has landed." Within moments, Neil Armstrong of Wapakoneta, Ohio, twenty miles from my grandparents' house, sets foot on the moon. It seems at once fake, like being woken up from a dream (which I was), and yet of dramatic importance even to a four-and-a-half-year-old. I look at my mom. She has tears running down her face. "Nothing will ever be the same," she whispers.

❖

My mother was right. The world did change. Soon thereafter I lost my father. He wasn't taken from us in a heroic/tragic fashion; in fact, he wasn't even dead. But when there is suddenly that emptiness in your home and in your heart, the loss feels very similar to death.

Like most boys, I idolized my father, even as a four-year-old. He was movie-star handsome, a cross between Paul Newman and a *Godfather*-era Jimmy Caan. Like the latter, he had a way with the ladies; like the former he was a product of the Midwest of the 1950s, set in his ways, cloistered, and with a premium on politeness and not rocking the boat to get your true needs met. He was athletic and strong, a champion tennis player in an era when few had yet discovered the sport. My earliest memory may be of him sawing his wooden Jack Kramer racquet in half at the handle so we could hit together, even though I was substantially shorter than the tennis net.

He and my mother were "pinned" in college at DePauw, true school sweethearts. My mother was an English major and boasted William Faulkner as one of her professors. She was bookish and

beautiful, from a small town in Ohio. Her father was the arche-
typical self-made man. The youngest of nine children, he left
home at eleven years old to escape his family's grinding poverty.
Starting as a butcher's apprentice, my grandfather eventually
worked his way up to owning the entire grocery store, parlaying
that into two successful restaurants. By the time my mother was a
little girl, her dad was the only man who could afford a Cadillac
in all of Shelby County, Ohio. And so she was raised in nouveaux
privilege, a sheltered world where only good things happened and
where life clearly rewarded those with the proper intentions. With
her arresting beauty, she not only looked like a princess, she was
treated like one.

My father, on the other hand, was from Indiana, a place of
hard-nosed pragmatism. He loved to fight, to brawl—a trait that
served him well as a four-foot-eleven high school freshman, and
less so as a five-foot-nine newlywed. But together, they made a
handsome couple and were married on the eve of my father's
departure for law school at the University of Virginia.

What makes the equation of man and woman so eternally
mysterious, glorious, and explosive? It almost seems as if each
decade has its own unique "battle of the sexes." The field of conflict
is ever changing, as are the players, but the carnage and confusion
are always fueled by the enduring quest for sex, love, and emotional fulfillment. (This list is in varying order according to experience and gender.) In the '80s we navigated the legacy of the then
decades-old free love movement, as well as a status-seeking ethos
powered by booze and coke and a vague sense that this sexual
smorgasbord wouldn't (and shouldn't) last forever. And with the
arrival of AIDS, it did not.

My mom and dad faced different challenges. They wanted
to escape the uniformity and banal conventions of the '50s, but
didn't have the road map later created during the upheavals of the
late '60s. On a practical level, sex was still the domain of married

couples only (in theory) and the pill didn't exist. Indeed, on their wedding night both my parents were virgins. On the first night of their honeymoon, as my mother fought an anxiety attack waiting in the hotel room, my dad escaped to the hotel pool, avoiding the inevitable by swimming lap after lap after lap. (And I wonder why whenever I'm stressed, I head to the water!) At some point, however, they must have figured it out, and on March 17, 1964, I was born at the university hospital in Charlottesville, Virginia.

For the then standard three days of my mother's hospital stay, my father was forbidden to hold or touch me. As my mother and I bonded, my father and I remained separated by the glass of the observation window, looking at each other across the distance, the first notes in a theme that would be played out for the rest of our lives.

When I was six months old, my dad graduated from law school, and we left Charlottesville for Dayton, Ohio. (Later in life as my love of history, of tradition, politics, and government became a constant, I began to wonder if I wasn't imbued with these passions by virtue of being born in the town Mr. Jefferson built.) My parents chose Dayton because it was then a bustling, growing city, home of a number of major businesses, including National Cash Register, Dayton Tire, AC-Delco, and Mead Paper. We moved into a nice three-bedroom house, whose floor plan I can still remember, in a leafy suburb. My dad joined a law practice; my mother gave up her job as a high school English teacher and stayed at home to raise me. They were the quintessential young, upwardly mobile midwestern couple of the mid-'60s. They discovered fondue, the cast album of *Camelot*, and gin and tonics. (Later it would be *Jesus Christ Superstar* and pot.) They had a close circle of like-minded friends.

According to family lore, at one of these fondue parties, thrown by my parents to introduce a young dentist to their circle of friends, my mother's naïveté was unveiled for all to see, in a fashion that seems almost impossible today. Attempting to drum up new business for the dentist, she told a hushed room that she loved going to his office because "he was so gentle when he put his prick in my mouth." She went on with enthusiasm to recount how she was never scared when he "puts his prick in," that sometimes "it feels good." My father, by then likely more well versed in such matters, burst out laughing in the horrified silence, simultaneously enraging and confusing my mom.

"What did I say?"

"Um . . . well . . . Barbara . . ."

"What? I'm just talking about his prick and . . ."

"Barbara," he began to explain, but gave up as she looked at him with a mixture of blithe indulgence and dawning reproach of what was clearly a deviant mind. Meanwhile, my dad (and every single other fondue eater present), swallowed his laughter and attempted to steer the evening back on track.

To me, this snapshot of their early marriage is revealing. My mother and father were moving in different currents toward different worldviews. So much so that when I was old enough to have such thoughts, I couldn't imagine that they ever had anything in common. But they were becoming themselves and, over time, this meant they were becoming increasingly dissimilar: Dad crystallizing into a dashing, successful, gregarious, hot-headed up-and-comer, and Mom becoming an earnest, thoughtful teacher, always slightly off the public frequency, beginning to occupy her solitary spot outside conventional wisdom and custom.

There were other warning signs that all was not well with them, but I was far too young to be aware. Claw hammers were thrown, lipstick was found in places it shouldn't be, and the painful clichéd narrative of being married too young to someone you don't really know because they don't know themselves headed toward its climax.

My dad started working late, my mom and I spent more and

more time at my grandparents' (without my dad), and it became normal that my dad's presence in the house was minimal. One day when I was four years old, my mom told me I would be having a brother. Looking back, I might have assumed as much, as the third bedroom had been redone in a Dumbo, the flying elephant, motif. "I'm going to name him Chad," she said. I remember thinking that the name "Chad" reminded me of the word "Chap-Stick." I didn't get it and I asked her to reconsider the name. Invoking her parental prerogative of not having to explain herself to her four-year-old son, she told me that the matter was closed.

My brother was born on January 15, 1968. I have no memory of Chad's birth, although I know my dad fainted dead away when he was told about it in the waiting room. Apparently, not letting him hold his newborn had some wisdom to it after all.

Baby Chad came home, my father did not. At least that is my assumption, as he is absent from my memories of this time. But these recollections are fuzzy and likely distorted. I believe it's not because I was so young as much as it is because the house was so filled with unhappiness; my mother's, my father's, and as a result, my own. I had already begun to tune out reality, to retreat to a private world and block out any pain. From this period of my life I have only two distinct memories—both events are unique; impossible to experience more than once in a lifetime: a stopping of time after which nothing will ever be as it was. One is my mother waking me up for the moon landing. The other memory has played out in my mind again and again over the course of my lifetime. I knew the moment it happened that all I had known was over; it has taken forty-three years to begin to understand the ripples that have emanated from that day. The shattering, dull wounding, the mistaken lessons, and also, the circuitous road that opened up that day, leading me to eventual happiness and fulfillment that would have been impossible to achieve otherwise.

Again, it is just my mom and I. I'm five years old. Chad is not there, and I am waiting for my mother to finish her errand at the lumber store. It's a big place, brightly lit, with giant stacks of two-by-fours and other cuts of wood, all in rows, one after the other. I'm sitting on one of these big stacks, watching my mother at the cashier. I'm sipping chocolate milk through a straw. It's summer and even though I am wearing shorts, it's hot and humid in the giant store, and I'm restless. I'm also thinking that there has been something bothering me, I've been sad and uncomfortable, anxious now, for a while. When feelings well up I push them down, lose myself in make-believe, play, cartoons, toys. I can't name this thing that is bothering me; I'm not old enough to know that I should even try. And today, in the sticky Dayton summer it's upon me again, this unease, this feeling of something bad about to happen. Usually chocolate milk from Mom can make it go away. Today it won't.

I'm watching my mom walking toward me. Later in life her hair will turn brown, but now she is still blonde, with a perfectly shaped nose and clear blue eyes. She seems tiny in this giant store, alone. Inside me something clicks. I see our life together very clearly, in all its reality for how it is and is not what I want it to be. Everything falls away, all other thoughts, all other feelings. Just a question forming now, for the first time, triggered by my mom walking toward me in a lumber store. She looks at me and smiles. I blurt out, "Is Dad ever coming home?"

My mom pauses for just a moment, then answers. "No, he isn't. We're getting a divorce."

I have spent my career on high alert to clichés, excising them from scripts and speeches whenever I could. I'm deeply suspicious and rarely entertained by conventionally accepted turning points in a plot, of events that are meant to seem earth-shatteringly dramatic when in fact, to me, they are merely predictable.

There is no hoarier cliché than a child's psyche rocked by divorce. And for much of my life I have not only resisted this notion, but have had a sort of vague disdain for anyone who pinned their adolescent or adult challenges on their parents' broken lives. To do so is to substitute another's life mistake for your own. And so later in life as I came to face my own shortcomings, I rarely considered the effect of a lost father on a four-year-old boy. That understanding would only come later, as I confronted my alcoholism and, more clearly, when I had two sons of my own. Anything painful surrounding my parents' breakup I sealed off and buried, left unexplored and undisturbed, like nuclear waste.

My mother was unprepared for my reaction to her unvarnished, truthful answer. At the mention of "divorce," my body felt as if I had been shot, shot full of terrible stomachache and a swirling, spinning-out-of-control desolation. I began to cry. Clerks and customers passed us by, oblivious, before my mom hustled me outside as I began to deteriorate. "Do you know what divorce is?" she stammered. I remember thinking, you idiot, what do you take me for . . . a *kid*?! "Of course I do!" I snapped. "I watch *Divorce Court*!"

By the time we reached our navy-blue station wagon I was inconsolable. All I wanted was my dad. In the onrushing, awful vision of life without him, I was confused and scared. When would I see him again? Would I *ever* see him again? If so, for how long and under what circumstances? I told my mother I wanted to see him, *now*!

It must have been a weekend because the first places we looked for him were the tennis courts. I can take you today on a tour of all Dayton's various tennis facilities; this terrible pilgrimage is so etched in my mind. And as I sat desperately looking out the window, hoping to see him on a court, in passing cars, or on the street, I thought to myself bitterly, that's what I get for asking the question. And with that I began to plot how to avoid any similar pain for the rest of my life. To avoid being emotionally bushwhacked on any level whatsoever. And somewhere in my unconscious, I vowed to never ask a question if there was *any* possibility of a painful or even uncomfortable answer, to disassociate from conflict. I began a life of avoidance of potential disharmony at all costs. Unknowingly, I set out down a road that cost me dearly.

I never did find my father that day.

## CHAPTER 3

"I want to french you."

"You . . . you want to what me?"

"French you! I want to french you!"

I'm sitting underneath a stage platform, in the dark, with a cute girl dressed in a Jitterbug costume. We are rehearsing a community-theater rendition of *The Wizard of Oz*. I'm about ten years old, she is thirteen.

"What do you mean 'french' me?"

"It's kind of a kiss. Don't you *know* that?"

I nod earnestly, but I have no idea what she's talking about. I do know that she's older and makes a very pretty Jitterbug. But "frenching" is not in my vocabulary, and I'm petrified of what is clearly about to go down.

"Um, I think American is better," I say. But Julie the Jitterbug has had enough of my dithering and she promptly proceeds to stick her tongue down my throat. Ho-ly shit! I think, almost gagging. What is she *doing*? She's wiggling it around in my mouth and I'm horrified and intrigued all at once. I've never had a kiss of any consequence and now I'm getting a mouth probe here in the darkness of the Dayton Community Theater.

If I hadn't fully grasped the sexy, subversive allure of the theater until then, this little vixen, smelling of perfume and greasepaint, has put me immediately on the path of greater understanding. After a moment I gain my sea legs.

"You're cute," she says, finally taking a break.

I take that to mean that our rendezvous is over. I mumble some excuse and climb out from under the platform and make my scheduled entrance as Coroner of Munchkin City. I'm way too young to appreciate the timing of my opening line: "As coroner, I must aver, I thoroughly examined her . . ."

⚜

A few weeks earlier my mom and her new husband, Bill, had taken me to see a friend of theirs in a production of *Oliver!* It was a transformational experience. I watched kids my own age playing the orphans and was knocked cold. It would've made a great scene in a terrible Disney movie: A young boy sits in a darkened theater and is thunderstruck with a vision of his life, of his destiny, and in an instant, he discovers his passion. Some kids hear the Beatles for the first time and are set on the road to rock stardom; my trip to Hollywood began with a (probably bad) local production of *Oliver!*

I was still flush with excitement, giddy, as we walked through the lobby afterward. On the wall I saw a sign-up sheet for *The Wizard of Oz*, and I asked my mom to sign me up. She and Bill looked at each other. "Why not?" They had no way of knowing how deeply affected I'd been, how electrified I was by the age-old connection of actors, material, and audience. The control, the power the actors seemed to possess while illuminated in the spotlight. And when they reached out to the people in the seats, they were heard, they were understood, and the alchemy of the theater experience transported all bystanders out of various pressures of their daily lives. Next time *I* would be up there; that was a club I wanted to belong to.

My parents' divorce finalized, my mother had married Bill, and my dad was around for weekends of movies, pizza, and adventures exploring the woods. Our lives seemed to be stabilizing into a new, pretty good routine. But then Bill's job required that we move into Dayton city limits proper, out of the leafy, bucolic suburbs. Bill was a profoundly principled, decent man with a deep interest in social justice and politics. He was the guy driving the VW bug and listening to left-leaning talk radio, as far back as 1970. He believed strongly in diversity, had an inveterate suspicion of the status quo and suburbia in general. As a result, he moved us to North Dayton, then an area of tough economic circumstances populated by proud, rough, gigantic Irish families, who were always on guard for any encroachment of the African American community that surrounded them. The racial tensions were thick in my new neighborhood, and things were getting worse every year.

It was a culture shock. Until I enrolled in Van Cleve Elementary School for the second grade, I had never met kids who had no parents at home, had never heard the term "food stamps," or seen people beaten to a pulp on the playground for a quarter. Black or white, everyone was completely unlike anyone I had ever encountered. This exposure was all part of Bill's design for equality and enlightenment. I might have been more interested in these ideas if I hadn't been so busy avoiding getting my ass kicked on a daily basis.

My newfound passion for acting wasn't helping matters. This

was Dayton, Ohio, 1972. Not Beverly Hills 1982. There was no *People* magazine yet. No *US Weekly*. No *Entertainment Tonight*, no MTV, no Disney Channel, no Nickelodeon or E! channel. In Hollywood there was zero premium placed on youthful actors other than one-offs like Tatum O'Neal or David Cassidy. With the exception of forerunners like *The Brady Bunch*, movies and television were the exclusive domain of stories about adults, acted by adults. Kid actors played the children of the stars, passing in and out of a few scenes, if they were lucky. In other words: the modern entertainment industry, in which that scenario would be forever inverted, had yet to be created.

The notion that some kid from Ohio could become a successful child actor was ridiculous on its face, particularly to the kids of North Dayton. It was another reason I was different, another reason I felt alone, not to mention it was the constant source of misunderstandings, hurt feelings, and more than a few fights.

But it was a small price to pay for having an interest that consumed my imagination. I "tried out" (I hadn't yet heard of the term "audition") for any child part at the community playhouse and local traveling repertory theater, in college plays, you name it. It made me feel like my life had direction, that I was no longer adrift in the pain and uncertainty of divorce and a bitter move to a tough neighborhood. Onstage I felt a confidence and sense of accomplishment I rarely felt anywhere else. If I happened to be in a production with other kids, though, I could tell I was different. They were in the play to have fun, and to do well, for sure, but it could just as easily have been a Little League team or summer camp project to them. I had fun, too, but I looked at every play as a step on a ladder that would lead me to my future. I was just too young and unsophisticated to know what that future would look like, or how to get it.

❖

My heart is pounding. I am trying to calm my nerves by telling myself that this is how the "real" actors do it, every day of their lives, but I am only eleven and I've never had a professional "audition" before. My mom and I are driving up to Columbus so that I can take part in a statewide tryout for the Midwest's biggest traveling summer stock circuit, the Kenley Players. I may even get to meet John Kenley himself, the legendary producer/owner, who brings some of Hollywood's top stars to a circuit that includes Dayton, Cincinnati, Columbus, and Warren in Ohio, and Flint, Michigan.

To me it is the height of the theatrical world to see Sandy Duncan in *Peter Pan*, Shirley Jones from *The Partridge Family* doing *On a Clear Day You Can See Forever*, or Dom DeLuise in *Under the Yum Yum Tree*, when they play huge fifteen-hundred-seat memorial halls for a week in each city.

At the hotel in Columbus I stand with about forty other kids. They are all holding eight-by-ten photos of themselves. I have no pictures and I'm embarrassed; clearly these kids are pros. A man wearing eyeliner asks us to do some rudimentary dance moves. I am fixated. Why would a man wear eyeliner?

One, two, kick ball change, he shrieks at us. I don't know what he's talking about. Kick ball change? Kick what ball? All around me kids are pirouetting, spinning like tops. I'm lost. My mom is nowhere to be found. She thinks it's important that I find my own way, so she is not among the lineup of other mothers holding their kids' photos, combs, and hairspray.

Next comes the singing. A twelve-year-old belts out "Gary, Indiana" from *The Music Man*, complete with a fantastic lisp. (Later, when I talk to him, I realize the lisp is real.) I get cold feet and decide to shit-can my bold choice to do "Where Is Love?" from *Oliver!* and instead fall back on my go-to musical audition piece, "Happy Birthday." I get through it fairly well and am immediately led to a huge oak door.

"Where are you taking me?"

"To meet Mr. Kenley."

I feel like I'm going to see the wizard. The minion ushers me into a huge suite. I've never been in a hotel room this big. There's a dining room table in it! A man rises from the couch and comes to greet me.

"Hello, son, I'm John Kenley."

Mr. Kenley appears to be wearing whiteface and red lipstick, like Cesar Romero as the Joker from *Batman*. He looks anywhere from 80 to 180 years old.

"So you want to be an actor?"

"Yes, sir," I manage.

"Well, we always need local actors and I hear you are getting a lot of experience in Dayton. You are in a song-and-dance group, is that right?"

"Yes, sir, we play birthday parties and stuff like that. We even just did the opening ceremony of the new courthouse square in downtown Dayton," I say.

"What is your group called?"

"Peanut Butter and Jelly."

Kenley eyes me. "Mmmmmmmh," he says.

For the first time it occurs to me that Peanut Butter and Jelly is probably not a very exciting name. He offers his hand. It is translucent white and utterly smooth.

"Good luck, son. We will keep you in mind."

My moment with the master behind me, I ride down in the elevator with my mom and two women who proceed to tell us that Mr. Kenley lives during the winter months in Florida as a woman named *Joan* Kenley. My mind boggles. I look up at my mom, who rolls her eyes and makes a clucking sound, which she does whenever she thinks something is entertaining but highly unacceptable. (I would elicit that cluck often later in life.) As we walk through the lobby, I see a man wheeling industrial traveling cases with the name Liza Minnelli stenciled on them.

My mom lets me ask the guy what's going on. He tells me he is a "road manager" for Ms. Minnelli, who is giving a concert tonight.

I turn back to my mom. "I want to meet Liza Minnelli!" I announce. (Liza has just become a superstar in *Cabaret*.) In keeping with her ethos of letting me explore the possibilities of my own life, my mom says, "Well, Robby, why don't you try and find her?"

With that I'm off. I march right up to the front desk. "Liza Minnelli's room number, please," I say. I figure if I can meet a real actress maybe I can learn something about how to be a real actor myself. Incredibly, the man at the desk says, "Ms. Minnelli is in suite 528."

Mom smiles at me and I run for the elevators. In a moment I'm standing outside of the suite. I knock as if it's the most natural thing on earth, as if she would be expecting me. In most other areas of my life I am slightly behind the curve, retiring, sometimes unsure, but when it comes to anything to do with dreams of being an actor I am filled with what I would later learn is called chutzpah. I knock again. There is no response. Now I can hear the sounds of stirring behind the door and a male voice says, "Just a minute."

The door opens. A man with no shirt stands there, looking down at me. "Who are you?"

"My name is Rob Lowe. I want to be an actor and I was hoping to meet Miss Minnelli."

The shirtless man stares at me for a very long beat. "Come in," he says finally.

I enter the suite. A few bottles of wine, some burnt candles, and room service remnants are scattered about.

"Liza! Are you awake? You have a visitor."

He leads me to the living room. Liza is propped up on the couch, eating chocolates and drinking wine. "Well, hello there, kiddo," she says in her unique, crackly, high-ended voice.

Mr. Bare Chest tells her that I am a young actor who has come calling.

"Well, isn't that *marvelous*!" she says, batting her incredibly long eyelashes. "What's your name?"

I tell her and she introduces me to the man, who turns out to be her husband, Jack Haley Jr. I have just played a munchkin in *The Wizard of Oz* and here I am with Dorothy's daughter and the Tin Man's son! Liza asks me to sit and offers me one of her chocolates. Gracious and warm, she doesn't seem to mind for a minute that I have intruded on her privacy. Faced with this proximity to a true superstar at the height of her fame, I'm tongue-tied, but she draws me out, chatting with me about theater and music, asking me questions about myself. It is surreal.

When I sense that it is time to go, I thank them for letting me come say hi and she kisses me on the cheek.

"Good luck. Maybe I'll see you in Hollywood." She smiles and winks at Jack Haley Jr.

"Yeah, kid, see you in Hollywood," he says. As I say good-bye, there is no way of knowing that, in fact, I will see them both again in Hollywood.

The effect famous people can have on other people's lives is not to be underestimated. They can inspire us with their talent; make us feel like kings with their kindness, with a hello, a handshake, or an autograph. They seem like creatures from another race with supernatural abilities.

And the true stars understand that. Liza Minnelli certainly did. When you are around them, the ones at the top of their game, there is always the possibility that some of their magic could rub off on you.

❖

One day I hear that Telly Savalas from *Kojak* is coming to Dayton. *Kojak* is the biggest thing on TV, although truth be told, I prefer *The Partridge Family* and reruns of *Lost in Space*. That said, if Telly Savalas is going to be in Dayton, I want to meet him.

It is a brutal, gray, dark winter day and the wind whips through my CPO jacket as I walk to the bus stop for the journey downtown to Rike's department store. I take the bus everywhere these days, sometimes transferring between a number of different routes. It never occurs to me that I'm often the only kid traveling alone. I love the freedom and the sense of adventure.

It's Christmastime, so Rike's is busy as I screw around riding the escalators backward for a while before following the signs that say, TV's KOJAK TELLY SAVALAS LIVE, 4TH FLOOR, TODAY! I have no idea why Telly Savalas is in Dayton on the fourth floor of Rike's and I really don't care; I'm just thrilled to see this well-known actor in the flesh.

The line for Telly Savalas wraps around the men's clothing department and into women's handbags. I take my place and begin to wait, thinking of what I want to ask him. How did he get his start? Is acting fun? What's Hollywood like? I know that on his TV show, he is famous for always having a lollipop in his mouth, so I've brought him one of my favorites, a Charms Blow Pop, as a gift. As I move forward in the line, I can see him sitting behind a sort of card table, signing an eight-by-ten photo for each person who steps forward. It's almost my turn now and although I've been in the line for over an hour, my excitement hasn't waned.

An aide leans in to whisper something to Telly Savalas, who looks up and smiles at the man, relief clearly visible on his face. The man moves to the front of the line and cuts it off with a red velvet rope. "That's it, folks, thanks for coming." Savalas bolts like a rocket. He is gone, out of sight somewhere between the kitchenware and women's handbags. There is a murmur of upset from the remaining crowd in the line. I'm third from the front and deeply disappointed, but I understand how busy Mr. Savalas must be; I'm sure he has to get back to Hollywood and to *Kojak*.

"Excuse me, sir," I say to the aide. "I have a gift for Mr. Savalas." I fumble in my pocket and offer up my Charms Blow Pop to the man. "Would you please give this to him? I know he likes lollipops." The man looks at me and smiles. "Sure, kid," he says. I hand him the lollipop and turn to go. I figure that even though I didn't meet Telly Savalas, I saw a great actor in the flesh and witnessed what it's like to be adored by fans, and the excitement that ripples around a star's appearance.

I turn around for one last look. I see the aide to Mr. Savalas throw my lollipop in a trash can.

⚜

Around this time, my mom and Bill begin to fight almost nightly. Chad is too young to know the slippery slope that this can lead us down. With the day in the lumberyard seared in my memory, I am anxious and scared each night as they scream below my bedroom. I develop a way to mask the yelling and pounding noises so I can sleep. I discover that if I shake my leg in a certain way it vibrates my bed frame and creates a metallic shaking noise that drowns out any other sound. Soon I can't fall asleep without my shaking-leg trick and it becomes a tic that will stay with me for many years.

As their marriage deteriorates, so does my mother's health. She is in bed a lot, and yet I'm never told exactly what is wrong. She can be her normal interested, interesting, supportive self one day and mysteriously incapacitated the next, adding to the volatility in the house and to my ever-present sense that something bad can happen at any minute.

I escape by bus to the theater and throw myself into any play I can find, like *Oklahoma!*, *The Time of Your Life*, and *Stop the World—I Want to Get Off* (what an apropos title for me!). My dad, always the one looking to have fun and making sure we did the same, arranges for me to appear on a local cable-access kids' show, *Clubhouse 22*. I'd watched it for years and loved the host, a hip guy named Malcolm and his sidekick, Duffy the Dog. Walking into the television studio, I feel an electric charge I still get sometimes today. The bright lights, the smell of paint and freshly cut wood, and the thrilling disconnect between fantasy and reality that you feel when you behold a TV or movie set and its unique mixture of beautiful fakery and practical, unexpected reality.

On the air, I help Malcolm and Duffy the Dog pick a prize-winner from the mailbag and am shocked when Duffy later removes his giant dog head to reveal a very beautiful blonde woman. (Years later, when I discover that my dad had been secretly banging Duffy the Dog, I don't think I was ever more proud. If that's the connection that got me onto my first set, so much the better.)

I'd also finally found a gang of neighborhood kids to hang out with, building forts, throwing mudballs, and playing tackle football. Although they thought I was a "freak" for my "acting," we bonded over our love of the Pittsburgh Steelers, Pete Rose, and the Big Red Machine, and ignored our differences, like their proclivity for petty theft and the killing and eating of neighborhood squirrels. (I often found skinned, bloody squirrel bodies in my friend's kitchen sink. His family was from Appalachia—"briar" is the local pejorative for them—and squirrel meat was a traditional food source. It was all very *Deliverance*.)

Soon Mom was pregnant again, and in keeping with my tradition of harsh judgments on such matters, I thought, Pregnant? You're so old!

She was thirty-three. Micah was born that summer and I hoped it would make our house less volatile. It didn't. My mom and Bill repainted their bedroom walls black-brown. Even an eleven-year-old knows that this can't be a good sign. The thing was, I had a good relationship with my stepfather, and I wanted their marriage to last. Bill and I listened to talk radio, cheered Senator Ervin at the Watergate hearings, did door-to-door campaigning for everyone from George McGovern to Senator Howard Metzenbaum.

When Micah was a couple years old, my mother began to retreat to her bedroom for hours a day, every day. She wrote short stories and poems and kept a daily journal (which she would do for the rest of her life). But her mysterious illness was gaining a grip on her. She began to feel that Chad was also suffering from what she thought were "allergies." And so she checked Chad and herself into the country's leading hospital for universal allergics, Henrotin Hospital in downtown Chicago. There they were to fast, having nothing but water for two weeks, and then eat nothing but blueberries. The doctors would see how they reacted. Another fast would follow and another single food would be introduced, each more exotic than the next, culminating in caribou meat. Chad, seven years old and feeling perfectly fine, was terrified, but off he went, the first passenger on the first of my mother's grand expeditions into the rising dawn of self-fulfillment, self-help, and self-obsession.

Upon their release from the universal allergy hospital, both my mom and Chad seemed exactly the same. What had changed was our refrigerator. It was now stocked with buffalo and caribou meats, and we were regimented to drinking special water. We consumed handfuls of vitamins that made me want to vomit. Chad and I looked forward to the weekends when we got to be with our dad and gorge on hamburgers, milkshakes, and pizza. Not surprisingly, on those carefree weekends, Chad felt great.

❖

I'm playing Nerf football with my friends in the mud and slush of a mild winter day. It's tackle, as usual, and we light into each other without fear of injury, absolutely hammering each other. This is a daily ritual for our gang of friends, football in the cold, kick-the-can when it's warm; huge games with kids everywhere. I've got my uniform: a "breakaway" Steelers jersey over a sweatshirt and Levi Toughskins. I see my mom on the porch waving me in. "Gotta go, guys!"

"Come on, Lowe! Just a few more plays! You pussy!" they yell good-naturedly, and I am happy that in spite of our different backgrounds, we've become such good friends. I lope down the block to my house.

I cannot remember the specifics of what happens next. I have spent hours, days, and years trying. It is like the Rosemary Woods twenty-minute gap in the Watergate tapes of my childhood. I've come to realize that the first divorce and subsequent move was painful enough to block the second one out of my long-term memory. But the facts are clear enough: Mom and Bill are over, my mom will make us forsake Ohio and its gray "unhealthy" winters for a move to California. She has friends there that she met while in the allergy hospital. Unlike the conversation in the lumberyard, I have only vignetted memories of this entire chapter of my life. Clearly, I had learned my lesson well: I would black out, avoid, disassociate anything and everything beyond my comfort level. Saying good-bye to my home, my friends, my dad, Bill, and my grandparents, to leave for a place I had never been or seen, was just too tough for me to process properly. Years later, I would learn the filmmaking phrase for my random, isolated memories; it is called a "montage."

Cue the music, Elton John's "Goodbye Yellow Brick Road," as I kiss my grandparents and hop into the packed car. Bill is not there, he has gone, unable to watch, saying his good-byes and hugging us boys in the middle of the night.

My football gang is there, too, the kids of great hardscrabble North Dayton families: the Freemans, the Scarpellis, the Eiferts. They run alongside the car as we pull away. I want to jump out, tell my mom, don't do this; don't make us go, I'm scared. I want to stay *here* with my friends. But I say nothing, I'm frozen inside. My brothers and I watch as our friends begin to stop running, falling by the wayside, unable to keep up, as our car speeds off into the distance.

CHAPTER 4

I have never seen so many cars in my life. Our Volvo station
wagon is stopped dead in the middle of the biggest, busiest
freeway I have ever seen. It's eighty degrees in the middle of winter and the sky is the color of a baseball mitt. To my left, eight guys
in a pickup truck are blasting accordion music, like what you
might hear at a circus. To my right is a trailer hauling cars. One of
them is the Batmobile. Welcome to Los Angeles, kid.

My mom navigates the traffic jam as best she can with little
Micah crawling like an ape around the car, trying to remove the
oxygen mask she's taken to wearing. Her new hero, Dr. Wilson, of
the allergy hospital, has prescribed the mask and a number of other
remedies, as a way to prevent allergy flare-ups. The horrific brown
L.A. air suggests that the oxygen mask might be a sound idea, but
I have no clue why she is also wearing thick, white gardening

gloves. (Later I learn that they supposedly protect her hands from the toxins "out-gassing" from the plastic steering wheel.) Now, out my window I can see the Pacific Ocean. It is rugged, crashing, and huge. A sign says, "Welcome to Malibu, 22 miles of scenic beauty." I'm feeling a queasy mixture of homesickness and gurgling excitement, beholding this stunning, alien world.

Point Dume sits at the westernmost edge of Malibu. A breathtaking, palisaded promontory, it looks like a sawed-off volcano, jutting its jagged cliffs into the crashing surf below. Named after the Spanish missionary Father Dumez, who cowed the local Chumash Indians into Christianity, it is rumored to be haunted, and stories of ancient burial grounds and lost underwater villages are legend. At the moment I'm unaware of this unsettling history, although within months I will see the signs everywhere. But as we turn into a cul-de-sac of modest ranch-style houses, I only know that my mom has chosen Point Dume because it has the best air quality in Southern California.

Our new house is a rented, single-story ranch house, very plain, with three bedrooms, one bath, and a yard strewn with what look to be small moon rocks. Chad and I will come to despise this yard, as we will have to weed it of intruding crabgrass every weekend before we can go out to play. But the real showstopper is the tiny horse corral, which Mom tells Chad and me was constructed with the leftover wood from the set of *Planet of the Apes*. I can almost look down the gully behind it to see the beach where Charlton Heston discovered the remains of the Statue of Liberty in one of filmmaking's most iconic scenes. There's also an unsubstantiated rumor that the Captain and Tennille may have lived in our house. I am quickly sensing that, in Point Dume, there is adventure as well as Hollywood history at every turn.

An entire book could (and should) be written about Malibu in 1976. In the bicentennial sunlight of that year, it was a place of rural beauty where people still rode to the local market on horseback and tied up to a hitching post in the parking lot. Long before every agent and studio president knocked down the beach shacks to build their megamansions, Malibu was populated by a wonderful mix of normal working-class families, hippies, asshole surfers, drugged-out reclusive rock stars, and the odd actor or two. The town was extremely spartan. Its lone movie theater only got films months after they had played everywhere else. Its one record shop wouldn't have the latest record for weeks and weeks after you could find it all over Los Angeles. There was a taco stand, a donut shop, a biker bar, and one or two restaurants in all of its twenty-two miles. Although Hollywood was only a forty-five-minute drive away, at that time it might as well have been forty-five light-years. It's almost impossible now to imagine a Malibu without Wolfgang Puck, Nobu sushi, Starbucks, and paparazzi documenting every B-list celebrity who walks out the door with a latte, but it did exist, once upon a time.

As I'm settling into my new bedroom, which I will share with Chad, my mom tells me she has a surprise in the other room. Chad is convinced it's a puppy. He and I run into the living room, excited to see what she has in store for us.

It isn't a puppy.

From behind a stack of boxes emerges a dark-haired, dark-eyed man with a black beard. (Think one of the guys on the box of Smith Brothers cough drops.) Chad gasps. "Dr. . . . Dr. Wilson?"

"Hey, Chad-o!" he says, smiling. I look around the room. Dr. Wilson? The allergy hospital guy? What's he doing here?

"How do you like the surprise?" Mom asks cheerily, as if she's just presented us with a new jungle gym or, indeed, a puppy.

"Hey, Rob-o!" he adds warmly.

"Steve is going to be living with us!" Mom announces.

I look at her. She is beaming. Happy. After taking a moment to digest the announcement, Chad seems to be down with the program as well. And in a testament to the simplicity and resilience of twelve-year-olds, I take a minute and process this instant addition to our family and conclude . . . sounds okay to me, can I have the bed by the window?

Later that night as I sleep in my new room, I think about what's become of our family. I'm desperately homesick for my dad and grandparents. I wonder if my friends are playing football without me. I consider my mother. She must be a brave person to leave an unhappy marriage when so many people of her background stick it out. I figure she is to be admired for following her heart and doing what she thought was right for both herself and us boys. As the beautifully pungent aroma of the night-blooming jasmine wafts through my window, I begin to see my mother in a new way. A rebel. An artist. A dreamer. A searcher. I am sad for her too, worried because I have no idea what she is searching for and fear that neither does she.

Dr. Wilson, or Steve as we now call him, is an intellectual, awkward, kooky, but nice guy. He and my mom have a deep connection; they spend hours reading Carl Jung (Steve is now working in L.A. County's Mental Health Department as a shrink), listening to Phoebe Snow, eating hummus, and rubbing each other's feet. He treats Chad and Micah and me well, and I'm relieved to see my mom happy and out of her pajamas for long stretches of time.

As our first day of school approaches, Chad and I haven't seen many other kids. There are no pickup football games, no kids riding bikes in the street, no sounds of yelling, rough-housing, and mischievous camaraderie between the houses. Chad and I wander aimlessly, looking for people our own ages. Eventually I will learn that this is very different from the Midwest, where kids connect with each other via big communal activities like kick the can and street hockey. Malibu kids are isolated, solitary by nature, and when among their peers they form small, extremely tight cliques.

The surfers. The burn-outs. The brains. The nerds. There are also those who seem like ghosts, not belonging to anyone or any clique. The Lost Boys of Malibu. And indeed, their tragic narrative of freak accidents and death will play itself out throughout my teen years on Point Dume, lending credence to the stories of its haunted past.

❖

My first day of seventh grade at Malibu Park Junior High begins with me getting on the bus and sitting next to a kid I think I might be able to befriend. But then he gives me a look that makes me feel like an idiot for not sitting in an empty seat behind or in front of him. I make a mental note of the Malibu bus protocol. Never again will I sit next to someone unless every other seat is taken.

Things don't get any better upon arrival at school. Kids snicker at my clothes; I've worn my favorite Levi Toughskins, not knowing that *no one* wears long pants to school, ever. Under any circumstances. In the classroom I'm eager and interested, which is also frowned upon. The cool kids sit in the back of the class in their shorts and flip-flops and talk about surfing until the teacher tells them to shut up. I begin to watch the clock, hoping that P.E. will be different, but I get no break there either. I am hoping for flag football or baseball or kickball, but get volleyball instead. Not a lot of volleyball in Ohio. I suck and everyone notices.

At lunch a group of girls ask me what I'm "into." I tell them I want to be an actor. They stare at me. If I thought being forty-five minutes outside of Hollywood would make that concept acceptable, I was wrong. "Are you a fag?" one of the girls asks me. The others laugh as my face turns bright red.

A shaggy-haired blond surfer grabs the cute girl by the ass. "Who's a fag? This guy?!" he asks, looking at me and pulling her in for a kiss. The other kids ooh and aah at this overt show of sexuality, and I use the distraction to make my escape, back to my locker. Finally school is over. I board the bus home and find an empty seat away from anyone else.

Over the next few weeks I begin to get the drill. Although my bus stop is first and the bus is always empty, I am NOT to sit in any of the back rows. If I were to attempt that, the ripped, blond leader of the cool set, a surfer named Peter, would have me forcibly removed. That area of the bus and other specific areas of the grass where we have lunch are the sole domain of the volleyball stars, surf champs, and their girlfriends. I eventually find my place in this Darwinian landscape where I probably, then rightfully, belong: with the nerds and the other "pleasures to have in class."

One day as I'm killing time hanging out at the Mayfair Market parking lot, I see a bunch of kids running around in army outfits. They seem to be playing a sort of war game and are taking it very seriously. I ask the kid who looks to be the leader what's going on. He is a chunky blond, with a runny nose that he doesn't bother to wipe. He tells me that he is "filming" a Vietnam movie and he is using the market's loading dock as a set. He shows me his 8 mm movie camera and introduces himself. "I'm Chris Penn. I'm the director." Now this is exciting—kids shooting their own movie! I ask him who else is doing his movie, hoping he will ask me to be in it as well. "Well, I got my best friend, Charlie, my brother Sean, and maybe Charlie's big brother, Emilio."

"You mean you guys are actors, too?" I ask. I already know that none of these kids are in the cool crowd—they don't surf.

"Nah, not really. We just like making movies. Charlie's dad is an actor, though."

"Holy shit! A *real* actor?" I ask.

"Yeah, he's done a bunch of movies."

"Can I meet him?"

Chris laughs. "Are you kidding? He's been gone for almost

two years working overseas on a film about war somewhere in the Philippines."

Later I learn the movie's called *Apocalypse Now* and his name is Martin Sheen. But at this moment, I think to myself, now that's a guy I'd like to meet someday.

Chris tells me that when they make another movie, he'll call me, but for now "we don't have any parts for you." I stick around and watch as they film each other getting shot in every conceivable fashion, slapping ketchup everywhere for fake blood. The Mayfair Market as Vietnam. The magic of Hollywood.

At home later, Chad has exciting news as well. His elementary school is going to be used the next day for the filming of a TV series. I can't believe it. My intense loneliness and longing for my father and friends back in Dayton begins to fade into the background. This place isn't so bad after all.

⁘

The previous week at my brother's elementary school, Chad's teacher hid a kid in his class in a closet so he would not be kidnapped in an ugly custody dispute. As the kid's mom and a team of lawyers scoured the school, the sheriff was called to rescue the poor kid, who was ensconced, like Anne Frank, in a broom closet of the art room. The father arrived, as well, and the staff oohed and aahed, as he was a legendary rock icon, but the kids were more excited to see the sheriffs running around with their guns drawn. The incident was soon forgotten. If the same thing happened today, it would be on TV and in the tabloids for weeks.

I rush home from school to stand with Chad and watch a TV crew convert the principal's office into a hospital emergency room with the help of giant lights and a caravan of equipment and trucks. People are crowding around to get a glimpse of the three actresses as they repeatedly enter and exit the "emergency room."

They shoot the scene over and over and to us it's riveting each time. The three stars take a break and walk to their chairs. On the front are each of their names, Jaclyn Smith, Kate Jackson, and Farrah Fawcett, and on the back a cartoonlike logo of them holding guns and the title: *Charlie's Angels.*

Unlike Liza Minnelli, these gals have flocks of people surrounding them. There's no way to get close, but eventually I strike up a conversation with someone on the TV crew. He looks important to me; he is hauling a lot of cables and lights and listening to a walkie-talkie. I ask him a barrage of questions culminating with the classic "How do you think I can get into acting?" The man tells me I should write to the producer of *Charlie's Angels,* Aaron Spelling; he's the biggest producer in the history of television. "I'm sure he would like to hear from you," the man says with a smile. I run home and compose a letter to Mr. Spelling. It takes some time to find an address for him but finally I do, care of the 20th Century Fox Studios. I drop it in the mailbox and wait for his reply.

✤

As seventh grade came to an end, I couldn't wait to spend my appointed time back in Ohio with my dad. I would see my old friends and tell them of my California adventures, and I'd get my spot back in Peanut Butter and Jelly. It would be good to be onstage again, as I hadn't done any acting since I moved to California.

My dad and my new stepmother, Kay, had a baby boy named Justin about a week before Chad and I returned. We all shared a room and Chad and I took turns giving him bottles. I was happy to be back with this branch of the family, but could have done without having a screaming baby as an alarm clock.

When I called the man who ran Peanut Butter and Jelly, he

told me that the group wasn't doing any performances "at the moment" and there was nothing on the horizon. It was strange. I had known this man for years and had never heard him use this kind, patient, and encouraging tone of voice with me. It would take me years of working in Hollywood to recognize this truth: When someone in the entertainment business (even in Dayton, Ohio) uses this tone with you, nine times out of ten they're lying. And indeed he was. Peanut Butter and Jelly was playing all around Dayton. They just didn't want me back.

After a month, Chad and I returned to Malibu, and only then did I realize that I was already beginning to prefer it to Dayton.

Malibu summers were epic. Each day was cookie-cutter consistent: eighty degrees and sunny, no thick midwestern humidity and no rain—ever. I had made some friends and we would spend endless hours exploring the mysterious overgrown gullies that ran to the ocean and bodysurfing in the crystal waves that made Malibu famous.

A ninth-grade girl had taken an interest in me, and I often rode my bike to her house to fool around with her. Like Julie the Jitterbug, she took great pleasure in teaching me the finer points of what my parents would probably call "heavy petting." She was not, by any means, one of the girls in the popular set. In fact, I took a lot of shit for being linked with her, which seemed unfair to both her and me. We were both misfits in a way, which made us a good match. And let's face it, when a ninth-grader is interested in a seventh-grader, it's pretty cool.

As the summer drew to a close, I somehow got invited to the birthday party of the Queen Bee of Malibu Park Junior High "in crowd"—a stunning blonde, sometime teen model, and surf goddess. Pulling out of the driveway, I had my mom stop to check the mailbox, as was my custom since I wrote my letter to Aaron

Spelling. It had been well over six months, but I still held out hope. And today, amazingly enough, I was rewarded.

Dear Rob,

I was happy to receive your letter. You seem like a very nice young man and I would welcome you to visit me at the studio anytime, providing it is fine with your parents. Please call ahead though.

Sincerely,
Aaron Spelling

P.S. I have a funny feeling you might have my job one day!

I was floored. It was on 20th Century Fox stationery! It was better than a letter from President Ford, as at the moment, Spelling was probably more powerful and popular than Ford.

At the party no one cared. The cool kids of the seventh and eighth grades were much more focused on the top-secret gift the birthday girl was sharing with everyone. It was a tiny amber-colored bottle with a black lid, filled with some sort of white powder. I asked Peter the Surfer what it was. "It's coke, you idiot." I didn't know what he meant but knew enough to get that it was clearly a drug of some sort. By then, I was used to seeing kids smoke pot. A number of them had brought their parents' "water pipes" to school and often set up a rudimentary bazaar on the lawn at lunch where the devices were traded and sold. But this was different. Since I was an outsider anyway, no one invited me to join them and the amber-colored bottle in the bathroom.

❖

I never told my mom or Steve what I saw at the party. Parents were rarely seen in Malibu. The kids lived *Lord of the Flies* style, running their own programs without any apparent interference from an adult—ever. And so, like any good chameleon, I began to do the same. And Mom and Steve were perfectly happy to let both my brother and me have freedoms that would be unimaginable today. Chad and I would take the bus twenty-five miles to Santa Monica alone, then catch three other connections for the additional fifteen miles through the wasteland of downtown Los Angeles to go to Dodgers games.

At one such game, a group of fans got belligerent with Chad for wearing a Yankees hat (even though we were Cincinnati Reds fans). Things were getting ugly when a guy stepped in and rescued my brother and me from the mob. Turns out he was a Yankees fan himself. We thanked him profusely and he just laughed and said, "You are cool kids. Maybe you want to come visit me at work. I'm a head puppeteer on the Muppets."

"The Muppets! Hell, yes, we'd like to visit the Muppets," we exclaimed. And so, a few weeks later, we did.

It was my first time on a soundstage. As Mom and Steve drove us through the guard gate, I felt a rush of adrenaline, a stirring so profound I felt almost light-headed. I was entering the inner sanctum of moviemaking. My first step into the world I wanted so much to be a part of.

On the set we watched Frank Oz perform Miss Piggy. The legendary Jim Henson himself sat on his director's chair with Kermit the Frog on his right hand. They were shooting a beautiful, and strangely sad, music number called "The Rainbow Connection" for what was to be known as *The Muppet Movie.* Our new friend from the Dodgers game, Richard, operated Scooter.

A few weeks later we got another invitation from Richard. For the first (and, I think, only) time in the show's history, a puppet would fill in for Johnny Carson as the host of *The Tonight Show.* Kermit the Frog would have the honors, and we were invited to be in the audience. Obviously, we went.

Backstage, after the taping of the show, there was a small party. A gregarious man with a Santalike beard greeted me. He introduced himself. "I'm Bernie Brillstein, I produce *The Muppet Show*. I hope you've had a good time."

A full twenty years later, he would not only become my manager but a surrogate father as well. Bernie also represented all the cast of the hot new show *Saturday Night Live*. At the time, I repeated the entire content of each show every Sunday morning, verbatim, to my nonplussed mother. I worshipped Dan Aykroyd and Chevy Chase. I even won the Malibu Park Junior High talent show with my own version of Aykroyd's classic sketch Bass-O-Matic that year. So the sight of John Belushi staring at me from across the party froze me in my shoes. This time there would be no going over to him and striking up a conversation. He was the biggest thing on television and I was way too intimidated. But Belushi kept staring. Was he mad that a kid was backstage at this VIP party? Did he want me kicked out? I had no idea, but was about to find out, as he began to make a beeline for me.

"Hey, kid," he said gruffly.

"Um, yes, Mr. Belushi?"

"What're you doin' here?"

"We were in the audience tonight."

"Oh," he said. He was jittery, vibrating with a weird energy.

"What do you want to be when you grow up?" he asked, softening with a smile.

"I want to be an actor. Like you."

He looked at me for a long-drawn-out moment and, at once, I knew I had said something wrong. His entire face fell, and his mood darkened in an instant. Then he pulled me close and whispered in my ear in a voice so thick I almost couldn't understand him, "Stay out of the clubs."

I should have listened. Instead, I got my first agent.

CHAPTER 5

I am standing on the roof of a run-down barn in our backyard corral. Below me, Chris Penn and my brother Chad are setting up an 8 mm camera. Chris is directing me in our mutually produced version of *The Six Million Dollar Man*. Chris has learned from his father, Leo, a noted television director, the intricacies of special effects and has concocted a plan for me (as Colonel Steve Austin) to leap two stories to the top of the barn roof. Unfortunately for me, it will require me to jump off the roof, backward. The film will then be reversed, making it appear that I have leaped up instead of down.

Chad takes pity on me and drags a moldy old beanbag chair we found in the garage and places it underneath me to break my fall. High up on my perch I can see all the way to the ocean; there is a nice breeze at my back. I look down at the beanbag and think: I betcha Leo Penn ain't asking his stuntman to jump into any beanbag chairs! Any normal person would tell Chris Penn to come up and do it himself. Alas, I'm deeply competitive, an adrenaline junkie, and never back down from a challenge. I'm also happy he has finally included me in one of the Penn-Sheen movie epics they've been filming all around the neighborhood. If I were to defer, I'm sure Sean or Charlie or Emilio would get the nod for this plum role.

"And . . . action!" Chris yells, looking through the camera.

I glance at my brother, who turns away. *Fuck it, how bad could it be?* I think, and I spring out, off my toes, facing away, but aiming for the beanbag, trying to clear the roof's overhang. I hit the beanbag dead center. I feel a snap in my ankle, followed by a white-hot pain. Immediately I know it's broken.

On some level you have to be crazy to be an actor. You must have a masochistic streak to deal with the rejection in failure and the unrelenting scrutiny in success. You must be able to shut off your logical brain; the voice that reminds you "two-thirds of the Screen Actors Guild makes less than a thousand dollars a year, get a *real* job" or "don't jump off this roof, you moron!" But if acting truly is your calling, if it's really in your blood, you will have these tragic/heroic flaws in spades. And when you are filming a scene or a stunt, even for an eighth-grade home movie, and break an ankle, you won't ask for a doctor; you will ask: Did you get the shot? And if the answer is yes, there will be no more pain, only euphoria.

I had just acquired an agent. Looking for advice, I cold-called a girl in my neighborhood who had played Cloris Leachman's daughter on a TV show. She told me that no one goes anywhere in Hollywood without an agent. Fortunately my dad had an ex-client who had relocated to L.A. and was a junior agent at a small agency. I went to their office, located in a tiny building on Melrose Place (yes, there is a real Melrose Place) and met the woman who would become my first agent. Soon I was hopping on the bus after school, heading to Hollywood for my first professional auditions. Sometimes I would be on various buses for three hours (one way!) and in the audition for thirty seconds—literally. Since I was so inexperienced, the parts were really nothing more than background or "extra" opportunities or commercials. They would call your name, take a Polaroid, and send you on your way. But I didn't care; I did my homework on the rides home, wolfed down a meal, and went straight to bed, as it was always late by the time I made my way back to Point Dume.

In spite of being on crutches after my big stunt jump, I still managed to catch my buses into Hollywood for the occasional audition. So far, there were no takers. Maybe it was due to my amateurish eight-by-ten, which in those days was called "a composite" because it had a number of different photos on it, meant to represent different sides of your personality. Mine had photos of me skateboarding, and dressed up as a magician and as a soccer player. Unfortunately, the photographer who shot me didn't have any wardrobe or "props," and I didn't know to provide my own. So, as the magician, instead of from a top hat, I was shot pulling a rabbit out of a stupid-looking bucket hat like Gilligan wore, and holding a basketball, but dressed in my soccer outfit. Even then I knew my composite was a disaster, but my agent told me "no one cares about those kinds of things." It may very well have been the first time I was encouraged to discount my instincts in favor of expedience, but it would not be the last. I wish I had known what I know now; trust your gut always. After all, it won't be anyone but you looking like an idiot holding a basketball while dressed like Pelé.

❧

At school we all began to buzz about Halloween, which was fast approaching and was a big deal on Point Dume. It was a perfect excuse for the already wild and lawless bands of kids to run amok, dousing tires with gasoline and rolling them down the streets into crowds of unsuspecting children, filling gas tanks with sugar, and egging people in the face at point-blank range. Shaving cream was used as mace. It was Christmas morning for bullies.

And, truth be told, I was not immune to the thrill of low-grade anarchy myself. I also would be appropriately armed for my own defense if needed. Stocked with a dozen eggs and a full canister of Barbasol, I met up with a group of kids to make our rounds. It was a perfect, dry, breezy, moonless night. None of us wore costumes; that was for kids, not young men on a mission. If we felt like trick-or-treating, we might pull out a twenty-cent mask, if needed.

My first stop was the Sheens' house. Knocking on the door, I hoped I might get a glimpse of the by-now legendary Martin Sheen, who recently returned from his two-year odyssey of making *Apocalypse Now*. There were rumors that the movie had almost killed him and that he might have gone insane while shooting it in the fetid jungle of the Philippines. Although I'd spent some time with Charlie and Emilio making our amateur movies, they never discussed their father. I was even more curious about him when I learned that he, too, had begun his acting career in his hometown of Dayton, Ohio.

My friends and I waited at the door, but no one answered. So we moved on to other homes and an egg-throwing scrimmage or two. As we plotted our next move, a figure jumped out of a bush, scaring us to death.

"What ya boys doin'?" demanded a man dressed from head to toe in army fatigues and wielding a gigantic baseball bat.

"N-n-nothing, just trick-or-treating," we answered. The man leaned in to have a closer look. In the blackness it appeared that he might have war paint on his face, but it was hard to tell.

"This is *my* neighborhood. I am on patrol tonight! There will be no monkey business on my watch! Do you understand?" He looked at my friends, who said nothing.

"Do you understand!?" he said again, this time looking at me.

"Yes, sir," I answered, knowing that it was probably a good idea to use "sir" when confronted in the dark by a bat-swinging, army-uniformed dude with security on his mind.

"Good," he said, and he smashed his bat on the pavement, making us jump. "I'll be watchin'."

And with that he turned and disappeared into the darkness. When the coast was clear, one of my friends exhaled and chuckled. "Hey, Lowe, you said you wanted to meet Martin Sheen? Well, now you have."

✥

One morning I sat on the school bus, with my crowd of kids in the "economy class" area, and talked and studied as usual. But back in the VIP area, something was up. Over the din of the radio playing "If You Leave Me Now" by Chicago, you could hear crying and frantic whispering. I craned my head to see what the commotion was, but the bus was packed and I couldn't see. As we emptied out into the school parking lot, I saw the blonde surfer girl who'd had the birthday party with the amber bottle. She was the one who had been crying. The rest of the surf gang was skittish and ashen faced. What the hell was up?

By second period everyone knew. As usual, there was no adult or authority figure stepping up to give guidance or information, so the news spread kid to kid. Peter, the golden Surf God, was missing. There were dark rumors that he might have been in some terrible accident. By lunchtime, sheriffs were taking members of Peter's gang to the principal's office for questioning. By the final bell that day it was clear: Peter had disappeared and no one knew where or why.

Bad things happen to kids every day. It is the core-shaking truth. We don't like to face it. We will do anything to avoid it, and

we attempt to find comfort in the knowledge that it is, mercifully, fairly infrequent. But in the beautiful idyll of Point Dume,
above the forgotten Chumash burial grounds, there was a savage
undercurrent running through the lives of the boys and girls of
those endless summers. Some of the blame falls to the parents, the
checked-out, live-and-let-live generation who came of age at Wood-
stock. Some of it falls to the kids themselves—unformed, undisci-
plined, unsupervised, and wrestling with all the promise and angst
of their tender possibilities. But some of it, and maybe a lot of it,
came from environment. And Malibu, with its beautiful facade
covering its complex, dangerous underbelly, was an environment
with the energy field of seven supernovas. Peter was the first one to
be sucked into the vortex.

They had all ditched school the day before. Surf was up, sun
was out, and the party was on. At Zuma Beach they laid out
their towels. I probably could have seen them out the bus window if I had been looking. Peter, his girlfriend, and the others of
his group stripped off their clothes. Some of them swam. Some
of them baked in the Southern California sun. There was pot.
One of the kids pulled out a bottle of Quaaludes. Soon darkness
was upon them.

Under questioning late the next day, the order of events became
clear. They had all fallen asleep or passed out on the beach. All
except Peter, who, high on Quaaludes, went for a swim. When
they awoke, he was gone. They searched for hours. The kids would
have to be home soon and they began to panic. Peter's clothes
were lying on his towel where he had left them. In an effort to
avoid getting in trouble, they dug a hole. They collected his clothes
and towel and buried them. Their plan was to deny any involve-
ment in whatever might have happened to Peter. And the plan
held together for twenty-four hours, until someone cracked.

Peter was never found. Later, they created a small park in his
honor in front of the Malibu Cinema. His friends marked their

loss by creating a touching and profoundly creepy ritual: The cool crowd held "Peter's seat" empty on the bus each day, preventing anyone from sitting in his spot in back by the window. He was fourteen years old.

⁂

Although my mom's health seemed to be much better, she and Steve dug into her obsession with alternative medicines and holistic treatments. She devoured medical books and self-help books and began to delve deeply into analysis, reading everything from the otherworldly (*Seth Speaks*) to the scholarly (the entire canon of Carl Jung). Our dinner-table talks were peppered with phrases like "the collective unconscious," and Steve and my mom deconstructed their nightly dreams like another couple might rehash a good movie. Mom redoubled her journal writing and her dream diary, and began writing short stories, novels, you name it. She was now spending at least four hours a day, every day, behind closed doors, writing. If there was ever any finished project to read, we didn't know about it or were not allowed to read it. Once, when I asked my mom why she worked so hard at writing, but (from my perspective) had nothing to show for it, she said, "I don't write for a result. I write for the process and what it teaches me about myself."

Meanwhile, I wasn't acting at all (unless you count our homespun *Six Million Dollar Man*). There was no setup for local theater in Southern California. Back in Ohio, I could do summer stock and plays at the community and university theaters. But L.A. was different. (To this day the theater scene is an afterthought.) Until I cracked into "real" show business, I would have to be content to sit on the sidelines and be satisfied with chance encounters with people who were already in the game—the sort of thing that can only happen in and around Hollywood.

Steve's brother and sister-in-law visited us from time to time and told us stories of their adventures as starving artists in the bohemian world of avant-garde filmmaking and rudimentary animation. Both graduates of the prestigious CalArts, they were among a small group of animators pioneering a new process known as rotoscope, which in 1977 was the CGI of its day. For months they bitched about their latest job, a cheap, low-budget movie that they described as a "cheesy Western" set in outer space. Regardless of their complaining, a movie's a movie and I wanted to check it out.

On the big day, the family piles into our Volvo station wagon. (Whoever sold the American public on Volvo being the standard of safety and reliability never drove our car. It sucked!) We drive to a seedy, run-down industrial area of the San Fernando Valley, populated by Mexican "chop-shops," porn distribution warehouses, and abandoned garages. Finally we are let into a large cinder-block building through an industrial metal sliding garage door by a guy who looks like Jerry Garcia. Inside, my stepaunt and uncle are waiting.

"*This* is where you're shooting the movie?" I ask. The place looks more like a hideout for the Symbionese Liberation Army. Jerry Garcia explains that shooting for the movie itself is finished and this is where the special effects are being added.

"Why does it smell bad?" Chad asks.

Jerry and my aunt and uncle laugh. "Yeah, it does reek, doesn't it? It's the costumes. They are pretty dirty and gross at this point."

We enter the main area of the warehouse. Suddenly people are everywhere; the room is filled with energy. "Tonight we are shooting footage for the climactic battle scenes," somebody explains. In front of me is a giant platform about chest high and easily forty yards long and twenty yards wide. It is covered with monochromatic battleship-gray miniature towers, buildings, trenches, gun portals, and radar dishes. I see that it is constructed with spray-painted egg cartons, elements of model battleships and tank parts, and other pieces of toys and everyday items. But in the hands of these crazy hippies, it looks like the surface of an absolutely enormous alien planet. "What is this supposed to be?" I ask, amazed. My uncle looks at the gigantic layout and smiles. "This . . . is the Death Star."

"Action!" yells the cameraman. A specially built (the first of its kind in the world, I'm told) camera is lowered into the main trench of the Death Star. It moves at a snail's pace down the crevice running the length of the platform. "Later, we will speed the film up and add the spaceship flying over this shot we are making now," says my uncle.

"I wanna see the spaceship," I say.

"It's right over there," he says, pointing to another corner of the warehouse. And there, sitting in front of what I will learn is a "blue screen," is a six-foot-long model of the coolest spaceship I've ever seen. "It's called the *Millennium Falcon.*"

I run my hands over it. Chad stares, too, slack-jawed.

"Well, why don't you come look at some rough footage on the big screen?" Garcia says.

We file into a filthy, makeshift screening room. I'm introduced to my aunt and uncle's boss. "Hi. I'm John Dykstra. I'm the visual-effects coordinator. I'm just about to watch some scenes we're working on."

As the lights go down, I turn to him and ask, "What's this movie called?"

"*Star Wars*," he says.

Even though most of the effects have not been added, what I see on-screen makes the hair on my neck stand up. When the hero grabs the girl and swings out on a rope to safety, even though they're flying a foot off the studio floor, I don't need the bottomless Death Star shaft to feel the rush. When the villain appears in the black mask and helmet, I am riveted, even when he pulls out a cool handle with a broomstick on it and begins a sword fight.

"This is what I do," says my aunt. "I'm gonna add a laser over the broom handle. It's going to be a laser-sword."

"No, we're gonna call it a *light saber*," says Dykstra.

When the clips are over, we stop to see a small robot that is shaped like a trash can. Apparently the robot is a major character in the movie, and I think the name is cool, R2-D2. My brother and I also check out Luke Skywalker's hovercraft, which has mirrors covering the wheels underneath it, to give it a rudimentary effect of hovering. Later, even that will be "rotoscoped" out for better effect, to make it look like it's flying.

On our way out we pass the source of the terrible odor that has been wafting throughout the building. It is a giant, wooly-mammoth-looking costume for a character to be called a Bantha. It seems they are the horses of the future. But they stink like dead elephants. And, indeed, elephants have been wearing this gross stinky costume. "Yeah, the guy who rode it got thrown off. Almost broke his neck," says Jerry Garcia.

The next day at school I tell all my friends about this amazing new movie that isn't coming out for months but is going to be "the coolest thing ever." In my opinion (and I am hardly alone), *Star Wars* did change the world. The movie business was never the same; the era of the blockbuster and the tent pole was now on the horizon. And, following the money, as always, was Corporate America and the dubious model of "vertical integration." *Star Wars* made it attractive for an engine turbine company like GE to want anything to do with an inherently flaky artistic business that couldn't be decoded by bean counters, MBAs, or "bottom-line" hawks, as much as they continue to try. Luke Skywalker's photon torpedoes not only blew up the Death Star from the warehouse in North Hollywood, they ended an era when the movie business was run by people who, first and foremost, loved movies. Through all the years, and the changes they brought, I still feel lucky to have witnessed the birth of the movie that changed it all.

✧

We are going broke. My mom and Steve are increasingly at odds. He works for the county government as a shrink, he doesn't have a private practice like the big guns in Beverly Hills (I have no idea why), and my dad is always late with child support. I'm sure my dad's point of view is: Let the "new" dad hustle some money.

The tension in the house is overt. There is no attempt to keep those issues from me and my brothers and as a result I am anxious and melancholy. When I hear that my dad is ducking his financial commitments to us, I take it personally. Is there something I should do about this? Is this in some way representative of how Dad feels about us? It also sometimes occurs to me that perhaps I'm only hearing my mom and Steve's side of the story. I want to call my father, but I'm scared (long distance = expensive) and would have no idea how to begin a conversation about anything *real*, any interaction about our relationship. As always, I want to keep my head down and assume all is well. If there is an eight-hundred-pound gorilla in the room, I won't be the one to point it out, lest I be eaten by it.

Although my classmates at school are decidedly middle class, the few who do have money are the popular ones, so there is plenty of the kind of talk that comes from cool kids with cash: exotic vacations, new skis, fun restaurants, new clothes, and what kind of party to have when parents are out of town.

We can't afford restaurants much. If we do go out, the rule is: No desserts. There is never a vacation. And no new clothes: When I attend a bar mitzvah, I realize I don't own a belt and my mom gives me a camera strap to use. I am ashamed that I don't have proper clothes for this special occasion. I want to be respectful, and that's a hard look to pull off with a camera strap around your waist. But this is where my ability to ignore reality is a gift. I walk in like I'm dressed like James Bond. No one says a word, and in fact, one girl asks where I got the cool belt. Fake confidence on the outside, as I will later learn, often trumps truthful turmoil on the inside.

Armed with this confidence, I've begun to put my toe into school politics. I'm savvy enough to know that I can't compete with the handsome, older, and more athletic Emilio Estevez for "Boys' Vice President," so I choose an office that no one else wants: parliamentarian. (When I tell you I wasn't a cool kid at Malibu Junior High, consider this entry from that year's yearbook: "Evan is a babe, but you are gay, sorry, better luck next time!") At the last second, a kid even more nerdy than I am runs against me. I crush him.

As the first order of business, the new student council stages a skateboard contest fund-raiser. The winner is a great-looking kid, a year older, named Paul, who runs with a rough crowd from down in Santa Monica, or "Dog Town" as they call it. They are the pioneers of the mid-'70s skateboarding boom; Paul is the first person I ever knew to have his own poster. Looking at him doing one of the sport's first aerials, I think: I want to be on a poster!

A girl who I've been doing scenes with in my drama class, Holly Robinson, *is* popular. She's a bit of an icon, being one of only two black girls in the school and having a father "back East" who appeared on *Sesame Street*. Holly is the star at all the talent shows and even people like Linda Ronstadt make the pilgrimage to our school auditorium to hear her sing. (Later in life, Holly will have a Hollywood career of her own, starring in tons of television shows. But now we do our scenes together in front of the drama teacher, who, the rumor goes, once stored a body in an industrial freezer—which seems outrageous to me, as there is nothing to indicate that the poor man even owns an industrial freezer.) Holly has the hots for Paul and is talking to him after the skateboard-contest award ceremony. She's standing with her mother, Dolores, who is a fledgling Hollywood manager, and some guy I have never seen before. Holly and I are good enough friends now, so I walk over to say hi. Dolores knows I want to be an actor and she puts her arm around me.

"How is it going?"

"Okay," I say, trying to be optimistic in front of someone legit.

"Well, you keep pushing. You'll get there," she says.

I look at Holly, but she is looking at Paul.

"Oh, and I want you to meet my client," she says, gesturing to the guy standing next to her. "I want you to take a long look at this amazing young man. Take this moment in and remember it, because I promise you that this time next week, he is going to be the most famous person in America."

I look him over. He's not all that much older than me, really. Maybe nineteen or twenty. He's black, with big, sweet eyes. I'm not sure what the hell Dolores is talking about, but she is deadly serious, so I am paying attention.

"Hi, I'm Rob."

He smiles dazzlingly. "Hi, I'm LeVar."

By the following Friday, LeVar Burton was the most famous face in America. His performance as Kunta Kinte in *Roots* put him on the cover of *Time* magazine and changed the course of television history. It also showed me how quickly the rocket fuel of stardom can ignite, how unimaginably *giant* the g-forces can be as you are propelled into fame's orbit.

Looking back, I also wonder at the mystery of destiny and fate. I marvel at the mercurial forces of fortune and am reminded that one must be ever vigilant to stay on one's own path, without envy of others. As the four of us stood in the afternoon light that day, LeVar was a week away from his triumphant destiny, Dolores was just beginning her journey, one that would make her one of the business's first important black female managers (with clients like Wesley Snipes and Martin and Charlie Sheen), and Holly was just six months from starring in her first major TV role. Paul

was in every skateboard magazine in the country, had girls falling all over themselves, and his poster was on the walls of teen
girls and guys. I was still being called an "acting fag" at school
and struggling to break in to Hollywood.

But fortunes change. Within a month I got that first break, so
long in coming. And within a few years, Paul became perhaps the
most notorious of all of Malibu's Lost Boys when, high on PCP,
he stabbed his mother to death with a butcher knife and was committed to a mental institution.

## CHAPTER 6

"I hope you like my birthday present," she says, handing me a package. She is practically shaking with excitement, her green eyes gleaming. "I'm sure it's great," I say, although I can't imagine what could be worth getting in a box as small as the one she just handed me.

We are on what I am gradually realizing is a de facto date; she's cooked me dinner, just the two of us, alone in a mobile home overlooking the beach at Paradise Cove. It's taken me a while to figure this out for two reasons: (1) I'm not exactly Mr. Popularity with the ladies, and (2) she's my little brother Micah's sixteen-year-old babysitter. I've known her for a while, she's given me rides to school in her red Ford pickup, and being a "driver" and all, to me, she might as well be an adult. Like me, she is sort of a social outsider. Her obsession is horses and she goes to some strange granola-crunching high school that no one's really heard of. But she's always nice to me, has beautiful eyes, Farrah Fawcett hair, and, Lord help me, an amazing body.

Recently she has been relentless about wanting to cook me dinner for my fourteenth birthday. I say yes without much thought to it one way or another: she's a cool pal and I'll suffer a bad meal if she's gonna make such an *issue* of it. Also, we are going to celebrate my first two professional jobs in Hollywood. One is a commercial for Coca-Cola, the most expensive one they've ever done and, for the first time ever, made exclusively to be broadcast on the Super Bowl. The other is for some sort of blender and costars a former Miss America. I'm basically an extra in both commercials, but you'd have thought I was starring in a major motion picture. A pro gig is a pro gig, and I'm thrilled to have finally broken in. I'm paid twenty-five hundred dollars for the Coke commercial. I frame the check.

"C'mon, open it," she says, and so I do. I tear open the wrapping paper (Christmas patterns) and look at the tiny present. She grins and my heart pounds. It's a condom. A Trojan, just like the ones in my dad's sock drawer back in Ohio. Now I get it; the dinner alone, at night, secluded location. It's all a setup, her master plan; for my fourteenth birthday, I'm going to lose my virginity. I feel the slow, hot burn of what we today call "performance anxiety" flush through my body. I could, I suppose, not live up to my end of the elaborate plan. But it would be the wimp move, and I would never back down like that. It just feels a tad rushed, and contrived, and certainly not of my own making. It's clear that short of using the chicken exit like those on a roller coaster, I'm gonna have to ride this baby all the way, like it or not.

And what's not to like, really? Older girl, very cute, handpicks her prey and does all of the work. I guess I could've chosen my own time and place, but at the rate I was going, it could've been years till I got it together! I had no game at all. Any attention I ever got from the opposite sex as a teen was purely a result of the girl knowing the score, and acting on it. I had no killer instinct. That would come later.

Turns out, it's her first time, too; so together on a moonlit beach, we cross that wondrous, anxiety-filled Rubicon, cutting away the last vestige of childhood. I wasn't in love, she wasn't even my girlfriend, but she was kind, she was pretty, and she was my good friend. I was too young to know how valuable and rare that combination is. But after that warm March night in Paradise Cove, I was on the road to finding out.

⊕

Other than on summer vacations, I saw my father only for ski trips. We met in Snowbird, Utah, and his method of throwing Chad and me up on the top of expert runs and letting us figure it out made us very good. I looked forward to being with my dad; he was unlike any man in my life. Whereas my two stepfathers were cerebral and sometimes socially awkward, Dad had the UVA law degree *and* the charisma of an actor. Women loved him and he loved them. With other guys, he was funny, competitive, and a loyal friend. He also had no qualms about busting someone up at the slightest provocation. He knew that even though it may be politically incorrect in a touchy-feely world, sometimes you have to kick some ass.

When I was living with my mom and Bill back in Dayton, I had a pet bunny named Miss Bunn. One of the North Dayton hoods was jealous of my white rabbit and I returned one day from school to see its disemboweled body lying in a grotesque scarlet pool in our snow-covered yard. Miss Bunn had been sliced in half with a knife. My mother and Bill held no one responsible, treating it as a piece of bad luck, something that just *happened*. Had I been living with my dad, he would have tracked down the perpetrator and there would have been a second disembowelment.

Skiing helped me come into my own. I was also playing Pony
League baseball and finally outgrew my "last to be picked" athletic stage. The birthday at Paradise Cove, my two commercials,
and my widening circle of friends at school were all ingredients
in my slowly simmering stew of confidence.

I decided to enter the school's annual "Turkey Trot," a big deal
at Malibu Park. How fast can a race be with the words "turkey"
and "trot" in its name, I figured. Turns out the answer is very, very
fast. I was smoked by a kid a grade lower. The guy was a rocket; I
mean he ran like he was Superman. Turns out he would actually
become Superman, playing the Man of Steel on *Lois & Clark*,
alongside Teri Hatcher from 1993 to 1997. Dean Cain wasn't an
actor then, he wasn't even thinking about being one. In fact, he,
like Charlie Sheen, wanted to be a pro ballplayer. Dean was eventually recruited by the Dallas Cowboys and Charlie was a promis-
ing baseball player. In spite of the odd 8 mm home moviemaking,
I was the only one who was "going pro" as an actor.

And for every kid on a date with destiny, there continued to be
those on course for tragedy. The ranks of the Lost Boys of Malibu
grew at a steady rate. Shane, the sweet, goofy kid from my wood-
shop class, went home one day, snorted rat poison, thinking it was
cocaine, and died instantly. Sam, a young kid from Point Dume,
lost control of his 10-speed on the way home from school and
impaled his head on a tree. He bled to death hanging from the
trunk of a eucalyptus tree on Bonsal Drive. An older kid at school
dropped out suddenly and moved away entirely. We later learned
his dark story: Hitchhiking on the Pacific Coast Highway, he had
been picked up by a man, driven to a remote canyon, tied to a tree
naked, and had his pubic hair plucked out one by one with twee-
zers. There was also my brother Micah's friend, the animal lover.
Scuba diving at night with his girlfriend, he decided to rescue lob-
sters from a lobster trap. He got his hand caught in the mechanism
and eventually ran out of air sixty feet below the surface, while his

girlfriend struggled unsuccessfully to release him. And there was my buddy Tony, who heard a gunshot from a garage in Malibu West and rushed inside to investigate. He found a high school kid, his intestines hanging out from a self-inflicted shotgun blast. The kid muttered, "I'm gonna be sick, I'm gonna be sick," over and over as he lay dying next to his parents' station wagon. Within a few years, my friend Tony would be dead, too, from a weird new cancer. It would be another few years before they figured out what to call it. Sadly, AIDS was around way before the death of Rock Hudson.

Underneath the glorious exuberance of the counterculture ethos, the fantastical weather and dreamlike beauty, Malibu's malignant undercurrents were a hidden danger to adults as well. An elaborate escape lane had to be devised at the intersection of Kanan Road and Pacific Coast Highway after a number of trucks lost their brakes and careened down the hill, killing their drivers. The Point Dume school bus was traumatized by the sight of more than one driver's burning body crushed in the cab of his truck.

At Little Dume Beach, we mourned the death of the couple who kayaked every weekend from Paradise Cove to the buoy anchored off the point. They had been doing this for years until the foggy morning when they were both attacked and eaten by a great white shark. All that was found was their beloved kayak, with bite marks and signs of an awful struggle.

Why was hideous and untimely death so commingled with the experience that was Malibu in the mid-'70s? There were drugs, which weren't as understood as they are today, there was also the wild and rough nature of the personalities Malibu attracted. But more important, there was a price to be paid for a culture that idealizes the relentless pursuit of "self." Malibu was a wellspring of counterculture group think. To be counter to the culture, you are by definition willfully and actively ignoring the culture, i.e., reality. And when you ignore reality for too long, you begin to feel immune to, or above, the gravitational pull that binds everyone else. You are courting disaster.

✤

Money was still tight at home. Mom and Steve were at war with my dad. "If he can't make his child-support payments, how does he manage the ski trips?" Mom wondered. At one point, Steve called my dad to complain. "How about I fly out there, knock on your door, and kick your ass," my dad responded. Shaken, Steve hung up and asked Mom if he meant it. "Probably," Mom said.

I figured I could at least make my own spending money by getting some sort of part-time job. True to my passion, I found one at the Malibu Cinema, taking tickets, making popcorn, and threading the projector. The owner seemed gruff and fairly mean-spirited, but how bad could he have been to give a kid like me a legit job at my age?

I lasted about fourteen days. First, I was caught kissing Holly Robinson behind the Coke machine. Then came the Friday night opening of Dustin Hoffman's new opus, *Agatha*. (This was a time in Hollywood when an A-lister would still do a movie whose title didn't refer to his own character.) I had been struggling to learn how to properly thread the new projector. It was a complicated system where each reel was put on its own "platter" and then run through the projector at the proper moment. Obviously, placing the reels of film in the correct order was paramount. But somehow I bungled it. The audience erupted in confusion and rage as one moment Dustin Hoffman was in a rainstorm, hanging danger-ously off a rooftop, and in the next angle, he wore a tuxedo and danced the foxtrot. To make matters worse, in the next moment, the end credits began and when they were over, there was Dustin doing some sort of love scene. The full house asked for its money back. I was fired on the spot.

I didn't have much luck as a busboy either. I lasted three

weeks at the Nantucket Light before I was a casualty of "downsizing." It probably didn't help that I was known for sneaking free slices of mud pie in the walk-in freezer.

All along, I continued my journeys into Hollywood for auditions. The best my agency could do for me were meetings on commercials. TV and movie meetings were clearly way beyond both of our credentials. I had recently gotten a commercial for Carl's Jr., a West Coast hamburger chain. I was pumped because I loved hamburgers and the concept of being paid to eat as many hamburgers as I wanted sounded pretty good to my teenage mind. I also got a speaking part this time, biting into a burger and yelling "I've got taste!" over and over.

By the fourth hour, I was ready to vomit. My costar, a new local L.A. newscaster named Regis Philbin, was clearly a pro. After every bite he'd yell, "I've got taste!" and spit his mouthful of burger into a bucket he had strategically hidden underneath his chair. I had a lot to learn.

The commercial ran relentlessly that spring and did wonders for my social standing at school. Even some of the cool surfer set would call out "I've got taste!" when we passed in the halls. It wasn't quite enough juice for them to let me paddle out and try my hand at surfing (they'd still beat the shit out of me) or to earn a seat on the back of the bus, but it was a start. And I'd take it.

Everyone knows that the teenage years are a time of profound emotion. The moody, exuberant, passionate, lethargic teen is a figure that has a special place in the hall of fame of clichés—and for good reason. It's all true. When we ourselves are teenagers, we are living life as it comes. There is no point in reflection. We are so inexperienced, there is very little to reflect on. If we fail a big test, we just move on. We win an award and we smile and say thank you. We fall in love and it's a thrill. We get our hearts broken and we suffer. And we feel all of these highs and lows in our absolute core; it feels as if it's never happened to anyone else because it's never happened to *us* before. Only later can we look back in the comfort that perspective brings.

I'm writing this looking out the window at my younger son playing with his dog, David. He is exactly the same age I was at this point in this narrative. Every parent feels that wondrous, prideful pang when they see glimpses of themselves in their children. I'm no different. I'm looking at him now rolling on the grass, backlit by the afternoon sun. He is a boy-man, wanting everything the world has to offer and ready for none of it. Wanting a girl, with no idea of how to get one. Wanting to make a mark in the world but unsure of how to do it. I look at my boy and I'm looking at myself. I want to run out into the yard and tell my young self that it's okay, all will be revealed in time. I want to give the advice I know he needs to hear. And on the occasions when I do talk to my boys about love, career, family, and all of life's unknowable mysteries, I realize that I am also talking to myself. And I wonder: Would my life have turned out differently had I had this perspective?

My first love was Corrie, a china-blue-eyed blonde with a rosebud mouth. She, for some reason, had gone totally undiscovered by the ruling class in spite of her archetypal beach-bunny credentials. But that was good news for me, as there was no competition for this overlooked beauty. I was stunned when she indicated that she was interested in me. I was about to graduate from Malibu Park Junior High School, and she was a year behind me. Looking back, I realize that probably gave me a leg up.

It was intense and full throttle from the get-go, the kind of euphoric mutual connection that I hope my boys will not have to suffer. Every spare moment was spent together, and we drove our parents crazy shuttling us the fifteen or so miles to each other's houses. I was a fifteen-year-old walking hormone. And after years of disinterest from most of the female set, I couldn't quite believe that a girl like her could like a guy like me, someone who never really fit in. But she did—and it changed my life forever.

❖

The pilot comes on to tell us that we are at our cruising altitude of thirty-five thousand feet. I look around the plane and I want to throw myself out an exit and plummet to the ground. I am on my way to my annual sojourn in Ohio and I am miserable. I want to be back in Malibu with my new girlfriend. It is torture to go a full day without seeing her and now I'm to be gone for five weeks! I am sentenced to a summer of tennis in 90 percent humidity and walks to the Dairy Queen with my brother, while she will be lying out topless on the beach or sunbathing on her roof, covered in Crisco, while the local sheriff's helicopter circles her house. That scenario would make even Hugh Hefner insecure.

After a week back in Dayton, I'm dying. Even my ability to consume as many beers as I want doesn't dent my depression and longing. Corrie and I talk on the phone, but she's rarely home—it's the summer in Malibu after all. I'm stuck inside, avoiding the midwestern humidifying oven outside, staring at the phone, waiting for the moment we can connect.

Finally, the phone rings. It's my agent. He tells me there is an open audition (i.e., cattle call) for a new TV series I might be right for. If I can fly myself back to L.A. next week, he can get me to read for the producers. I jump at the chance. "One way or another, I'm coming back," I say.

My dad and mom have a moment of détente and take pity on me. They okay my return. As I pack to fly back to L.A., I'm giddy with excitement. This is what I've been dreaming of, what I've been wishing for with such passion. I'm going home to my girlfriend. And, oh yeah, I'm also going to audition for a new TV series. It's called *A New Kind of Family*. It is for ABC and the story focuses on two divorcées and their young kids sharing the same house. (Years later, this exact premise will be redone to great success in *Kate & Allie*.) I have never had a proper audition. For commercials, they basically just ogle you and send you home. Now I will have to attempt the horrific gauntlet that is The Hollywood Audition.

Apparently there is not yet a script, so for my reading I am given a scene from *Happy Days*. I will be reading the part of Richie Cunningham in a scene where he has a malt with Fonzie. Obviously, this has absolutely nothing to do with the premise of the new show or the character I would be playing. But what the hell? They're the experts, right?

Back in Malibu, if I'm not at the beach with Corrie, I'm studying my lines. I have no coach, no feedback from anyone whatsoever. I don't run lines with anyone and I prepare just like I have been since the days of Peanut Butter and Jelly. I also am still so green that I'm blessed by ignorance of the odds against me. There are probably hundreds of actors auditioning for this part and very likely there is a "list" of ten actors that the producers are likely to cast. I am too inexperienced to know that getting this part is akin to walking into a 7-Eleven, buying a lottery ticket, and winning the Powerball.

Mom is behind the wheel of our shitty Volvo, making a rare journey into the toxic summer smog of L.A. Although I am sometimes pissed that she won't give me a lift into Hollywood, I secretly admire that she finds it just as important to drive my little brother Micah to a playdate as to facilitate my budding career. My mom will never be in the ranks of eight-by-ten-clutching, armchair-directing, aggressively hustling stage mothers who haunt every waiting room in show business. Hers is a different kind of support. From her I get ownership of my own life and a confidence to go my own way. On occasions like today, when it is really important, she will hold my hand. But mostly she guides me from the sidelines, quietly. And the message to me is: *This game is yours to win*.

In Hollywood, it works like this: You don't get an audition for anything unless you have an agent. He or she gets a call from a casting director who is working for producers who are casting a role written by a writer. In movies, the writer is weak and has little to no say about anything having to do with the script they wrote. The producers have a big say (executive producers do not) and the director has the final word. However, in recent times, all of these players have been trumped by the desires of the "foreign sales" and "marketing" departments. These are the sole entities that choose the actors in 95 percent of all movies made today. In television, the writer is king, the director is weak and the producers are grunts, and the executive producers hold the power. Some executive producers write as well and that makes them "show runners," and they truly rule the TV roost. However, once they make a decision, they go to their bosses for approval, the vice presidents in charge of programming (although the actual title for this position changes year to year and network to network), who then vet everything for the head of the network, who is God.

So, if you are looking to get a part in a movie or TV show, regardless of how big or small the part might be, it is wise to think of yourself in a live-action version of the arcade game Frogger. Any one of these layers of folks can blindside you out of contention for any reason at all, and you must navigate your way over and beyond each gatekeeper you encounter. As I make my way through this process on *A New Kind of Family*, I, of course, have no concept of the agendas and personal fiefdoms I am conquering along the way. I just practice the same principles I use to this day. I know my lines, I give the character a point of view, and I keep it honest.

Mom pulls the Volvo into the headquarters of ABC, then located in Century City and known to me as the location of future earth in *Planet of the Apes*. We are early, so we get a soda and wait in the giant three-story lobby.

"How do you feel, Robbie?"

"Good."

"You want to practice?" (My mom always said "practice," like I was a baton twirler.)

"I'm okay, thanks," I say, as out of the corner of my eye I see the casting director approaching.

"You ready?"

I nod. Mom gives me a hug and I follow the casting director through giant double doors. As I walk away from my mother I am also walking away from my childhood. When I come out of those big doors, I will have a full-time job, and that job will subject me to pressures and scrutiny that some adults never face. It will fulfill my dreams and break my heart and lead me to experiences beyond imagining. I will never be the same. I'm fifteen years old; my life is just beginning.

## CHAPTER 7

The tiny agency that represents me has another young client who has just landed a big role. She lives in New York, is around my age, and is going to be in California for some meetings. My agent arranges for us to have lunch. My relationship with Corrie is the extent of my "dating," so I'm a little nervous even though this is not a romantic meeting. Any time a young teenager spends with a member of the opposite sex is fraught with expectations. Will she like me? Will I like her? Is she cute? Will she think I'm cute? What if I make a fool of myself?

The scouting report says that she's an extremely smart musical-theater actress who is taking Broadway by storm as the new "Annie." Those are big heels to fill, so she's gotta have some serious game. I'm nervous to meet her. I'm just one of four kids in a TV family but she's fuckin' Annie! After more consideration than you would use to choose the location of a multinational war council, I decide to host young Annie at a local Malibu restaurant called Paradise Cove—famous to me because I lost my virginity on the nearby beach, possibly famous to Annie because it is the home of Jim Rockford's trailer in the legendary TV show *The Rockford Files*. I also bring my girlfriend with me because I am an idiot.

My mom drops Corrie and me off at the restaurant and I see my agent waiting outside.

"Hi, Rob. Glad you could do this. She's excited to meet you."

"Same here," I say.

"Who's this?" my agent asks, with a smile.

"This is Corrie, my girlfriend."

"Oh."

I can't tell if my agent disapproves; it will take me years to understand the inner workings of agents.

"Well, come on in. She's waiting."

Sitting in a corner booth is a curly-haired, brown-eyed, slender girl with a shy smile.

"Hi, I'm Rob. This is Corrie. I've heard a lot about you."

"You too," she said. "I'm Sarah. Nice to meet you."

Soon we are eating french fries and talking shop. I am in awe of Broadway and can only imagine how difficult it must be to play a role like hers. Of course I mention nothing of my musical-theater experience in Peanut Butter and Jelly, instinctively knowing that I am in no position to compete in a "credit swap."

"How old are you?" I ask.

"Fifteen."

"Do you have a . . . a boyfriend or anything?"

"Not really," she says, glancing quickly at Corrie, who has been bored to death by our conversation. I begin to feel guilty. Corrie is a normal kid. She can't relate to Sarah and me. Why would she? She stays quiet as two young actors connect over a mutual passion.

As we say good-bye, Sarah takes my arm.

"Will you do this forever, you think?"

"Do what forever?"

"Acting, silly."

"I don't know. I hope so. What about you?"

"It's what I love," she says, her eyes glowing with sweet intensity. "I hope I can do it forever."

She says this with a solemnity that is so honest that it moves me. "Or at least until I'm an adult!" she adds, laughing.

We hug a good-bye and, as my agent drives her away, I wonder if I will ever see her again.

Twenty-one years later, I'm at the Golden Globes ceremony, nominated for Best Performance by an Actor in a Television Series—Drama for *The West Wing*. I don't win that night, and while I'm disappointed, I'm thrilled when Sarah Jessica Parker does win for her smash, *Sex and the City*. She said she wanted to do it forever, I remember as she walks up to the podium.

❖

There is not much to compare with the uproar that a successful child actor can cause in his family. Forget the esoteric touchy-feely discussions of the pluses and minuses of teen fame. The simple, logistical hurdles will kill you. What about school? Who is going to drive you back and forth? State law requires a legal guardian to be with you at all times; which family member will that be or do you hire someone to do it? If so, how do you find someone you can trust? My mom and Steve agonize over these decisions as Corrie and I celebrate the fact that I won't be going back to Ohio and . . . I just might become a TV star.

I cram as much time as I can hanging out at Little Dume Beach with my friends before I start shooting the show. Corrie

lathers on the Crisco oil, in her tiny leopard-print bikini. My
buddies and I just laugh and boogie board. The Surf Crew, now
calling themselves the Point Dume Bombers, are not impressed
with my new job and still threaten to pummel me whenever they
think I might try to actually learn to surf. I may become famous,
but I ain't gonna become a surfer.

My mom's commitment to giving all her boys equal attention
prevents her from spending twelve hours a day sitting on a set with
me while I shoot. Chad and Micah have schoolwork and Little
League and all the other activities of boys their ages. When Mom
isn't holed up for hours mysteriously writing God knows what in
her office, she wants to be at home for her two younger sons.
After meeting a number of candidates for the job as my guardian (including one of the Penn boys; I don't remember which
one, Sean or Michael, but one of them wanted to try acting and
thought being on set would be a good way to learn), we settle on
a big, shaggy-haired Bostonian named Clark. He drives a ridiculous old cruise-ship Cutlass, complete with big swatches of primer
paint prominently displayed across its body. We will make quite an
impression as we roll up to the soundstage. Clark is a huge sports
fan and not averse to buying my friends and me the odd six-pack
of Coors. I'm not sure what my mom's criteria for a guardian were,
but he certainly met mine.

The next step in organizing my life as a working child actor
was dealing with my education. I was always a fairly good student
with better-than-average grades. I actually liked learning (which
did nothing to help my social standing), so I hoped that I would
be able to easily handle the transition from school to private on-
set tutoring, which law required to be a minimum of three hours
a day. I was due to start high school in the fall (Santa Monica
High began with sophomore year) and I would have to get their
permission to stay enrolled while working. Many kid actors opt
to drop out of traditional school to avoid the difficulties of social

reassimilation and inevitable academic catch-up. I wanted to go to the same school as all my friends and be as normal as I could. After much wrangling, "Samohi" begrudgingly let me stay enrolled and accepted the state-sanctioned tutor as a legitimate proxy.

Rolling up to the soundstage for my first day, I feel the light-headed electric pulse that I imagine is common to any kind of dream fulfillment. A little over three years ago, I was a kid in Dayton, Ohio, having my showbiz illusions shattered by an aide-de-camp of Telly Savalas but still fantasizing about life as an actor. Now I'm about to work my first day as one of the stars of a show on ABC.

I meet the other actors and they all seem nice. The *real* star of the show is Eileen Brennan, a dry and very funny actress, who just finished filming her role in the soon-to-be hit movie *Private Benjamin*. I will play her son Tony. My TV brother is David Hollander, a show-business veteran, who has already starred in countless commercials and episodes of big TV shows as well as movies, including the current hit *Airplane!* Lauri Hendler, a savvy back-talker, is typecast as my savvy, back-talking younger sister. In a harbinger of things to come, I will play the good-looking, vaguely uninteresting, and extremely underwritten straight-man (boy) part.

The other family that will share the house with us consists of a beautiful brunette, who is known for being married in real life to the commander on the hit TV show *CHiPs*, and her daughter, played by a cute blonde who appears utterly uninterested in any form of acting whatsoever.

I'm given an embossed red script binder with the title of the show on the lower right-hand corner. I receive it as if I'm being handed an original copy of the Magna Carta. We read through the script, try on wardrobe, and then are assigned dressing rooms, which is like being given the best clubhouse any fifteen-year-old could ask for, complete with a phone! I'm introduced to the wonder of a stiff cup of coffee and a selection of twenty kinds of doughnuts every morning, a love affair that continues to this day. I learn the hierarchy of the set, who does what, and where my proper place is in the army of two hundred people it takes to make an episode of television. For the first time in my life, I do not feel "different." Even though I'm as green as a pine, I feel the satisfaction of fitting in—of *belonging*.

The lessons are coming fast and furiously. During a rehearsal I "step" on one of Eileen Brennan's lines (which means that I start talking before she's done with her line) and she gives me a withering look. I will never make that mistake again. I watch as she navigates the role of "star." One day she reads the latest script and goes ballistic, demanding the producers and writers come to the set for a script meeting. We are sent to our makeshift classroom as a very heated and tension-filled meeting goes on outside. It will be years before I properly appreciate the pressure she is under and how necessary it is for the star to fight every day (if they can) for the best writing possible. Eileen didn't win many of those battles on *A New Kind of Family*, as most actors don't, and I'm sure the show suffered for it. Most actors are very good judges of what "works," and yet they are always at the mercy of writers or producers, who can label them "difficult" or "divas." Meanwhile, if the show flops, it's always the star who takes the most blame. Which is not to say that there aren't moronic actors out there who will ruin *Citizen Kane* if given half the chance. But in general, I've learned, an actor who's made it to a certain level knows what works for him or her better than anyone else.

❖

*A New Kind of Family* was filmed before a studio audience of about two hundred people. They were tourists and folks off the street who were by turns excited and bored by the endless filming from seven thirty to midnight each Friday. When they could no longer be counted on to laugh at the jokes, a man would throw candy at them, which they would devour, and then they would cackle like hyenas, high on sugar.

A sit-com is basically a filmed play. You even have a curtain call (although unlike with a play, it comes at the beginning before you film). Even though it was my first big job, I had done enough theater to make me comfortable in front of the camera. We filmed six episodes leading up to our actual air date, and in early September 1979, our show debuted at 7:30 p.m. on Sunday night on ABC. I was too unsophisticated to realize that we had been put in the "death slot" opposite the number one show in all of television, CBS's ratings juggernaut *60 Minutes.*

They crushed us. I mean it was a bloodletting. There were lots of tense long faces the next week as we prepped our next episode. I was too young to understand the pressure. I was living my dream.

It's Friday night. The studio audience is full. The Doobie Brothers' "I Keep Forgettin'" is blasting over the PA system. This is the week we will turn it around. This is the show we will *kill it.* It is also the first episode we've taped since our show's debut. I come out for my preshow curtain call and the crowd erupts. They go absolutely bat-shit crazy. Up until this point, I've been greeted with midlevel, warm applause, so I'm stunned. I look around, not sure that this ovation is for me. Maybe the actual star, Eileen Brennan, is standing behind me. But she's not.

The cameras roll. I enter. Bedlam. I hear for the first time in my life that particular, unique, high-pitched, piercing, hissing, sonic screech that is the sound of screaming teenage girls. We play the scene. Every time I open my mouth the girls go ape. Just last Friday I was happy if I got a big laugh. This Friday, after one show on the air, I can't get one laugh because my new fans won't shut up! It is a stark lesson in the power of television.

Eileen Brennan, being a consummate comedienne and veteran actress, is having none of this. I can see in her eyes that she's livid. I hope she's not pissed at me; I'm just trying to get through the scenes. Finally, it's over and no one knows quite what to make of what has just happened. For my part, I'm at once shell-shocked, embarrassed, and (in truth) loving every minute of it.

As Clark and I arrive for work the next day, I head off to the makeshift classroom for my daily on-set schooling. I'm studying my tenth-grade French when a production assistant stops by with my very first fan letter.

"Here ya go, Rob. Got a bunch more up at the offices."

I don't know what to say, it's all new. Someone has written a fan letter to *me*.

"Oh, and one more thing . . . from now on, no one under the age of eighteen will be allowed in the studio audience," he says mildly as he heads out.

I don't know whether to be upset or even whom to be upset with. I *do* know that this new edict marks the end of my ear-splitting receptions. I turn my attention to my fan letter. I open it carefully, excited to read it.

Dear Mr. Rob Lowe:

I enjoyed you very much on the TV show The New Kind of Family. You are a great actor. Can you please send me an auto-graphed photo of yourself? If possible in a bathing suit or in your underwear.
Sincerely,

Michael LeBron
#4142214 Pelican Bay Prison

In our second week, our ratings are even worse. (Although today any network would absolutely kill to have our numbers. In

1979, if fourteen million people watched you, you were at death's door. Today, a huge smash like *Two and a Half Men* averages about that.) Our executive producers are two smart and energetic women, both of whom are married to powerful husbands who run movie studios. This is their first big producing job, and they go on the offensive to boost our ratings, orchestrating a press barrage, personal appearances, and a trip to New York to compete against actors on other ABC shows on *The $10,000 Pyramid*. (That's right, *The $10,000 Pyramid*—can you imagine that amount of prize money today? You've made it all the way to the final rounds and you've won *almost* enough to buy a used car!)

The network doesn't want to be known as a home for idiot actors, so they gather their young stars for a "game show" audition, to pick out who goes to New York. I religiously watch *Pyramid* and am no slouch at charades, trivia, or similes (thanks, Mom), so I'm chosen to go to New York.

On the big day, I draw a cute twenty-something actress from *Eight Is Enough* as my partner. We will play Tony Danza, a young ex-boxer who is a huge hit on the smash comedy *Taxi*, and a sultry brunette, about my age, from ABC's other big new comedy hope, *Out of the Blue*, starring some young comedian the network thinks will be the next Robin Williams. (He won't be.)

I love Dick Clark, the host of *Pyramid* and already a TV legend—and I will continue to. But the man is absolutely mangling my introduction.

"Ladies and gentlemen, please welcome Ron Loeb!"

I stop. He stops. I go back to enter again.

"Ladies and gentlemen, Rob Lone!"

This goes on for a good ten minutes until finally the game begins. The woman from *Eight Is Enough* reads me the clues.

"Okay, um, okay . . . it's . . . it's . . . something the astronauts . . ."

"TANG!" I shriek.

*Ding!* Yessss. I don't know what's gotten into me; I'm in the kill zone and I can't miss.

"Okay . . . okay . . . um . . . um . . . It's a . . . It's a . . . um . . . they're really old. They are really old . . . um . . ."

"THE PYRAMIDS!" I yell. Come on, girlfriend, we've got ten grand to win.

*Ding!*

We easily beat Danza and his little minx partner in straight rounds. At the final round in the Winner's Circle, I figure we have to cut our times down. I'm treating this celebrity charity show like it's Wimbledon.

"Let me give the clues."

"You sure?" says Eight Is Enough.

"Yes."

Dick Clark has my name right now. "Rob, for ten thousand dollars, here is your first clue . . . GO!"

It appears in the screen in front of me.

"Founding Father. Flew kite."

"Benjamin Franklin!"

*Ding!*

"Cordoba."

"Ricardo Montalbán!"

*Ding!*

And so it goes. We win with ten seconds to spare.

I donate my winnings to the Cleveland Amory Fund for Animals and the Wilderness Society. As we all squeeze together for the "good-bye shot," Tony Danza's young partner surreptitiously puts her hand on my backside. And keeps it there. "See you on the plane," she whispers.

On the flight home, I have what is to be the first in a long series of lessons about the temptations of actresses. Although Corrie's waiting back in Malibu, the excitement and glamour of the enfolding romantic drama in the first-class cabin quickly over-power my fifteen-year-old male willpower. What happens on the plane isn't anywhere near Erica Jong territory, but I'm definitely not going to be sharing any traveling stories with my girlfriend.

❖

Back in L.A., the battle to save our show continues. I'm sent to Riverside, California, for a personal appearance. Even at fifteen I don't see how walking through the Riverside fairgrounds will boost our ratings enough to put a dent in *60 Minutes*. But I like snow cones as much as the next guy, especially when they are free. So, off I go.

There is a line of mostly young girls waiting to get autographs. This time I am on the other end of the line, and I'm not sure what the protocol is. I make a rookie mistake.

Dear Marie-Sue:

Thanks for watching *A New Kind of Family*. I hope you like it. Good luck at UCLA in the fall. Go Bruins!
All my love,

Rob Lowe

I will learn that this is not the way it's done—too much time, too many people to get through. In spite of wanting to connect personally, you have to keep it simple. "Just write Marie-Sue and sign your name," the network handler tells me afterward.

Later, on the way to the car, I see them. They are swarming, gathering in the shadow of the Tilt-A-Whirl, twenty to thirty girls who look to be between twelve and sixteen years old. They are whispering, pointing, and staring at me. One starts to shake. Another lets out a sort of whimper and runs with her feet in place like she has to go to the bathroom. Another pushes the girls in front of her to the ground and runs toward me. The girl on the ground screams, then they *all* scream; low at first, then building to a point where it sounds like a sonic knitting needle is puncturing my eardrum. And then . . . they charge. I don't know it yet, but I will come to learn that being charged on the African savannah by a rhino is only fractionally more dangerous than being bull-rushed by a gang of fourteen-year-old girls whipped into a lather by hormones, group think, and an overdose of *Tiger Beat* magazine.

"Hi there," is about all I manage before they are all over me. One girl grabs me by the arm, another by the hair. One girl is literally untying my shoes while another steals the laces. The network representative does nothing. "I bet this doesn't happen to Morley Safer," he says. I can only hope this kind of mauling will help our ratings, but something tells me it won't.

On the long drive back from Riverside, I have a lot of time to ponder the conflicting emotions welling up in me. On the one hand, how cool is it to be mobbed by a bunch of girls my age? It's any guy's dream, right? And it is part and parcel of being a star. Right? All true, more or less. But on the other hand, the whole experience feels a little shitty. And feeling shitty about something that's meant to be exciting makes me feel worse. The girls' reactions seemed almost programmed, like they were both the performers and the audience in a teen-angst drama that had nothing to do with me. It certainly wasn't about what a good actor I was. And if I was such a hottie to them, why didn't I have the same effect on those who knew me well at school? And so the first wisps of an idea appear on the horizons of my consciousness. And the idea is this: If you *really* knew me, you wouldn't like me nearly as much.

## CHAPTER 8

The network has shut down our show. It's not canceled, they say, it's on a "creative hiatus." I have no idea what that means, but the practical ramification is that I get to make my first appearance in a real high school.

I still don't have my learner's permit, so I take the bus the twenty-two miles from Point Dume to Santa Monica High. It's a huge monolith of a school, with thousands of students of all races, backgrounds, and economic standings. There are also gangs, although not on the level of rival school Venice High, a few miles down the road. I have a lot to navigate, particularly coming in a few weeks after everyone else, and it doesn't help that Corrie and I are having trouble. She watched *Pyramid* and saw the cute actress put her hand on me. She has retaliated against my tacit flirtation on national television by hanging out with a rough, young surfer (who will in later years become Malibu's resident paparazzo, causing Barbra Streisand to take out a restraining order against him). It is the beginning of the end for us.

If I was expecting a reception from the girls at "Samohi" like the one I received in Riverside, I was mistaken. When I walk the "Quad," there is no indication that my TV career was noticed. The Mexicans don't care, the whites don't care, the blacks don't care, and the Malibu kids never cared. Part of me is disappointed and part of me is relieved. I am just like any other sophomore newbie. I dive into the subjects I love (history, marine biology, French) and grind it out in the ones I don't (anything math-related). I spend time with my small clique and try to fit in with this huge new pool of faces. And, I wait. I know our show's fate is hanging in the balance, but I try not to think about it.

Soon, I get the call to come back to work. As Clark drives the harrowing road between the Pacific Coast Highway and the 405 freeway that has killed so many truckers, I notice that he seems out of it. When he passes a car by driving on the shoulder of the road, I know something's up.

"You okay?" I ask.

"Mmmm. Long night. Sorry."

We pull up to the soundstage, and I can see all the producers and even some network executives milling around. We are late, so Clark pulls right up to them at the stage entrance. I open my door and wave hello. Clark opens his door and vomits on his shoes.

It's all downhill from there.

As I get my usual morning coffee and doughnuts, I notice a young black girl with pretty eyes grabbing the last glazed twist.

"Hi. I'm Janet."

"Hi. I'm Rob."

"Nice to meet you. Have you met Telma yet?"

"Who?"

"Telma! C'mon. I'll take you to say hi."

I have no clue who this girl is or why she's on our set. But I go with her to meet Telma, who turns out to be a tall, dark beauty who could be Janet's mother. It is then that I notice that the two actors who play the members of the other family living with us on the show aren't anywhere to be seen.

"Have you guys met Gwyn and Connie?" I ask.

They both look at me blankly as a production assistant ushers us to our seats around the table where we read through the scripts.

Janet and Telma sit in the seats usually occupied by the two missing actors. What's going on here? As we read the first scene it all becomes clear. Janet and Telma are replacing the missing actors. In the script there is no explanation of what happened to the original family that was living with us, or why these new folks have moved in. To this day, I have no idea what happened. I can only assume someone at the network felt that our ratings would improve with the more dramatic concept of a black and a white family living together. Amazingly, they thought viewers would simply accept the switch without even a good-bye to the previous family.

Janet comes from a big family with a ton of show business savvy. She is painfully shy but we are about the same age and we become confidants. On the day when our show is mercifully canceled, we console each other.

"I'm done with acting," she says.

Ever the optimist, I fill her head with a rosy vision of her acting future.

"I tell you, I'm done. I'm going into music. If my brothers can do it, so can I."

I wish her luck, hug her and the rest of the cast good-bye, pack up my dressing room, and leave. *A New Kind of Family* shot thirteen episodes, five of which aired in 1979. *60 Minutes* survives to this day. Next to me as I write this is today's newspaper. In it, I see a photo of my old friend Janet. The caption reads, "Janet Jackson sells out opening night of new world tour."

⌗

You think star athletes have a tough re-entry when they retire? Try going from endless free doughnuts, screaming girls, and a starring role on television to tenth-grade driver's ed. It's almost as if my show never happened. It certainly didn't lead me to any new jobs, at least temporarily disproving the old adage about just getting your foot in the door. In fact, with money so tight at home, I go back to work on the weekends as a busboy at the Nantucket Light. (You'd think I could have at least landed a gig as a waiter.) On the positive side: It's easy to keep your head on straight when you are signing an autograph while clearing someone's lobster dinner. I go back to the life of any other teenager, except for the few times when someone yells out *"A New Kind of Family!"* while I'm getting gas or walking down the street. But that is very rare. I guess our bad ratings didn't lie.

Back at school, friends are trying out for the school's tennis and baseball teams. Charlie Sheen has an absolute bazooka for an arm and wants to be a pro ballplayer. We are constantly in his backyard batting cage or playing "tennis ball baseball," the Malibu version of stickball. Every once in a while his dad, Martin, will join us, cigarette dangling from his mouth, and completely crush a ball out of the park. He laughs at us and then, maddeningly, runs the bases backward. Charlie's brother, Emilio, still wants to be an actor, and has taken their original family name, Estevez, to ensure he is not riding his dad's coattails. Emilio is a few years older than me; he's got a car and is really making the rounds, auditioning for tons of roles. Charlie and I (and often my brother Chad) still make the occasional 8 mm movie together, but now that I've been to the "bigs" I see little point in backyard movies. I'm a pro now; I'm moving forward—not backward.

My mom's health has taken a turn for the worse. She is in bed most days, and even when she's up and about, she remains in her pajamas. I hate seeing her like this, in the grips of something she can neither understand nor explain. Both she and Steve feel her bad spells are from reactions to everything from smog, perfume, household cleansers, mold, and food, to air-conditioning, paint, dust, water, and plastics. We finally replace our terrible Volvo and the new car sits outside the garage, all windows open for six weeks "outgasing" before Mom will enter the vehicle. She doesn't use her oxygen mask and gardening gloves to ward off the "fumes" like she used to, but instead has become a sort of recluse. There are never dinner parties at our house. She and Steve do not entertain friends. They don't go out to dinner or the movies. Mom remains a whip-smart conversationalist, a lover of books, and a loyal supporter of my brother and me, and from time to time she even surprises us with her former adventurous spirit. But mostly, she's just checked out, and I miss her. To this day, I have a terrible, visceral reaction to a woman in pajamas.

When engaged, my mom is a fairly astute advisor, but she's got two younger kids to worry about and she's battling her own issues. Dad is two thousand miles away. So there is no "career planning." There is no "Team Lowe," full of lawyers, agents, publicists, personal trainers, and the like that would today assemble around a fifteen-year-old kid with a little bit of success under his belt. There's just me.

Eventually, however, I'm "poached" from my little agency (where I was one of the few up-and-comers, despite my current status in the hospitality business) by a much larger, more sophisticated agency. That's the way it works in show business (and in life); if you have some success, you often outgrow those who were there in the beginning, but you give them a shot to grow with you. If they can't—or won't—you move on.

My new representatives are able to get me my first movie

auditions. Now I am competing with kids who have much more experience, most of whom are over eighteen and, by law, able to work full-time on the set without any child-labor restrictions. Like for a boxer moving up a weight class, the prize will be bigger, but I'm not sure I can compete. My first movie audition is for a film about the music business in the late 1950s called *The Idol-maker*. I don't even make it past the first meeting.

My boss at the Nantucket Light is not impressed with the odd tourist asking for an autograph and eventually fires me for my ongoing penchant for pilfering the occasional mud pie. I protest that I'm hardly the only dessert thief in the busboy ranks, but to no avail. My spirits are lifted, however, when ABC signs me to a holding deal (which means that they will keep me "in house" until they figure out what to do with me). It's not a ton of money, but it's enough to buy my first car, which I do, on my sixteenth birthday, a white Mazda 626.

It's a lifesaver on the one hand—now I don't take the bus for two and a half hours every day to school—and a curse on the other, as Mom has me driving my little brother Micah to and from kindergarten. It's hard to look cool in your new car with your six-year-old brother in the backseat. I am also delegated to grocery store duty, which I hate with a passion. I stagger around the Mayfair Market for hours trying to find all the obscure items on my mother's list. But it still beats pulling the weeds out of our gravel front yard by hand.

Each day at lunch, I check the bulletin board just off the Quad to see if my agents have an audition for me. Finally I do land my next job. It's a test show or pilot for a possible new TV series on ABC called *Thrills and Chills*. It's about a family of animal trainers, acrobats, and daredevils that form their own traveling circus. I play the young, crazy motorcycle jumper—think a teen Evel Knievel in spandex.

The first day on the set, the director, Ron Howard, who was at that point still playing Richie Cunningham on *Happy Days*, takes me aside. He's only directed once before, a low-budget B-movie called *Grand Theft Auto*, and he seems as nervous as I am.

"Rob, I need you to really tear out on the bike after your last line. I mean as fast as you can, really crank it," he asks.

I'm cooking like a sausage in my skintight purple spandex, but with this request my blood runs cold. Clearly no one has told him that I can't ride a motorcycle (I only just learned how to drive a car!), let alone "really crank it." I always assumed a stunt double would do the motorcycle work. I break the news to Ron with as much dignity as I can muster. In a mark of what a great director he will become, he just smiles, reassures me, and figures out another way to shoot the scene. I say my last line, something like, "Let me show you what this baby can do! Outta my way!" and two elderly crew members hiding just off camera attempt to roll me out of the frame. It seems to take forever.

*Thrills and Chills* never made it on the air. (It never made it onto Ron Howard's filmography, either.) To my knowledge, the producers didn't even bother to show it to anyone. I've certainly never seen it. Although he's always gracious when we meet and is one of my favorite directors, I've never worked again for Ron Howard.

⚜

In a way, ABC's *Afterschool Specials* were ahead of their time. They could definitely be cheesy, but they dealt with taboo issues like drug addiction, anorexia, and teen pregnancy. And they got great ratings. For a brief and shining moment, I was the King of the Afterschool Special. I did a number of them under my ABC contract, the best being "Schoolboy Father." In it, I had a baby out of wedlock with the tortured and ill-fated young actress Dana Plato, from *Diff'rent Strokes*. I think it won some sort of Daytime Emmy Award, although honestly I'm not sure. I've long since dropped it from my résumé, mainly because I don't want to be reminded of my David Cassidy hairdo.

A night I will never forget: watching "Schoolboy Father" with my then would-be girlfriend's father. My romance with Corrie had fizzled out. I had set my sights on a stunning doe-eyed brunette named Jennifer whom I had met along the beach at the Malibu Colony. My lack of mojo with girls has been fairly well documented in the previous pages, but with some early acting successes and a driver's license to boot, I had upped my game. Nonetheless, I was intimidated. Jennifer attended an elite private school and her mom, Dyan Cannon, starred with Warren Beatty in one of my all-time favorite movies, *Heaven Can Wait*. Warren Beatty was a hero of mine: funny, smart, romantic, and great in both comedy and drama. He was the real deal.

Jennifer had an on-again, off-again boyfriend who was something of a tough-guy idiot. He was just the latest in a string of guys who never cut me any slack, so when he lipped off to Jennifer one day at the Malibu Colony beach, I lit him up, yelling, "Why don't you shut the fuck up and leave her alone." The next thing I knew, we were rolling around on the ground and people were pulling us apart. Jennifer must have appreciated the chivalry because when, a few days later, I gathered up my nerve and asked her out, she said yes. (It was like a plot from one of my *Afterschool Specials*!) "Schoolboy Father" was going to air the following week, and Jennifer suggested that I come to her dad's house in Beverly Hills so that we could watch it together. I was hoping for Dyan Cannon's house, but whatever.

It's the first time I drive on my own from Malibu into L.A. The Pacific Coast Highway is always a potential death trap, and as I transition up Sunset Boulevard, I feel a surge of accomplishment. When I make it to Beverly Hills, I look for the prettiest yard I can find, pull over, steal some flowers, and make my way up the winding road to the top of Benedict Canyon to Jennifer's father's house.

Cary Grant greets me at the front door in a white terry cloth bathrobe. I have a vague awareness that Jen's father is an old-time movie actor, but I'm ashamed to say that I knew more about "Cary Granite" from *The Flintstones* than Cary Grant the Film Icon. In my defense, he hadn't made a movie since I was an infant.

"Hell-o, young maaan. Jenn-i-fer is in her room. Would you like some milk?" he says in his Cary Grant voice. He leads me through a stunning white-on-white modern home with breath-taking views of the city.

"Are you in Jenn-i-fer's graa-ade?" he asks.

"No, sir. I go to Samohi."

"Aaaah, well. I see," he says, as if making some sort of calculation.

We walk into an all black-and-white kitchen, with industrial stainless steel appliances. He grabs two glasses and moves to the single best design feature ever put in a home—a restaurant-style milk dispenser protruding from the front of a gigantic refrigerator. I want to stick my face under it.

"Here you go, young maaan," he says, filling our cups.

Later, he and Jennifer introduce me to the wonders of shepherd's pie, handmade by Cary's beautiful young wife, Barbara. It instantly becomes one of my favorite dishes. To this day, I've never had better.

Cary and Barbara leave Jennifer and me in private. We talk about our schools and people we know and we laugh, but there is not going to be anything romantic between us. It feels more like a friendship. Soon, it's time for my show to air, so we head to the biggest TV in the house, the one in Cary's bedroom. Jennifer and I sit at the foot of the big bed. I'm still not used to seeing myself on TV and I'm nervous.

Just as the show begins, Cary pops his head in. "Young maaan, would you mind if I watched with you?"

"Not at all," I say, proving unequivocally that ignorance is bliss. And so, the single greatest movie star of all time takes a seat with us to watch a sixteen-year-old rookie in his first starring role.

When the show is over, I'm not quite sure what to think. (This sort of reaction continues; only rarely do I know right away how I feel about a finished project.) In Cary Grant's bedroom, as the credits roll, no one says a word. Then, finally, from Cary, "Young maaan, you're quite goood. You remind me very much of a young Warren Beatty."

Driving away, down his long, winding driveway, I suddenly see him, running down the hill, chasing me in the big, white bathrobe. "Young maaan! Young maaan!" he calls, rushing up to my driver's-side window.

"I thought you might like to have these!" he says, slightly out of breath. His arms are filled with products from Fabergé, where he sits on the board. He fills my car with boxes and boxes of Brut aftershave and soap on a rope.

"Thank you, Mr. Grant," I say.

"Enjoy them," he says behind those famous big, black glasses. "Good luck in the moo-vies. You're going to do great."

As I pull away I can still see him in my rearview mirror, standing in the long driveway and waving. I keep my soap on a rope (in the shape of a microphone) for years after.

⚜

When I learn that someone is doing a remake of the Warren Beatty–Natalie Wood classic, *Splendor in the Grass*, Cary Grant's words ring in my ears and I feel I might have some sort of inside track. It will be a television event starring the biggest young actress on TV, Melissa Gilbert, the star of *Little House on the Prairie*, and every young actor wants the Warren part. I read for the legendary casting director Lynn Stalmaster. I think I rocked it, but by the time I've driven back to Malibu, my agents have called; I didn't get the role. Jesus! I'm the right age, I'm the right look, and I had a great audition. I'm perfect for the part, but if I can't even get out of the first round on *this*, what does that say about my future?

When I was in Ohio I could always go to work in a college production of a good play. But there aren't those options available in Los Angeles. I want to act, not audition. I want to continue to learn my craft. But for now what I really need to learn is that there is very little rhyme or reason for who gets what in Hollywood. There are plenty of dedicated, talented actors destined for jobs they hate, chasing in vain a dream that will never come. Soon I'll have to start thinking about college and possibly reconsider my life's direction. I've had just enough success to keep me chasing the dream, but not enough to ensure a career. I promise myself I won't be one of the deluded ones, being the last to know that my moment didn't come, and that I should've hung it up long ago. I'm going to be seventeen soon. Am I already a has-been?

❖

Luckily, I've made some great friends despite the time I've spent on my career. Jeff Abrams and I follow Magic Johnson's arrival in L.A. and shoot hoops whenever we can. Jeff's a huge Bjorn Borg fan, while I'm a Connors man, and we spend hours on the tennis court, attempting to learn the new "topspin" forehand. Along with Chris Steenolsen and Josh Kerns, we hang out and steal booze, go to beach parties and on road trips in Josh's gigantic hand-painted "road beast"—a 1969 Impala. Good students and serious about school, we are hardly pro-level hellions, but we have some fun. Also in our orbit are the Sheen brothers and the Penns. Chris is still making "Nam" movies and Sean is more of an enigma; he's older, into surfing and getting serious about acting himself. In history class I bond with a hilarious, madrigal-singing maniac named Robert Downey Jr. No one is funnier or more brilliant at stream of consciousness banter. Charlie Sheen is also one of a kind. While his brother is serious and always has his eye on the ball, Charlie, a Polo preppy clotheshorse in a world of O.P. shorts and surf T-shirts, is a wonderful mix of nerd (he's a member of the AV club and won't go near the ocean) and rebel (always ready to ditch class to go to the Dodgers game to root for our beloved Reds). He is also a conspiracy-theory freak, who sometimes wears a bulletproof vest under his clothes to school, and together we debate everything from the likelihood that the moon is hollow and whether the trilateral commission killed JFK to the authenticity of the moon landings. Also, coming from Hollywood royalty, he has all the toys you can imagine. At my house we are still saving money by not buying desserts; at Charlie's house, it's never-ending Häagen-Dazs, brand-new BMWs, a lagoon pool with underwater tunnels, and a lit, professional-grade basketball half-court. I sometimes feel like a bit of an Ohio rube with no toys of my own and no access (like Dodgers season tickets) to offer my friends in return for their generosity. No one seems to care or notice except me.

Apparently there is an amazing part in an upcoming movie that Robert Redford is directing. Emilio is preparing for his audition. I hear the mysterious Sean Penn is also gung-ho about the part. They say the role of Connor in *Ordinary People* is the kind of role that changes your life. When I don't even get a meeting on the project, I'm devastated. At a time when all my friends are choosing which colleges to apply to, or finding an easier path in the business than I am, I'm wondering if Hollywood saw what it needed from me and decided I wasn't up to a career of substance or longevity. For the first time since I was an eight-year-old, I start thinking about finding something else to do with my life. Luckily, I've applied to UCLA and USC and have been accepted to both.

A kid named Timothy Hutton gets the Redford movie and it does change his life. He goes from unknown to Academy Award winner in nine months, with one shattering performance. Some of my other peers/competitors are also doing well. Sean Penn is filming a surf high school movie called *Fast Times at Ridgemont High* and then will team up with Tim Hutton for *Taps*. I am unable to get a meeting on either film. Maybe it's time to throw in the towel and be grateful for the amazing adventure I've had. I call my agents to tell them that I'll be enrolling in either USC or UCLA and will be unavailable for any further acting roles. They are disappointed, but understand. When I hang up I feel the loss of all the possibilities I had hoped would come my way. I'd thought that if I worked hard enough and believed hard enough, I could will myself into the life I had wanted for so long. I was wrong. And so I join the ranks of all the other confused, scared seventeen-year-olds standing on the brink of adulthood, looking into the hazy distance for a navigable road to the future.

Then, just after Christmas 1982, my phone rings. My agents are calling with a question: "Do you want to give it one last shot? We've gotten you a reading. We think it could be a big movie. It's called *The Outsiders*."

CHAPTER 9

A vicious winter storm sends driving rain into the streets in front of Francis Ford Coppola's personal movie empire, Zoetrope Studios. Thunder and lightning crackle as I hunker down in my Mazda, parked just outside the front gates. In my hand I have the five-page scene I will be reading. I have it memorized now; anyone would. This will be my fourth audition for *The Outsiders*. Originally I met with Janet Hirshenson, the casting director who was seeing every male actor in Hollywood between the ages of fifteen and thirty. She has been good to me in the past, and even though I have never gotten a job on her watch, she has brought me back whenever she felt I might be right for a part. After I made it past Janet, I read for the film's producer, Fred Roos. Fred cast all of Francis Coppola's early movies as well as George Lucas's. Among the actors whom Fred Roos would discover were Carrie Fisher, Mark Hamill, Harrison Ford, Ron Howard, Richard Dreyfuss, Robert Duvall, Laurence Fishburne, Diane Keaton, and Al Pacino. He was intimidating as hell; his face betrayed absolutely no emotion. I didn't know whether he loved or hated me, but he kept bringing me back.

I turn the car radio on. I need to relax; with each level of audition the pressure has built. I try, but I'm not hearing the music. I'm not even hearing the rain. I look down at the scenes. I look once, twice, and then again. Each time I make more mistakes, forgetting lines I knew just hours ago. I look up into my rearview mirror but I see no reflection. In five minutes, I'll be reading for Francis Ford Coppola and I'm starting to choke.

A bunch of sixth-graders had the idea to make *The Outsiders* into a movie. The kids at Lone Star Elementary School in central California wrote a letter to the biggest, most famous director they could think of, petitioning him for his services. Although the book was (and still is) required reading in middle schools across the country, Coppola had no idea of its existence, let alone the massive built-in following of *The Outsiders*. The book began as the high school English project of a Tulsa teenager, Susie Hinton. She wrote a spare, moving, and authentic story of teen alienation and want of family. Set in the early 1960s in the slums of Tulsa and following the orphaned Curtis brothers and their gang of "Greasers," the book (as well as the movie) was the forerunner to cultural youth sensations like *Harry Potter* and *Twilight*. In fact, when young Susie changed her name to S. E. Hinton in order to hide her gender and to ensure young male readers and old male editors that she could handle the subject matter, somewhere in England a very young Miss Rowling may have taken note.

The guard at the Zoetrope Studios gate directs me to stage 5 and hands me a map. "Go right on Marlon Brando Way. Follow it to Budd Schulberg Avenue and it's just next to the commissary." I wonder why I'm reading on a soundstage and not in an office. I look for a place to park and run through the scene again in my head. My nerves are threatening to unravel all of my preparation. I try to quiet these inner voices that are telling me that my success so far has been nothing but a fluke, but they are gaining strength and I can feel it. I park the car and jog through the rain to soundstage 5. I can't believe what I see. There must be twenty-five other actors huddled under the overhang at the stage door. A lot of them are famous, some of them are dressed head to toe in full Greaser regalia. Most of them are smoking and all of them look older than I do. It's like the Screen Actors Guild version of the prison yard. Posing, fronting, and intimidation. I look for a friendly face. I see Emilio Estevez wearing an almost ridiculous pompadour.

"Dude! What the fuck is going on?" I ask. A reading for a director is supposed to be a low-key, private meeting. This looks like a public cattle call with every important young working actor in the universe.

Emilio, ever the old soul, smiles and shakes his head. "Hey, it's Francis."

Working for Coppola had almost killed Emilio's dad. The stress, the hours, and the heat of making *Apocalypse Now* had given Martin Sheen a heart attack in his midthirties. He barely survived, and it changed him. Martin, usually full of life and laughter, was strangely quiet on the subject of all of us competing to work under the great master. In fact, he rarely speaks of *Apocalypse Now* or Francis at all. But for his sons and their friends (as well as film fans worldwide) it is the stuff of legend: Francis replacing Harvey Keitel supposedly because the actor bitched about not having a trailer; Martin flying in on a day's notice for a ninety-day shoot and staying for 360 days of shooting over the course of two years; Brando showing up so fat and bald that they could only shoot him in shadow and making Francis read *Heart of Darkness* aloud to him in its entirety before he would begin shooting; hurricanes threatening lives and destroying sets; the Phillipine military pulling all the jets and helicopters to quell a coup; Dennis Hopper electing to live (and party) in the jungle with the natives instead of staying at the hotel; Playboy Bunnies being written into the film on a whim and wrecking a marriage or two in the process; sickness everywhere; a tapeworm poking its head out of Martin's driver's mouth, gagging the man until he pulled the wiggling, pulsing worm out of his own body on the side of the road; dark tales of stunts gone wrong and actors being asked to do dangerous and reckless things. But to watch Eleanor Coppola's own recollections in her brilliant and frightening documentary *Hearts of Darkness* is to suspect some of the legends are true.

The stage door opens. Another group of actors emerges from the soundstage. They all look bummed, out of it. One guy, though, has a huge, toothy, wolflike grin. He whispers to Emilio and me, "Francis sent these guys packing, but he asked me to stay." Emilio gives a high five to his buddy, a new young actor from New Jersey who has been staying at the Sheens' house while he auditions in L.A. "Fucking Francis, I mean the guy is unreal! He just sent 'em away! Said it right in front of everyone!"

I start talking to the kid from back East. He's open, friendly, funny, and has an almost robotic, bloodless focus and an intensity that I've never encountered before. His name is Tom Cruise.

It will be survival of the fittest for all of us. We will need to intimidate, dominate, and crush our competitors for these roles of a lifetime. But there's no reason why we can't try to stay friends while we do it.

"What part are you reading for?" I ask Tom.

"Christ, up until today, it was Sodapop, but Francis has everyone switching parts and bringing us all in and out while everyone watches everyone else! I just got done reading Darrel."

"But you're not old enough to play Darrel," says Emilio, mildly panicked.

"That's what I thought. Plus I hadn't prepared that part," says Tom.

The three of us stand under the overhang, out of the rain, trying to calculate how the various age pairings Coppola is trying will affect our chances. If Darrel, the oldest part in the movie, is played by Tom Cruise, I'm screwed.

"Okay, next group!" a man says, ushering us into the darkness of stage 5. And for the first time, I can hear the blasting sounds of Italian opera . . .

✢

Francis Ford Coppola won his first Oscar in 1971, as the screenwriter for *Patton*. He then took a dime-store pulp novel and, despite countless attempts to have him fired, created *The Godfather*, giving us Pacino, reintroducing us to Brando, and winning the Oscar for Best Picture. He made its sequel in an era when to do so was considered a shameful, soulless, explicitly commercial folly. *Godfather II* made history by being the only sequel to also win Best Picture, a record that remains to this day. He mentored his young protégé, George Lucas, through his breakout, *American Graffiti*, after having used George to shoot pickup shots on the first *Godfather*. Like Lucas, Francis deeply distrusted Hollywood and lived and worked in San Francisco, away from the bullshit and the schmooze. And like Lucas, when massive success came, he created his own personal fiefdom, filled with murderously loyal counterculture artistic geniuses. The Zoetrope group made its own rules and broke them at will. It was the center of the bull's-eye in the nexus of artistic achievement, prestige, controversy, and mystery.

But as Tom, Emilio, and I take our seats along with the twenty or so others on stage 5, Zoetrope Studios is fighting for its life. *Time* magazine has just put Coppola on its cover for a story about the cost overruns on *One from the Heart*, his latest movie, a groundbreaking special-effects-filled musical meditation starring Nastassja Kinski. Financial power plays are everywhere, with Chase Manhattan Bank threatening to shut Zoetrope down and foreclose on the studio. Francis's artistic/financial high-wire act is the biggest story in the entertainment industry.

Our chairs are against the walls of the soundstage. There are too many of us, though, so some actors sit on the ground. The only light is an illuminated area in the center of the floor, which appears to be exactly the size of a boxing arena. A table and four chairs have been set up in the light. Just beyond, in the shadows, I see Francis for the first time. He is wearing a beret and fiddling with a state-of-the-art video camera, recording everything. On the table next to him is an old-style record player. My tastes run toward Tom Petty and Bruce Springsteen, so I'm a little foggy on the genre of extremely emotional Italian music emanating from the turntable. Francis has an assistant with him, no one else, and she turns down the music.

Francis walks to the edge of the illuminated area and looks out at us. No small talk, no introductions. He gets right to it. "Hi. I thought we'd all get together today and sort of run through things," he says casually, as if auditioning while thirty of your competitors watch is the most normal thing in the world.

"Some of you may be asked to play different roles than you have prepared and some of you won't. This is really just an opportunity to explore the material," he says mildly. *Explore* the material? Is he serious? I look over at Tom Cruise. The only "exploring" he'll be doing here today is to try to find a way to bash my brains in and take my role from me. And from my perspective—right back at him! This may be an abstract artistic exercise for Coppola, but for every single one of us young actors huddled in the darkness, this day will be the difference between continuing the struggles of our daily lives and seeing those lives changed forever.

Francis points for three actors to step into the light. "Say your name into the camera and what role you are reading for," he instructs.

Quietly I ask the actor next to me how long this has been going on. "I've been here five hours already," he says. The chosen actors face the Sony prototype video camera, which looks to me like something from *The Jetsons*.

"Hi, I'm Dennis Quaid. I'll be playing Darrel."

"Hi, I'm Scott Baio and I'm playing Sodapop."

"I'm Tommy Howell and I'm Ponyboy."

They take their places around the makeshift "kitchen table set." Francis turns up the opera. They start the scene.

They are good. Quaid is doing it all from memory and he's a major guy and he will be tough to beat. The Tom Howell kid, I've never heard of; he looks like a baby and is so low-key it seems like he is not even trying. But he also seems real, there's nothing forced about his performance. Baio is a huge TV star on *Happy Days*, so if Coppola wants stars, he's got a shot. He was also terrific in Alan Parker's *Bugsy Malone* with Jodie Foster.

Like everyone else, I'm watching, judging, looking for any edge I can find to help my own audition when I'm finally called.

I run through a matrix of possibilities. Do I play it from memory, like Quaid? If I do, Francis may think I'm so prepared that it's a final performance with no room left for improvement (or his direction). But being "off book" also shows nerve, craft, and dedication. Do I stand on it emotionally and really crank up the conflict that's there to be exploited in the writing? Or do I play it understated, withholding something? When great actors do this (like Pacino as Michael Corleone) it's riveting; when lesser actors do it, it's dull. I watch Tommy Howell—it's clear he is in heavy contention for Ponyboy—and he stays in first gear almost all the time and never "pushes." I consider my biggest dilemma, one that every actor at any level struggles with; at the end of my big scene, I have to break down and cry. How much is too much?

And behind that unanswerable question is the one that makes any actor's heart stop—what if I can't cry on cue?

And that's all it takes. In that one nanosecond of doubt, I feel the blood rush to my head, and my chest begin to tighten. I don't know if I can cry during the scene but I sure as hell could cry right now. In the lit arena the actors are killing it, knocking it out of the park. When they finish, another group takes over, and another, and then another. No one flames out. No one sucks. It is unheard-of to actually sit and watch your competition, and there's good reason for this protocol: it makes the pressure almost unbearable.

I'm getting more unnerved by the minute. An hour goes by. I watch a stream of the elite enter the set; the guy who starred in *Caddyshack*; the blond kid from *On Golden Pond*. A young actor with big teeth and curly hair reads Ponyboy; people are buzzing about the supersecret movie he stars in about to come out from Steven Spielberg called *E.T.* I look over at Tommy Howell to see his reaction to this guy's reading. Tommy is stone-faced, cool as ice.

"How *old* is that kid?" I ask Emilio.

"Tommy Howell? He's fifteen."

There's a commotion at the stage door. The storm has stopped, the sun's come out, and its blinding light streams in as a man dressed like a homeless person enters. He has long, filthy hair, a three-day beard, and ripped, stained Mad Max leather pants. He is also on roller skates. Francis makes a beeline for him and they huddle in the corner.

The other actors point and whisper, "That's Mickey Rourke!" says one of them.

"Who?" I ask. I've never heard of the guy, but he is being worshipped like the love child of Laurence Olivier and Jesus Christ.

"He's the next James Dean," someone says. All around there are nods of agreement.

*"Really?"* I say, looking over. "He sure as shit looked a lot better in *Rebel without a Cause.*" We all chuckle quietly, beginning to bond over being thrown together into this extraordinary pressure cooker.

It's getting late, nearing 4:00 p.m., and I've been waiting and watching for hours. Francis seems to be tiring; he no longer swaps guys in and out like hockey players changing lines on the fly, he's now reading names off a list.

"Rob Lowe? Is Rob Lowe here?" he asks, squinting into the darkness.

Adrenaline explodes in my chest.

"Um, yes. Hello, I'm here."

"You're playing Sodapop," he says, without looking at me.

I walk into the glare of the lights. I'm blinking, trying to focus. I've been sitting in the dark too long; I'm disoriented. I can't see Francis or the camera or the other actors watching but I can *feel* them, just beyond the light, compressed into an omnipresent being.

My heart is a jackhammer. It sounds like someone is running up a flight of stairs in my head. Something is wrong. I remember the problem. I have forgotten to breathe. I try to exhale slowly so no one sees me do it. I've got to mask my discomfort and cover my nerves at all costs. The other actors gather around me. Tom Howell is Ponyboy and a guy named John Laughlin from *An Officer and a Gentleman* plays our older brother, Darrel.

"Why don't you guys take a moment and begin when you're ready," says Francis. I've got the first line of the scene, so it will be up to me when we go. I look the other actors in the eyes; we've never met, never even said hello. Now we will be the Curtis brothers, now we will manufacture the memories, the relationships, and the rapport of these characters' lifetimes, in an instant. I've got my pages in my hand; they've been there since I sat in my Mazda in the rain. But I let them fall to the floor. I will go from memory—

let the chips fall where they may. I know this fucker cold. I won't let the fear overtake me, not now, not today. I say a quick prayer: "Keep it simple. Keep it honest. Let it rip." I start the scene.

I've never agreed with the conventional wisdom that "actors are great liars." If more people understood the acting process, the goals of good actors, the conventional wisdom would be "actors are *terrible* liars," because only bad actors lie on the job. The good ones hate fakery and avoid manufactured emotion at all costs. Any script is enough of a lie anyway. (What experience does any actor have with flying a spacecraft? Killing someone?) What's called for, what actors are hired for, is to bring reality to the arbitrary.

I know nothing about being an orphan. I was only a baby in the early 1960s. I've never been to Tulsa, Oklahoma, and I've never met a Greaser. But I *do* have brothers whom I love. I know what it means to long for a parent who is no longer in the family. I have met my share of rough kids and have felt that I didn't belong, and when I remember my old gang of friends back on Dayton's north side, my personal truths provide enough emotional ammunition for me to play Sodapop Curtis.

Like a skater approaching the point in his program where he has to land a triple axel jump, I know the moment for my "breakdown" is coming up fast. I'm trying to stay "in the scene," not stand outside of it, up in some corner, looking down in judgment like the characters in an episode of *Bewitched*. But part of me can't help it, the stakes are too great and I know if I don't land this jump, I mean really stick it, this audition is over and, with it, practically, my career as an actor.

"I hate it when you two fight," I say, beginning the final speech. "It just tears me up inside."

I look at Tommy Howell. I don't know him from Adam, but I see his eyes are moist. That's all I need, that tiny peek at humanity and empathy from a fifteen-year-old stranger. It sets me off.

Behind it, the pressure and the nerves and the stakes, and the need to be liked and accepted and chosen, build into a wave that I cannot stop if I want to. The emotions explode. At the end of the scene, Howell and Laughlin and I are huddled in the glare; they are holding me as I weep.

⚜

After the audition, I hear nothing for weeks. No phone call comes in to my agents. I know I shellacked it in my reading, but after Francis sent the other actors back to the shadows, he asked me to read a different part, the role of Randy the Soc (it's pronounced "Soshe"—more than a few actors had their tickets punched by calling them "Socks"). It's a small part with one big speech but I can see that physically I would be right for it. I pray that I'm still in the running for Sodapop. Other than Ponyboy, Sodapop is the most coveted role in the movie. The part is huge, romantic, and, with the big breakdown scene at the end of the movie, unforgettable. I'm worried I've lost it.

I spend all my free time four houses down at the Sheens. Cruise is still camping out in the guest bedroom, but neither he nor Emilio have heard about their auditions either. We work out, play hoops, call our agents, call up girls, hide our booze from Martin, hit baseballs with Charlie and Chad, anything to try not to lose our minds with anticipation.

I have settled on USC as my college. If I don't get a part, I will enroll and study film. I've been toying with following my dad into law or pursuing marine biology. But in the end, my heart is stuck on reaching people with stories on film. If I can't be in front of the camera, I'll be behind it.

Finally my agent calls.

"Do I have the part?"

"No."

My heart sinks.

"But they want you to fly to New York and read again."

I can feel the blood coming back to my face. I'm still alive in *The Outsiders* sweepstakes.

"What part am I reading? Soda or Randy?" I ask, holding my breath.

"Both."

I try not to be disappointed that Randy is still an option.

"Pack up. You leave day after tomorrow."

I put down the phone. It rings in my hand. It's Emilio.

"Dude, did they call you? Are you going to New York?"

"Yeah! I made it. What about you?"

"We're going, too! Me and Cruise!"

"What parts?"

"I'm going for Soda, Randy, and maybe Darrel, depending on ages," says Emilio.

"What about Cruise?" I ask.

"Soda, Randy, Darrel, and Dallas."

"Holy shit," I say. This thing is clearly still a wide-open free-for-all.

I hang up, excited that my friends are among the chosen. We are competitors and it will likely come down to one of us versus the other. And if it does, we will try to blow each other out of the water with zero regrets on all sides. But until then, it's down to the Sheens' Gilligan's Island pool to celebrate.

On the plane we sit with the other two "L.A. finalists," Tommy Howell and Darren Dalton. Together we try to predict who will get what role. We also find a cute stewardess and work her relentlessly for alcohol.

It's a night flight with lots of empty seats, so it feels like we own the plane. By the time we land we are connected like a less dangerous, teenage, show-business version of the Dirty Dozen. We are all thrown together by fate, required to work together to achieve a goal that will be a highlight of our lives. Along the way any one of us could fall. You don't want it to be you, but you don't want it to be your new brother either. There is also a group waiting to knock us out entirely, the "New York" actors. Their reputations precede them—tough, intense, serious hard cases. We make our plans to battle them, to come out of this together, leaving the others in the dust. We are the L.A. Greasers. After surviving the three-day, thirty-hour battle at Zoetrope Studios, we feel like Hollywood's finest.

We check into the Plaza Hotel. I am taken aback at the luxury and spectacle of the lobby. Last time I was in New York, Dad and I stayed at the Sheraton. The front desk tells us we will be sharing rooms. In a flash, Cruise is on the phone to his agent, Paula Wagner.

"Paula, they are making us *share*," he says. He is certain that this is not right and wants it fixed ASAP. The rest of us are staggering around like happy goofs, but this guy's already showing traits that will make him famous; he's zeroed in like a laser—all business and very intense.

"Okay, then. Thank you very much," he says like a fifty-year-old businessman getting off the phone with his stockbroker. "Paula says it's fine."

After sorting out our rooms, we decide to pile into a cab and check out the sights.

"Forty-second Street," someone says.

The cabbie's eyes widen as he turns to look at the group squeezed into his backseat—a fifteen-year-old, a seventeen-year-old, and the three "adults" weighing in at around nineteen years old.

"You boys sure you want to go down there? Ain't nothin' but women and trouble to be found there."

"Yes, we're sure!" we howl, and laugh, banging on the Plexiglas divider like animals.

We are all seriously dragging the next morning as we arrive at "Zoetrope East." Any effects of our long night are mitigated by the growing tension of the East Coast versus the West Coast acting brawl that is moments away.

This time the auditions are called what they actually are: screen tests. And unlike at the L.A. audition, the group from New York is much more select, maybe fifteen guys in total. We lounge together in a giant loftlike waiting area in some dingy office building somewhere near Broadway. I'm freezing—having little travel experience, I have not packed correctly for New York in the winter. It doesn't help that I'm jet-lagged and hungover. I find a spot on the floor next to a radiator and take a nap (to this day, when I feel too much stress I want to fall asleep).

"Dude, wake up," says Emilio, banging me in the ribs.

I try to clear my head as I roll up off the floor.

"Francis wants us in the studio."

It's a small, hot space. The basic setup is exactly like L.A., except for—inexplicably—Carly Simon, wearing a sort of catsuit, curled up in a corner. I also recognize Matt Dillon, already a huge teen idol and the star of S. E. Hinton's first movie adaptation, *Tex*. It hasn't come out yet, but it's supposed to be good. Matt is in front of the camera reading the part of Dallas. And by reading, I mean reading. He is holding the entire script, eyes locked on the text. After a while, however, he puts it down and begins paraphrasing. Soon he's ad-libbing completely and making up dialogue while the other actors try to keep up.

I don't know if Francis asked him to freelance like this or not. If he did, then clearly Matt has got the part locked up. If he didn't, then Matt Dillon has dangling, clanking, scary-big elephant balls.

Next up is a tiny kid I competed against a few months back for a part on the hit TV show *Eight Is Enough*. It came down to the two of us for a new starring role they were adding to that show.

We both went to the network reading in a boardroom packed with stone-faced executives in business suits. He came out on top.

Now he's reading the part of Johnny, the tortured, doomed Greaser. Like with Tommy Howell, it is clear that he is the front-runner. When he's done I call over to him.

"Ralph! Hey, Macchio! It's me, Lowe."

Ralph comes over to say hi. "Hey, man, good to see ya."

"How many times have you read for this?" I ask.

"A lot. Matt and I have been doing this for *days*."

"Have you read for any other parts?"

"Nope. Just Johnny. Matt, too. Just Dallas."

I see Francis looking around the room. "Rob? Rob? Can you come read the part of Randy?"

This is what I was afraid of. I feel like I might pass out.

"Um, sure. Uh, no problem," I manage.

I quickly look over the scene. If I do well now as Randy, Francis might want me for that part, opening up Soda to one of the other finalists who have been on the periphery until now, like Tom Cruise. Maybe I should tank the reading, I think briefly, but knowing I'm incapable of it.

I finish playing the scene at full throttle. I'm praying I don't get this part. No one wants to be a Soc in a movie about Greasers. It's 110 degrees in this sweatbox of a studio as Tom Cruise is called to the floor. Now I have real issues; he's giving *my* role a try. He begins Sodapop's big breakdown scene at the end of the movie. I watch him and think, that's it, I'm done. He's clearly a force to be reckoned with, and is more focused and ambitious than I ever thought about being. (And that's saying something.)

But then . . . Tom has stopped. Stopped the scene! Right in the middle of the monologue! A hush falls over the room.

"Um, I'm sorry. Um, I'm really sorry," he says, looking directly at Francis. "This just isn't working for me."

Holy shit! Not working for *him*? I thought Francis Ford Coppola was the judge of what works and what doesn't. There is a low murmur among the actors. Francis lets him try again. When he's done, I know the Cruise missile threat has passed.

"Rob, give Soda a try, please," Francis asks blithely. But I know that right now, right here, in this moment, a life-changing part is mine for the taking. What Francis is really asking is: Rob, do you *want* this part? I do the scene and crush it. The answer is yes. Yes, I do.

## CHAPTER 10

A suspenseful two weeks later, it's official. I'm offered the part of Sodapop Curtis, the romantic, sweet-natured, loving middle brother. Tommy Howell surprises no one by getting the lead role of Ponyboy, and Matt Dillon fulfills expectations by getting the role of the tough hood, Dallas. My instincts proved right about Ralph Macchio: he will play the tragic mascot, Johnny. The other roles remain uncast.

I'm elated. It doesn't seem real. I'm going to make a *movie*. And in my first movie, I have one of the starring roles. My first director will be one of the greatest who ever lived. And not only did I survive one of the longest, most competitive casting searches in years, I was one of the first to be cast.

I celebrate with my family. I contact USC and tell them I won't be enrolling. I start to think about what it will be like to be away from home, on my own for the first time, while we shoot on location in Tulsa, Oklahoma. I also am anxious for my new brothers in arms, Emilio, Tom, and the others with whom I bonded over the last few months. They are all still hoping to get one of the remaining roles, but so far they have heard nothing.

I have no idea what to expect. My apprehension is probably similar to what any seventeen-year-old feels as he packs for freshman year at college. But in that case, you could ask your dad, "What do I need to know? What advice do you have?" and Dad tells you. But obviously I can't do that, as no one in my family has any experience in this new world.

So I walk down to the Sheens' house, looking for Martin. We crack open the vanilla Häagen-Dazs and I ask him every question I can think of. He is gracious and patient; I am vulnerable and a little scared, but excited. By the time we finish our ice cream I feel more prepared for what I might encounter. I thank him. At the door he stops me.

"One last thing . . ."

"Sure, Martin, what is it?"

"Don't let Francis make you do anything you're uncomfortable with."

I consider that last unsettling piece of advice as I jog back home, through the gathering fog, to pack. I am on the cusp of something and I feel a mixture of emotions: I'm proud, scared, cocky, insecure, anxious, and confident, all at once. And truth be told, after the long adrenaline-filled audition process, I'm also feeling a little let down. (I will later learn this is a hallmark of alcoholism; we call it the Peggy Lee Syndrome. You reach a goal you've been striving for, only to feel, "Is that all there is?") If I'm gonna make a career of this, I will have to sort myself out.

My bare feet are hurting slightly as I trot down our driveway. Chad and Micah are playing horse and my mom is calling us all into the house for dinner. A wave of homesickness rises up, but I haven't even packed a suitcase. Looking down, I notice a tiny cut with some blood on my right foot and I realize, I am going to have to build up my calluses.

⊕

There are giant praying hands outside my airplane as it descends into Tulsa, Oklahoma. The massive sculpture from Oral Roberts University seems to be sending a message. My future is at hand. It is unknowable. It is an adventure. I don't know where it will lead, and I might as well pray!

I'm flying alone. Tom and Emilio were offered parts at the last minute and are driving out in Emilio's pickup. Tom is playing my best friend, Steve, and Emil, Two-Bit Matthews, another of the Curtis brothers' circle of friends. The Sheen family's complicated history with Francis runs so deep that before he accepted the role, Emil literally put the script under his mattress and "slept on it" before finally saying yes.

The plane comes in for a bumpy landing on an early spring afternoon in the beginning of March 1982. It's two weeks before my eighteenth birthday.

The Tulsa Excelsior sits smack in the middle of downtown. This will be my home for the next ten weeks. At the front desk I'm handed a new shooting script, crew list, an envelope with a wad of cash, per diem, and a key to room 625. "You are right next door to Tommy Howell and across the hall from Mr. Macchio. Welcome to Tulsa," says the man behind the counter.

I look up and recognize Diane Lane coming through the revolving door of the lobby. At only sixteen, she already seems like a legend. She has starred with Laurence Olivier and been on the cover of *Time* magazine. Oh, and she may be the prettiest girl on the planet. She will play Cherry Valance, the queen Soc. Too shy to introduce myself, I watch as she breezes by with her chaperone. With all the teen testosterone on this movie, she'll need one!

I head up to my room, which is very plain and very simple—a desk, a small refrigerator, and two twin beds. But to me, it's the greatest setup I've ever seen. It's like my own first apartment—and in fact, it is. I'm out of the house, away from my parents, living on my own, and because I'll be eighteen in a week or so, for the first time, I have no guardian. This new sense of freedom is powerful enough to knock me to my knees, right here in room 625.

"Hey, man, is that you?"

I recognize Tommy Howell's voice as he unlatches the door between our adjoining rooms.

"We did it," I yelp, as we hug in celebration.

"Man, I am so glad you got Soda," he says.

"Thanks, man. Who's with you? Do you have a guardian?" I ask Tommy.

"No, it's just me!"

I'm a little taken aback. Tommy is just fifteen, but I ask no questions.

"Put your shit down, let's go eat," he says.

I throw my suitcase in the corner and we head for the elevator. It stops on the fifth floor.

"Hey, guys!" says Darren Dalton, a tall kid who got the part I was praying I wouldn't get, Randy the Soc.

"Why aren't you on our floor?" I ask.

"Dude, our floor is Socs *only*. We have these amazing suites, free room service, gym privileges—it's so cool!"

"Yeah, Francis wants us segregated," Tommy informs me. "He's given them more per diem, better rooms, and these embossed leather script binders."

"Aah, I see, he's trying to create a class system on the set, trying to make us Greasers jealous," I say.

"Well, it ain't working," cackles Tommy. "If anybody's jealous, it's them about us, since the Greasers are the fuckin' stars of the movie!"

Tommy and I laugh and high-five, busting Darren's balls. On *The Outsiders*, ball busting will become a fine art.

Coming back from dinner, we come upon an amazing spectacle. There must be fifty girls around our age congregating around the Excelsior lobby. I remember the body language and the low-level hysteria from being mobbed in Riverside and I recognize them at once as fans. But of whom?

At that moment, Matt Dillon saunters past and the girls sway en masse like willows in a spring breeze.

"Um, hey. What's shakin'?" asks Matt in his patented, laconic cool-guy fashion. It's a little hard to hear him, as he's carrying a gigantic boom box that's playing an obscure song by T. Rex.

None of us really know Matt well; we are the L.A. group after all, and he is the embodiment of the "New York actor." He is already well established as a fledgling matinee idol and, more important, has Tulsa wired from starring in the movie *Tex*, which he shot there six months ago. He knows the rub on all the levels. We had crossed paths at the New York auditions but now we make our introductions in earnest. Matt is funny, wry, and has a sort of jaded charisma that none of us possesses. As we talk, the girls twitter and whisper in the background.

"Aaah, man, I'm *tired*. See ya at rehearsals," he says, hoisting his boom box to his shoulders. He crosses to the elevators and passes the gaggle of fans. Then something remarkable happens. He stops dead in his tracks and whispers to a pretty brunette. She listens for a beat, then turns to the four girls she's standing with and whispers something to them. Matt fiddles with the volume on the boom box. The girls caucus together for a total of four seconds till the brunette leaves her friends behind and joins Matt for a walk to the elevators. He puts his free arm around her. At the last second, just before they enter the elevator, she turns back to look at her friends. Her expression is one I've never seen before. It's like she has a thought balloon over her head that reads: "Holy

Sporting a Steve McQueen haircut at
two years old in Dayton, Ohio

Chad and me with our father,
Chuck, in Glen Helen Park,
Yellow Springs, Ohio, 1971

Always working: selling
the *Dayton Daily News*,
Ohio, 1975

With the first writer
I ever knew:
my mom, Barbara,
in Malibu, 1977

With my favorite Cincinnati Reds
fans: my brothers Chad, Micah,
and me on Point Dume in 1979

Me with Chad, Micah,
and our mom in
Malibu, 1978

ROBERT LOWE
3-17-64

Ann Wright ASSOCIATES, LTD.
8422 MELROSE PLACE, LOS ANGELES, CALIF. 90069
Telephone 655-5040

My first professional acting "composite."
Why am I dressed for soccer but holding a basketball?

My first big break: *A New Kind of Family,* 1979. Being upstaged by a dog. (©American Broadcasting Companies, Inc.)

The Greasers. *The Outsiders,* 1983. Cracking up at Macchio's joke. (Warner Bros./The Kobal Collection)

President Bartlet and Sam Seaborn. Backyard at the Sheens' pool, 1984.

The three amigos: Nastassja Kinski, me, and Jodie Foster
on location for *The Hotel New Hampshire*
(Photograph by Steve Schapiro)

Trying to compete (and failing) with the iron man, Patrick Swayze, on the set of *Youngblood*, 1984

Wild '80s fun: Drinking kamikazes from the Stanley Cup with Wayne Gretzky

Using everything I learned from Clarence Clemons and the E. Street Band: *St. Elmo's Fire,* 1984 (Columbia/The Kobal Collection)

The highway patrol officer getting more than he bargained for and a seat on Michael J. Fox's lap. Pulled over on the "Clean Water Caravan," 1986. (Daphne Zuniga, Robert Walden, Whoopi Goldberg, Jane Fonda, Rosanna Arquette, Judd Nelson, and Morgan Fairchild are among the crowd.)

Michael J. Fox and me on the roof of the Greyhound bus, escaping the throngs on the "Clean Water Caravan"

With Senator Lloyd M. Bentsen Jr. on the campaign plane during a swing through California (Photograph by Diana Walker: Time & Life Pictures/Getty Images)

James Spader, Lisa Zane, and me in character for *Bad Influence*, 1989 (Epic/The Kobal Collection)

Sheryl keeping a close eye on me in Australia during the *Bad Influence* press tour, 1990

The beginning of a beautiful journey: on the beach with Sheryl in Fiji, 1991

Wedding day: July 22, 1991

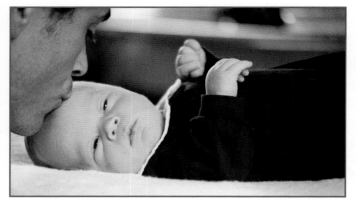

A kiss from a proud dad for Johnowen, 1995

Back at home after a long day on the set, Matthew and me headed to dreamland

My boys, Johnowen and Matthew, in 2002 (Photograph by Lyndie Benson)

My favorite face in the world, my favorite soul, my best friend: my wife, Sheryl

A weekend in the country: in the kitchen with Sting, his wife, Trudie, and Pavarotti, Wiltshire England, 1992

Rehearsal break on the set of *Suddenly, Last Summer*: me, Sheryl, Richard E. Grant, and the dearly missed Natasha Richardson. London, 1992

Laughing with Chris Farley on the set of *Tommy Boy* (Photo courtesy of Paramond Pictures. © Paramont Pictures Corp. All Rights Reserved)

With Lorne Michaels on the beach in Amagansett

Rehearsing with Martin on the set of the pilot of *The West Wing*

With "the maestro," my friend and the creator of *The West Wing*, Aaron Sorkin, at the Emmy after party, 2001

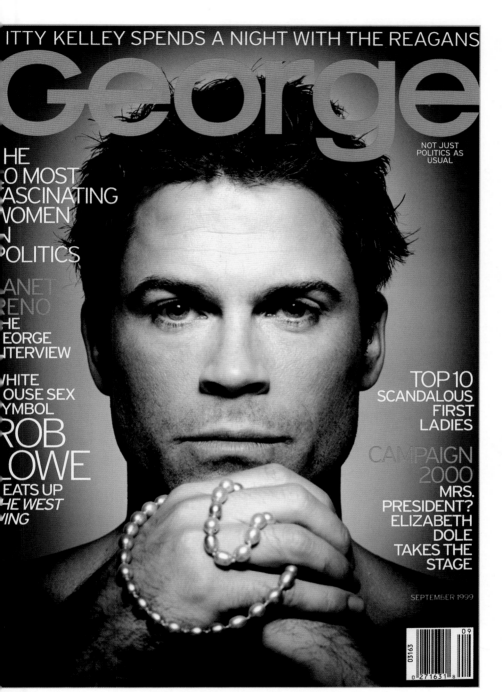

ITTY KELLEY SPENDS A NIGHT WITH THE REAGANS

George

NOT JUST
POLITICS AS
USUAL

HE
O MOST
ASCINATING
VOMEN
N POLITICS

ANET
RENO
HE
EORGE
ITERVIEW

VHITE
OUSE SEX
YMBOL
ROB
OWE
EATS UP
HE WEST
ING

TOP 10
SCANDALOUS
FIRST
LADIES

CAMPAIGN
2000
MRS.
PRESIDENT?
ELIZABETH
DOLE
TAKES THE
STAGE

SEPTEMBER 1999

03163

0 271631 8

09

JFK Jr.'s last *George* magazine cover, 1999
(Courtesy of Hachette Filipacchi Media/Photograph by Platon)

Accepting the SAG Award for Outstanding Performance by an Ensemble in a Drama Series for *The West Wing*, 2002 (Photograph by M. Caulfield, WireImage)

Life imitates art: meeting the real deal at the White House Correspondents Dinner, 2000 (The William J. Clinton Library)

President Clinton crashing our staff photo during a visit to the West Wing. Chief of Staff John Podesta and the president's personal secretary, Betty Currie, on the left. I'm holding Matthew.

President Clinton holding his gift
from Johnowen on the South Lawn
of the White House, 2000
(The William J. Clinton Library)

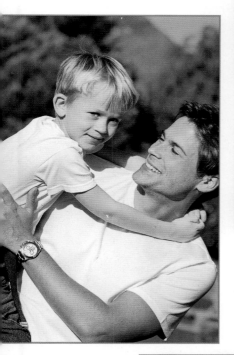

Wrestling with Johnowen in the
backyard in summer 2002

Family photo:
Micah, Matthew,
Chad, Johnowen,
me, and my mom,
Fourth of July,
2002

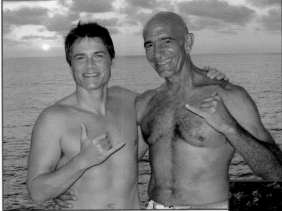

On a surf safari with my best
pal and Miramax partner,
Tom Barrack, 2011

In the backyard with Sheryl
(Photograph by Lyndie Benson)

My proudest achievement:
my sons, Matthew and Johnowen, today

shit! How lucky am I?!" Matt yawns, and the elevator doors close. The entire transaction takes less than forty-five seconds. So *that's* how it is, I think, and take note. Matt Fuckin' Dillon. My hero.

Rehearsals begin the next morning in an abandoned elementary school. The classrooms are used as the film crew's production offices, the auditorium/gymnasium as our rehearsal space. I've never rehearsed anything but a play, and there is no real rehearsal in television. Since we are playing two of the three brothers at the center of the film, Tommy Howell and I are already beginning to connect in a way that will hopefully pay off emotionally later when we need it in our performances. We stand in a corner of the musty, dirty gym with Tom and Emilio, who pulled an all-nighter driving from Point Dume.

"Who is playing Darrel?" asks Cruise, who had auditioned for the part of the eldest Curtis brother.

"We still don't know," says Howell. It's been a bit of a soap opera, the search for this last actor in *The Outsiders* puzzle.

"I heard they offered it to Mickey Rourke but he turned it down," Emilio says.

"I heard he turned down *all* the parts," says Ralph Macchio.

Someone proffers up a tidbit that Fred Roos has pulled the casting rabbit out of the hat by finding an actor who never auditioned with us in L.A., a much older guy who did a movie where he danced around on roller skates.

"What's this guy's name?" I ask.

"Patrick Swayze," says Emilio.

Minus the mysterious Mr. Swayze, who will arrive later, the entire cast begins what will end up being over two full weeks of rehearsals. Only years later will I learn that this lengthy, luxurious preparation was due to the movie's funding collapsing. While behind the scenes the future of *The Outsiders* hung in the balance, we blithely submitted to Francis's unique methods of preparation.

On the first day, we read through the script, get haircuts, and have wardrobe fittings. We cut off early, as Francis wants us up by 8:30 in the morning for a meeting at the house we will use as the main set.

The next day we pile into vans and are driven into the terribly run-down, desolate neighborhood where 80 percent of the movie will be shot. When we arrive at the small, beat-up two-bedroom home that will be the Curtis brothers' house, Francis stands in the weed-filled dirt yard, waiting.

"Hi guys. Gather round," he says in his relaxed, earnest, and brainy way. Sometimes Francis sounds a little like Kermit the Frog but with a deeper register.

"I want us to meet like this on the spot where we will work, and to be together. I feel like we should do this every day. And now, I'd like us all to begin our day with a half hour of tai chi," he says.

I don't know what tai chi is. I look around for a deliveryman. Maybe it's some sort of Asian takeout—which would be great because I'm starving. But as I scan the horizon, I see it's just us— Francis and his Greasers—standing around in the dirt. Francis begins swaying and gesticulating in slow motion, almost like he's underwater.

"Tai chi is the art of energy transformation," he says. "It builds concentration, strength, and balance. It puts your body in harmony with its environment." We all form a line and begin to follow his movements, and that's when I recognize the motions as the ones Martin Sheen did in front of the mirror at the beginning of *Apocalypse Now*. As the exercises drag on, I think: Martin's character was in Saigon; my character is in Tulsa. Why does a '50s Greaser know or care about tai chi? But if the world's greatest living director thinks we should stand on our heads to prepare, we should probably do it.

Patrick Swayze arrives in time for the next day's rehearsal. He walks into the gym as cool as you want, wearing tight jeans and a tattered, sleeveless Harley-Davidson T-shirt revealing his massive, ripped arms. (This is his uniform, he never changes it, and if I looked like him, neither would I.)

"Hi, I'm Buddy," he says, squeezing my hand with such enthusiasm that it could snap like a twig.

The guy is *yoked*. I mean he is literally made of iron. He's very high-strung, amped, and ready to storm the battlements at the drop of a hat. He's a Texan with a legitimate drawl, so he's a great arbiter of "Okie" accents. Buddy is also a decade older than the rest of us, and married, so on that level he might as well be a Martian. But that, too, serves him well as the older brother Darrel, who is farther down life's road.

"Hey guys, I had a notion that you are all acrobats," says Francis, entering the gym sipping an espresso. "In fact, I'd like you all to go down the hall for some training," he adds, heading over to greet Swayze.

"You bet, yaaaaawoooo!" hoots Swayze, clapping his hands and yelping like a wolf. I love his enthusiasm. He makes Tom Cruise look lobotomized.

The seven Greasers file down the hall to a classroom that has been turned into a rudimentary tumbling area. There are parallel bars, rings, and a trampoline. The only thing missing are safety mats. Instead, someone has placed a bunch of two-by-two squares of Styrofoam on the floor.

Swayze immediately takes charge.

"I was a gymnast in high school," he informs us. (His list of previous accomplishments will grow to include ballet dancer, bow-and-arrow specialist, motocross expert, horseman, guitar player, singer, songwriter, construction worker, carpenter, and artist, to name a few.)

Along with a local guy from the University of Tulsa, he begins to teach us a standing back flip. I am one of those guys who love sports and the adrenaline rush of a physical challenge, but when it comes to flips, I'm a pussy. I don't flip. I don't even dive into a pool—straight cannonball for me. The thought of falling midflip onto the ground conjures up images of rolling around in a wheelchair like Raymond Burr in *Ironside*. No thanks. Cruise, not surprisingly, is all over it.

"How about this!" he says, almost pulling it off without even being spotted. He wipes out, but tries it again immediately. Now Howell and Emilio have their blood up. They don't want to be upstaged, so they begin digging in earnest. *Splaat!* One goes down. *Thunk!* Another hits the deck, making the sound of a side of beef hitting the pavement. Eventually some of the guys figure it out and then, mercifully, it's time for our next assignment back in the rehearsal hall.

Francis tells us that we will be shooting the entire movie on video, in front of a green screen in the gym, before we begin real, principal photography. Later he can use new Sony technology to put in any background he chooses. But before we shoot, he asks us to do a lengthy improvisational exercise that culminates with us attempting to go to sleep on camera. Now this I can do. When it comes to sleeping, I should be in the goddamn Olympics. "Very good job, Rob," he says, and I'm thrilled.

Diane Lane and the other Socs, led by the teen idol Leif Garrett, arrive to do the big drive-in sequence. The minute Diane enters the room, a competition for her attention commences. Matt Dillon clearly has the inside track and soon we all know that we have no chance. Francis appears to dote on Matt as well—he's clearly grooming him to be the James Dean of the movie.

For his part, Leif Garrett has embraced Francis's attempt at class warfare. We all like Leif; he's so jaded from his years as a teen cover boy that he's hilarious, but he is determined to be superior to us, just like his character, Bob, would be. This, of course, leads to merciless ball busting.

On the day all the Greasers pose for a photo shoot in full costume in the shitty gym, Leif comes to watch. The local kids have been running roughshod through the production offices for days, stealing anything they can get their hands on. (It really is a horribly poor part of Tulsa, and who can blame them.) We are all posed together under the flashing strobe as a production assistant finally goes off and drags a local ragamuffin away for pilfering the candy bars and other goodies that are laid out, just off the set.

"Keep your goddamn hands off the food, it's not for you, it's for *the actors,*" the assistant yells.

"Yeah, Leif, you hear that," calls Macchio to Leif, who is standing at the snack table, "those are for the *actors!*" Garrett is mortified. A hush falls over the room until we all burst out laughing. I look over, cracking up at Ralph, who now looks a little scared. Flash! Snap! The camera captures the moment. That frame of film will become the poster for *The Outsiders.*

That night we are divided into groups and sent out to spend the night with "real Greasers." And when I say spend the night, I don't mean go have a long dinner and hear some stories. We are meant to *sleep at their houses!* I'd always hated overnights with kids I didn't know very well. So the thought of bunking with a Hells Angel that some production assistant found off the street has got me rattled. "Um, what are the odds they could be murderers?" I ask Tommy Howell.

Francis has chosen Tom Cruise as my roommate for this adventure. He and I are delivered like two sacks of mail to a slightly tired-looking duplex way outside of town. Tom's unrelenting enthusiasm for anything, however ridiculous, plus a few hours to calculate the mathematical improbability that these folks are axe murderers, has made me kind of intrigued about our experiment.

We are greeted at the door by a middle-aged couple.

"You boys must be the actors!" says the man, offering his hand. He is almost fully tattooed.

"Yes, sir. I'm Tom Cruise."

"Hi. I'm Rob Lowe."

"Well, come on in, boys," says the woman, who looks like any other midwestern housewife. Clearly, my darker fears are unfounded, as this couple could not be more welcoming. We share dinner in the tiny kitchen and swap stories about our lives as young actors in Hollywood with their stories of being Greasers in the mid-'50s in Tulsa. We talk late into the night until everyone tires.

"Well, boys, I better tuck ya in for the night," says the woman, leading us to a foldout bed that Tom and I will share.

"Thanks so much, ma'am," says Cruise, who is always unrelentingly polite and formal with adults or anyone of authority.

"See you in the morning," I add.

"You betcha!" she says, shutting out the light.

Cruise and I lie there on the bumpy cot, saying nothing. Neither wants to disturb the other's chance of actually falling asleep in this bizarre circumstance. I'm trying to assimilate all of the information, experiences, and lessons that are hitting me every day like crashing waves. I have made it to this point in life on instinct and hard work. But after a few days on *The Outsiders* I know I have so much to learn, and for once my mind won't go to sleep. I know I'm hardly alone. Other than Matt Dillon and Diane Lane, all of us are just getting started in movies. But I'm competitive, and if anyone is going to come out of this most ready for the future, I want it to be me. Oddly enough, there is something comforting about knowing that my cot mate feels exactly the same way.

"Cruise? Cruise? You awake?" I whisper.

"Yeah, man," he answers.

"Me too," I say, as we both stare at the ceiling, waiting for tomorrow and what will come next.

❖

In keeping with the theme of toughening us up and having us interact with the genuine articles, the next morning finds us gathered to play some local tough guys in a game of tackle football—on cement.

I huddle up the Greasers. I am in my element. Back in Ohio I spent countless days like these drawing out buttonhooks and go-routes with my gang of North Dayton toughs. Our opposition is really no different, although I'm a tad unsettled by my suspicion that some of them wouldn't mind sending a Hollywood actor to the hospital.

I look at Team Greaser. Clearly I'm going to have an issue with Dillon. He has the boom box playing Bowie and is wearing his ever-present motorcycle boots. He yawns and scratches his chest. I know a blocker when I see one.

"Matt, play line," I say.

"Cool, man," he replies, lighting a Marlboro.

Macchio is tiny, so I have to hide him somewhere as well. Cruise and Emilio are fast as all hell and gung-ho, so they'll be receivers. Swayze, of course, wants to play all positions and probably could.

"Hey, Soda," he says, calling me by my character's name, "see that big dude with the goatee? I'm gonna knock his block off on the first play."

He's got a look in his eye that I will come to know well, and I figure I better let him do what he wants.

"Go for it, man."

Tommy Howell has been walking the parking lot, kicking away rocks, and otherwise just sort of checking out our playing field. Being the son of a longtime Hollywood stunt man, Tommy is evaluating the risk/reward equation of the matter at hand.

"I think these guys want to hurt us," he says.

"Me too," I answer.

He looks at me like, How the hell did we end up in this situation?! We take our positions, hoping for the best.

"Red rover! Red rover! Thirty-two. Thirty-two. Hut. Hut!" I bark, doing my best Terry Bradshaw.

Cruise and Emil blow their guys out of their shoes (Estevez was a track god at Malibu Park and hasn't lost a step), but the Tulsa Tough Guys have blitzed, disseminating my line of Dillon, Howell, and Macchio. Swayze, however, has totally shit-canned his man, who lies on the ground, wiggling like a fish.

I'm forced to roll out. I look for my receivers but there are guys in my face. Someone hammers me from the blind side and I'm down, hard.

The Greasers return to the huddle.

"Man, that was fucked up," says Dillon lazily.

"Ya gotta listen to me. Listen to me! I'm telling ya, when I was growing up in Texas I played a guy who . . ." begins Swayze, with a vintage story of his youth and Pop Warner Football. I can't follow the rest because I'm trying to clear my head.

"Let's just all go long," interrupts Cruise, calling the play universally reserved for teams who are desperate.

"Old Yeller! Old Yeller! Hut! Hut!"

Everybody goes long. Everybody gets knocked silly. The Tulsa hoods try to hide their satisfaction at the beat-down.

"Y'all almost had us on that one!" says the one in the Levi cutoff shorts.

We attempt to regroup in the huddle.

"Okay, I'm takin' over here," says Swayze, wild-eyed.

"No. No, you're not," says fifteen-year-old Tommy Howell. His quiet tone and earnest demeanor have us all listening.

"These guys are looking for a story to tell their girlfriends. 'Honey, you shoulda seen it, we popped those Hollywood actors good!' Well, that's not going to happen on my watch. I'm done. I quit. 'Cause if I break a leg doing this, I'm out of this movie in two seconds and on the next flight home. And I'm not gonna lose this part over a stupid fucking exercise. It's over. Francis can fire me if he wants to," he says, walking away.

We all look at each other. There is no denying his logic.

"Hey guys, we forfeit. Congrats. Great game," I say.

If there is any dissent among the rest of Team Greaser, no one is saying anything. The Tulsa roughnecks look stunned as we clear out, but they, too, say nothing. As we pile into our van to drive away, I think I can make them out laughing at us. I'm sure they thought we were just a bunch of scared Hollywood pansies.

❖

On the night before principal photography begins, Francis has one last task for us. He wants the three Curtis brothers to spend the night at the house we will be shooting in, and do a marathon improv session. He will observe with *The Outsiders* author, S. E. Hinton. Swayze, Howell, and I are petrified. It's one thing to improv a scene or two, but to do *hours* of it? In front of the director and author!?

Back in our van, we huddle together, working out a framework. We decide that we should cook a dinner, figuring it will eat up a lot of the clock and give us something to talk about as well. Problematically, neither Tommy nor I can boil an egg, but as usual, Swayze has experience in the field.

"I'll cook us a steak. You two make a salad," he says.

Later that afternoon we gather at the house. Francis and S. E. Hinton sit on the couch in the living room, saying nothing, just observing. S.E. (or Susie, as she is called) has become our den mother. She is a firecracker—smart, sarcastic, and a real guy's gal. All the Greasers love her. And we should. She created us. Now she watches her Curtis brothers cooking in the tiny, run-down kitchen. (This improv will later be incorporated into the film as Ponyboy makes a breakfast of chocolate cake.) Tommy, Swayze, and I laugh, bicker, and banter like the brothers. Francis seems pleased. As the evening wears on and we run out of inspiration, Swayze bails us out again by pulling out his six-string. The three of us break our 1960s timeline to sing Springsteen songs until late into the night. Eventually Francis has seen enough.

"Okay, guys. That's all for now. If you would rather sleep at the hotel, maybe that's best."

Relief washes over us. We pile into the van and head back to the comparative luxury of the Tulsa Excelsior. On the ride, Francis tells stories about shooting *Apocalypse Now* and *Patton*. I'm hoping to hear more, to hear about *The Godfather* and Pacino or what's going on with *One from the Heart* or any of the other extraordinary chapters of his great life, but we've arrived at the hotel.

"Break a leg tomorrow, boys," Francis says. "See you on the set."

Some actors take acting classes. Some go to schools of drama like Yale and Juilliard. Not me. I learned on the job. And my most influential teacher was Coppola. His lengthy, sometimes bizarre rehearsal process for *The Outsiders* was my most memorable course. I learned more about preparing a character (how he walks, talks, dresses, eats, sleeps) in those two weeks than I probably would have in two years elsewhere. It also happened at the perfect time—the end of my senior year of high school. Just as any kid about to go to college begins to think seriously about how he wants to earn a living, I was learning the tools of my trade—and being paid to do it.

There were days when I would've liked to have faced lower

expectations and less pressure than learning at this particular level demanded. It's much easier to expose yourself, to take chances, and to allow yourself to fall on your face when you are not being groomed for a Warner Bros. spring release. Crashing and burning in an elite private acting class would have been a very different experience, and part of me envied those who were schooled in that fashion. But that was not my path. Having a movie or two to "warm up" in small roles while I got my feet wet might have had an advantage or two, but let's face it, it's good to be a lead. But as I sat in the makeup chair before our first shot on our first day of shooting, I was completely unprepared for the intensity of what was to come.

Like all the Greasers, I have chosen a "uniform" for my character, one that will be different from the seven others and easily identifiable in the many group shots the movie will require. (This is an important lesson when working in ensemble casts. Be unique. Be noticed. But never do it in a way that is showy or attempts to pull focus in a dishonest way.) I'm in my black work boots (they are heavy, and will make my walk slow and plodding) and white T-shirt with an open flannel shirt over it. My collar is up. My hair is slicked back.

I am in awe of Emilio's bold choice for his "look." He will wear a Mickey Mouse T-shirt throughout the movie. Francis likes it so much that not only does he pay Disney exorbitant rights so Emil can wear the character on his shirt, he writes a scene where we all watch Mickey on TV. That's how you make a mark. Make a strong choice for your character, and if it works, you never know where it will lead. (And indeed, Emilio's relentless ad-libbing and ideas took a peripheral character and made him a focal point.)

My first shot in the movie has all of us together in the dirty yard where we practiced tai chi. Ponyboy has been beaten up by the rich kids and we rush to the alley to save him. As the Socs' car pulls out, I elect to do a diving spin move over the hood that I remember from the credit sequence of *Starsky and Hutch*. I calculate that Francis has rarely, if ever, watched TV, so he won't notice my blatant lift from my childhood heroes. I'm right.

"Hey, Rob, do that again," he says.

Cruise and I chase the Socs out of the alley over and over. Maybe fifteen takes each time. I begin to notice something about Tom that I will subsequently come to know well about certain actors. Although they are always prepared and ready, the second the camera rolls they instinctively ramp up to a whole new level of intensity. Like bulls when they see the color red, they are in a very special zone.

After we rescue Ponyboy, we walk him back to the house, with all the others joining us in one long, uninterrupted shot, which is called a master. It is a lengthy scene, pages long, and all of us have lines to deliver while we walk along and over a raised bed, which the camera is gliding around on, called a dolly track. Sometimes it's two feet off the ground, but you can't look like you are stepping over anything, which is an art that we will all become quite good at.

As Matt Dillon's character, Dallas, arrives on the scene, I observe another phenomenon—the power of charisma. Matt is not revved up; he is not blazing like a nova. He is relaxed and confident. He can just stand there and the camera loves him. I have watched actors on a set and they look just fine, then shifted my eyes to look at them on the monitor hooked up to the camera, and suddenly they look otherworldly, *amazing*. Matt is one of those guys.

Francis is really grinding us, but we love it. On *The Outsiders* we will shoot a minimum of twelve takes to get a scene, maybe more. Often we will do twenty or thirty. To keep us energized and in the mood (not that we need it), he plays Elvis Presley's "I Want You, I Need You, I Love You" from giant speakers before every take.

On any movie or TV show, you shoot a minimum of twelve hours a day. On movies it's usually more like thirteen and on *The Outsiders* we would average fourteen hours. So at the end of day one, I'm tired but exhilarated. This is early in all our careers, so we share tiny dressing rooms and cram together into vans to be driven home. On the ride back, I'm introduced to a tradition I will come to embrace with tremendous gusto—the complimentary cooler full of beers. (If for some reason you might not realize that the era of AOL Time Warner is different from those old days of working for the Brothers Warner, consider that they had no issue with a fifteen-year-old drinking their beers on the clock!) Being teenagers, we hoard as many bottles as we can hide in our clothes, after drinking as many as we can in the van. Later, we start the tradition of the Greasers' "Caps" drinking game back at the hotel. Like with all else on my first movie, I am learning how after hours are done in the big leagues. Work hard on the set, and then play hard at the hotel.

❖

It takes an army to make a movie. Camera crews, lighting crews, wardrobe crews, makeup crews, hair crews, painters, builders (called grips), a crew to provide the props, a crew to provide the furnishings (the art department), electricians, special-effects people, stunt performers, stand-ins, the accountant, scheduling and finance (called the unit production manager), catering and someone to provide snacks and drinks (called craft service), and the team of walkie-talkie-armed Gestapo that police the second-by-second momentum of shooting: the assistant director staff. But no one, and I mean no one, has more juice and is more loved and feared than the Teamsters. They come as advertised—they can make or break any production. You simply do not fuck with them. But in his typical fashion, Francis has other ideas.

I'm crammed into my tiny trailer with Emilio, Cruise, and Howell when we hear Francis screaming at his longtime producer, Gray Frederickson.

"Get rid of them! I want them gone!"

"Um, Francis, we can't fire the Teamsters," responds Gray, evenly.

"Yes we can! I want them gone. Today!" yells Coppola, livid.

"What's the deal?" I whisper to the guys.

"I think it's about the budget," says Emil, who knows these things.

"Francis, if the Teamsters go, so do the cars, trucks, and trailers," argues Gray.

"I don't give a fuck!"

"But if the trailers go, the actors have nowhere to change clothes or keep warm or out of the rain."

"So what!"

"Well, they are all Screen Actors Guild members and they are contractually provided with shelter."

"Well, fuck them, too! I'll make this movie with University of Tulsa film students," yells Francis.

Oh boy. Last week we were worried about getting injured and being sent home. But this new scenario has us all *really* freaked. I look at Tommy Howell, who is wide-eyed. I remember the *Apocalypse Now* documentary where Francis is as least as concerned with continuing to shoot as he is with Martin Sheen's heart attack. I think to myself, this is one tough industry.

Eventually the director and producer move off and we can no longer hear them. At lunchtime the Teamsters (and our trailers and ourselves) are still in place. By wrap at the end of the day, it's like it never happened. Francis is back to his jovial, opera-listening mode, but I've seen how hairy it can get and how quickly it can happen. I'm beginning to see that show business at this level is full of emotion, threats, and warlike conflict, usually followed by smiles and hugs. If you weren't crazy for wanting to get into movies in the first place, you could quickly become so once you got there.

B ack at the hotel I punch Tom Cruise in the face. I hit
him squarely in the nose, and *hard*. I see his eyes water
and blink, so I know he's stunned and in pain. He goes
into a rage and begins to pummel me mercilessly in the chest and
ribs. It's getting way out of hand, and finally Emilio and Tommy
Howell step in and stop the fight.

We've taken to these nightly sparring sessions in the sixth-
floor hallway as a way to kill time, blow off steam, and prepare for
the upcoming "rumble" sequence in the movie. We wear headgear and mouthpieces; the gloves are pro-grade (all equipment
provided by Emilio and Tom, the masters of fitness). Most of the
time it's pretty friendly, but every once in a while . . .

"Hey, man, you okay?" asks Cruise, coming back to reality.

"I'm good. Sorry about the face shot," I say.

"Well, now you know what'll happen if you do it again!" he says, grinning his grin.

We high-five and begin to help the others pack up the equipment. Soon we are planning the next session of our "R and R," the nightly flyby of the lobby to check out any potential girl activity.

Since I first observed Matt Dillon's master technique, I have been wondering how I might fare on my own. I have been dating Melissa Gilbert back in L.A., but her mom thinks I'm after her for her fame and won't let her visit me. I'm also beginning to feel the unique effects of shooting on location—a euphoric and toxic mix of excitement, boredom, anonymity, recognizability, and loneliness. After a few weeks of walking by frenzied, available girls who look exactly like the cute girls at Samohi who always ignored me, I'm ready to have some fun.

And so begins a time-honored tradition of entertainers on the road—sometimes you chase girls, sometimes they chase you (literally), sometimes it's just to flirt, and sometimes it's more than that. But it's always fun and both principals in the equation seem to get exactly what they want out of it. We are all teenage boys, so you can imagine how enthusiastically we take to this pastime. Only Swayze, who is married, seems content to watch from the sidelines with a wry smile.

For most of us Greasers it's a perfect setup. My situation is complicated somewhat by my long-distance relationship with my girlfriend and there are times when I feel bad about that. But I begin to learn another great lesson: nothing quiets the inner voice you want to ignore better than a couple of beers. And between the open cooler on the van ride home each day and Francis's food-and-wine festivals at the end of each week, I'm getting a lot of practice at quieting my conscience.

❖

You really know you've arrived in the movies when you are given your own stuntman. These are the guys (or in our case, boys) who will take the blows and make you look like a stud. Even looking at your stuntman is a cool experience; he is dressed in your clothes, has the same haircut and style, and is your same weight and height. In essence, he is your tough, fearless doppelgänger.

Buddy Joe Hooker was (and is) the most legendary stuntman ever. A hit movie was made about him called *Hooper*, starring Burt Reynolds. He is the stunt coordinator on *The Outsiders* and will help Francis design all the car sequences, knifings, fights, and, of course, the big rumble between the Socs and the Greasers. He's dressed head to toe in white (including his cowboy hat) and is smoking a tiny cigar as he stands in the muddy vacant lot that will be the set for the big brawl.

"Hey, Lowe, come meet your guy," he says, gesturing to an exact replica of myself as Sodapop Curtis.

"This is Reid Rondell. He's one of my best," says Buddy Joe, who knows his stuff.

Reid and I shake hands. Soon we are talking like old friends. He's a lot like me, the same age, and has been doing his thing since he was a little boy. He gives me my moves for the fight sequence, shows me how to throw a movie punch that looks great on film but doesn't "land," and he shows me how to get "hit" by one as well. We work in our own corner of the field. All around us, the other Greasers are doing the same thing with their stuntmen. The most dangerous thing you can ask is for two actors to "fight" each other (as Cruise and I know), so each Greaser will fight his stuntman dressed as a Soc, which means I will fight Reid.

"Let's kick ass! Let's make our fight the best one in the entire rumble!" says Reid.

We try to come up with cool elements for our beatdown. We also scout what the other Greasers are up to, to see where we stand. It's just like the audition process all over again—lots of camaraderie, but very competitive.

The rumble scene is a few days off and the company has switched to filming all the night shoots in the movie. This means breakfast at four o'clock in the afternoon, shooting at sunset, lunch around one in the morning, and finishing at sunrise. The first few days are magical: the crazy hours, the giant lights and exotic equipment, the buzz of adrenaline that comes from pulling an all-nighter, all in the company of your band of brothers. Then reality sets in. Your body begins to revolt. You are too wired to sleep at sunrise, can't sleep enough during the daylight hours to get the rest you need, and are always hungry at the wrong times. You start to feel like a vampire—you miss all of everyday life while you try to recuperate in your manufactured, light-sealed room/cave. As anyone who has pulled the graveyard shift will tell you, it becomes a serious grind.

It's around three thirty in the morning and Francis has asked that an entire section of the front of the house be removed for a shot he wants. As the grips continue this major piece of engineering, we try to kill time and stay awake. At one point I find myself alone with Francis, sitting in the living room. Coppola has been an enigma throughout the filming. He's always pleasant and clearly wants the best for me and everyone else on his crew, but he is also aloof and can play favorites (which as an adult I understand was his prerogative, but as a teenager I did not). Like everyone else, I do whatever I can to please him, make him proud, and to be in his good graces. Now, since it's just the two of us, I try to make conversation.

"Francis, I'm sure you hear this a lot, but *Godfather* was on in the hotel and we all watched it for the hundredth time. What an unbelievable movie."

"You know, Rob, to me *The Godfather* is like that lamp," he says, pointing. "It exists. It's right there. People have opinions about it," he continues mildly. "The real *Godfather*, for me, is the experience I had making it."

It would be many years and many projects before I fully understood what he meant. If you are fortunate enough to be part of a hit, particularly a transcendent one, all emotional ownership is transferred from you to the audience. They judge it and embrace it; project their own hopes, dreams, and fears onto it; take their personal meaning from its themes, and with these investments it becomes theirs. The significance of your participation pales in comparison to the significance the project has on their imaginations. And so, you are left outside of the phenomenon. Just as Paul McCartney can never experience the Beatles, Francis Ford Coppola can never experience *The Godfather*. It becomes a lamp.

❖

Coppola's reputation as an innovator is well earned. For large chunks of the filming of *The Outsiders*, he watches from a monitor, covered in a blanket, or sometimes from blocks away in a specially designed Airstream trailer nicknamed "The Silverfish." Since movies were first made, directors have been close by on set, sometimes right in your face, next to the camera, observing. Not Francis. He is a pioneer of video hookups and on-set monitors, and there are days when we rarely see him on set as the cameras roll. Back then, it was surprising. Today, it is commonplace—all directors have their heads buried behind monitors and no one actually watches your performance "live."

Tonight, standing in the unseasonably cold spring rainstorm, part of me wishes I was able to sip an espresso in my own Silverfish. But mostly I'm just trying to stay warm by the huge bonfire that has been built as part of the scenery for the rumble sequence. Like with all great movie productions, on *The Outsiders* the artistic is also the practical. The fire is really only there so the actors don't try to leave the set to get warm in the shitty little trailer huts parked blocks away.

Same with the vicious, cold driving rainstorm all of us Greasers are standing in. Some directors would wait out the bad weather before shooting such a lengthy—three to four days—and important sequence. But Francis won't wait, and in fact, he uses what nature gives him to dramatic effect. He asks the great director of photography Steve Burum (whom I will work with again on *St. Elmo's Fire*) to light the rain in the most unusually stunning way possible.

As usual, I'm huddled with Tom Howell and the rest of the Greasers. We don't really mind being soaked in the mind-numbing cold because we know how great it will look on-screen. What none of us realizes is that if it doesn't continue to rain for the next few nights of shooting, rain will be created to match this storm, with fire hoses spraying even colder water up into the air.

It rains until lunchtime on the first night and then stops. Out come the fire hoses, which instantly give you an ice cream headache.

Reid Rondell and I go through our choreographed fight moves. Swayze is doing some sort of ballet dancer warm-ups that look very challenging. Cruise is tugging at a front tooth that he will later have removed by a local dentist to bolster the authenticity of his fight's aftermath. Under a tarp, Matt Dillon's boom box plays Tommy Howell's favorite mix tape—Adam Ant's "Stand and Deliver," Soft Cell's "Tainted Love," and Oingo Boingo's "Only a Lad." When I hear those songs today, I still feel wet, cold, and extremely pumped.

On the last night we shoot my part of the fight. Reid and I slug it out and in the end it goes pretty well. I feel particularly good about making it look like I took his punch in the face. What I didn't know then was that you are better off "selling" a punch you throw than a punch hitting you. And so, if you watch the rumble sequence today, two things stand out: the rain comes out of nowhere and Sodapop kinda gets his ass kicked. Ah well, live and learn.

As the weeks of shooting roll on, I settle into a groove. All of the actors have bonded deeply (think of your new friends in your first semester away at college) and we show up for each other on set even if we aren't needed. We play elaborate drinking games nightly (I am the undisputed champion of Caps) and share reconnaissance about the local girls (Tommy Howell being the undisputed king of local outreach by a mile). He and I share an adjoining room and never close the door, an indication of how close we are becoming. The script calls for Ponyboy and Soda to have a bond that is deeper than brotherhood. And after weeks of pressure, fun, hard work, and long hours, that relationship is now real.

Tonight, the music coming from Howell's room is so loud it's keeping me awake.

"Shut the hell up! We have a seven a.m. call time," I yell.

"No, man! I'm going method in the scene! I'm supposed to have been up all night, so I'm going to *be* up all night," says the fifteen-year-old Marlon Brando.

"Good luck with that," I say, plugging my ears and eventually falling asleep.

At 7:00 a.m. my alarm goes off and I go into Tommy's room.

"Still awake! Didn't sleep at all. I'm *so* ready," he says.

"I need my coffee," I yawn, as we pack for the set.

We shoot the scene. It's postrumble, all of us up all night, nursing our wounds. It's long and complicated and takes all day. Finally, around 5:00 p.m., we get to my close-up. (Anytime you are in a large ensemble, your close-up is a very important shot. Good actors are excellent not only in their own close-ups, but also, almost more important, off camera while others are shooting theirs.) As he does during every shot on *The Outsiders*, Francis blasts "I Want You, I Need You, I Love You."

"Action, Rob!" comes his voice from the big speakers (he's in the Silverfish today).

I start the scene. Somewhere in the middle, Ponyboy has a line that's a cue for me. It doesn't come.

Wow, that's a dramatic pause Tommy's taking, I think, as I wait for his line. The camera continues to roll. My back is to Tommy. I don't want to turn around and look at him, and I have a pretty good idea of what's going on. I look over at Swayze, who is staring at Howell. Then I hear it. Snoring. Tommy is literally passed out, sleeping right in the middle of my close-up! So much for the Method.

✤

The big emotional-breakdown scene between Sodapop and his brothers got me this role. Now, in the last few days of shooting, it's time to do it for real.

As on any movie, at the end, everyone is on edge. The actors are contemplating what they have (or haven't) been able to accomplish, the director is clawing to shoot as much as possible before time runs out; the crew is exhausted and being driven into the ground. But I'm feeling pretty good. I've watched the other actors take center stage and excel. Now it's my turn. I've done this scene with giant pressure in New York and L.A. I've been to this emotional well before and I know there is water.

We shoot in a neighborhood park breathtakingly lit by Francis and Steve Burum. Masses of equipment surround the perimeter. Coppola wants it to be windy, so a Ritter fan with blades the size of a turboprop is standing by. I'm laughing and joking with Swayze and Howell, trying to quell the emotion I can already feel, just under the surface.

A technician cranks the giant Ritter fan and points it at the rows of towering elm trees. The blast is powerful enough to bend the branches. In the beautiful, eerie light it looks like a storm is brewing.

"Action, Rob!" Francis yells. Five cameras shooting different angles and sizes roll. The crew of fifty or so people watch quietly as I race into the park, chased by my two brothers. As I reach the baseball backstop, they tackle me in the pool of light created to play the scene. At the end of this very long take, I dry my eyes, feeling pretty good. Francis sends us back to go again. Once more, I'm tackled into the backstop. After another eight or nine takes, I'm starting to tire emotionally, but I know I've given 100 percent. I'm glad we had five cameras to capture every moment.

"Hey, buddy, good job," says Swayze, giving me a long, hard hug.

"Thanks, man," I say, punching him in the arm.

Francis comes ambling out of the darkness.

"Hey, how ya feel?" he asks, putting a big paw on my shoulder.

"Good. Um. Good. You?"

"I think it's time to do your close-ups," he says, full of encouragement.

I can feel my legs go to rubber and my pulse skyrocket.

"Um. None of the cameras were close-ups?" I ask, trying not to panic.

"Oh, no. They were all extremely wide. Now we'll punch in and really get the emotion!" he says, walking off to set the shot.

Standing alone now, I know I'm in deep trouble. Through take after take I have poured my heart out, cried my eyes dry for the last hour. I have nothing left, and I'm terrified. I've wasted all my emotion on giant wide shots where you probably can't even see my face. I feel like an idiot.

I don't dare tell anyone. I begin to pace, to wind myself up to refill my tank. It will take them a while to reset the cameras; maybe that'll be enough time for me to regroup.

Soon they're ready. No need to run through the park and be tackled now. I throw myself to the ground on my own. The camera is two feet from my face. It's not a good sign that as I begin my "breakdown" speech, all I can think about is that I've probably said these words over fifty times on camera, but this will be the only version that will matter. I try to wrestle myself back into the scene, but I can't; I'm thinking one thing and one thing only: I can't possibly duplicate what I did in the wide shots. And it turns out to be true. Where I wept before, there is nothing, no tears, and no real emotions. So I do what all actors do when they have nothing authentic left to offer: I begin to act.

I can feel everyone around me tighten up. It's obvious that it's not happening for me. The take ends.

"Let's go again," says Francis.

"I hate it when you two fight," I say to my brothers (please, God, let me get this, let me let go, I need to cry again, this is for *everything*). Howell and Swayze are willing me to the finish line but I can't get there. I'm actually more locked up than I was in the previous take.

"Okay. Let's all take a ten-minute break," offers Francis. The crew wanders off to smoke or get coffee.

"Hey, c'm'ere!" says Tommy Howell. "I wanna talk to you."

We step off the set into the shadows to be alone.

"What's going on?" he asks.

"I . . . I . . . I . . . can't . . . I . . ."

"Fuck that, man. You *gotta*. You can *do* this! This is what it's all about. Right now! You, me, and Swayze!"

I'm looking at my feet, getting lectured by a fifteen-year-old.

"I don't know what to do. I didn't know to save it for the close-up. Nobody told me," I say lamely.

Tommy grabs me by my face, hard.

"Look at me," he says, his eyes shining. "I love you. You're my brother. We're gonna get you ready."

And then come the most loving, generous, wise moments I've ever shared with another actor. He starts a narrative, a hushed, hypnotic story of our life together as orphaned brothers. He tells me about our mother, how beautiful she was with her blonde hair, and about the day she nicknamed me Sodapop because I was always so happy. He asks me to remember Dad and how much we miss him—his strength, his laugh—and reminds me of the pony he surprised us with at Christmas. As he winds down, he pulls me close to him and whispers: "There's no one else like you in this whole wide world, Sodapop Curtis. You're my brother and I love you so much. You're all we have left."

"Come on, guys," calls Francis. "We've got about twenty minutes before the sun's up."

"Don't listen to that," says Howell firmly. "You're ready now. Go nail this fucker like you know you can."

We walk back onto the set. I'm full now—full of the emotion I need, full of love and of unending gratitude for this amazing friend. His compassion and leadership will remain unmatched in my professional experience.

Francis rolls the camera. I do the scene. This time, there are tears. When it's over, I hug my brothers as the sun breaks over the horizon.

CHAPTER 12

The letdown that ensues when returning home after making a movie on location is something that all actors struggle with, particularly young ones. Fighting a stuntman, shooting a potential blockbuster, and living in your own hotel room is always going to trump doing chores, being back in your old bedroom, and answering to your parents. You've been on a high for weeks on end and now it's back to "normal" life surrounded by people who can't really relate to what you've just experienced. So while I still hang out with my girlfriend, Melissa, and my high school buddies, I'm spending more and more time down the block at the Sheens. Emilio and I are inseparable and in constant touch with Cruise and Tommy Howell. We all have a suspicion (and a hope) that we've just been a part of something special, something that may eventually change our lives. That no one else knows this makes it seem like we are living with a secret that we would like to share, but can't, sort of like having a super-power that's not come online, or being a president elect. For the moment, our lives proceed as usual, but in a few months every-thing—we think—will change. It's a frustrating, if exciting, dis-connect and, as I do with any situation that makes me feel at all uneasy, I have found a way to deal with it.

"Pass me a beer," I call to Emilio as we sit, going over a script. There are stacks on his desk and I recognize all of them. With *The Outsiders* in the can, the only others who share our suspi-cion that big things may lie ahead are a few key studio execu-tives. They aren't offering us movies, as the public, for the most part, has no idea who we are, but they want us to come in and read for major roles. At a minimum, my days of not getting the meetings I want are over.

Some of the Outsiders have already capitalized on the industry buzz. Francis immediately hired his favorites, Matt Dillon and Diane Lane, for his next movie, *Rumble Fish*. Tom Cruise is about to do a movie called *Risky Business*. I finished shooting *The Outsid-ers* and was starring with the great Gena Rowlands in a Hallmark Hall of Fame movie, *Thursday's Child*, within a week. In a measure of my small, but growing, status, CBS held the project until I was available to shoot it. (It would bring me my first Golden Globe nomination, for Best Performance by an Actor in a Supporting Role in a Series, Mini-Series, or Motion Picture Made for Tele-vision.) And now, as I sit sipping a Corona, Emilio and I are prepar-ing to read for a cool romantic comedy called *Class*. We are both trying for the same part, a boarding-school virgin who mistakenly falls in love with his rich roommate's mom.

As always, there is affectionate competition and industry chat-ter among our group. The consensus is that Cruise is taking a chance with *Risky Business*. The script is funny, but dark and weird; the director wrote it himself and has no experience. *Class*, on the other hand, clearly has a great shot at being huge. The director is coming off the critically acclaimed movie *The Great Santini*, with Robert Duvall. I work hard on my audition, awed to be traveling in the same creative circles as the Duvalls of the world.

In the Sheens' backyard there is a professional batting cage. My brother Chad and Charlie play all the time, still hoping to become baseball players. They rib Emilio and me mercilessly about being "serious actors!" As Emilio and I help each other run lines and prepare, we can hear the thwack of the bat in the distance. They have no patience for our show-business shoptalk. But we both have big momentum and are pressing the advantage.

❖

I'm led to a back area of the historic Beverly Hills Hotel. We wind through lush landscaping and fragrant gardens. I ask the girl taking me where we are going and she says simply, "The bungalows."

I come to find that there are a number of private cottages, some quite large, hidden away from the more downmarket riffraff occupying the main hotel building.

"Welcome to Mr. De Laurentiis's bungalow," says the girl, with a heavy Italian accent. She leads me into a large living room, where a fire roars in spite of it being well over a hundred degrees outside. "Champagne?" she asks, and even though I rarely, if ever, turn down such an offer, I decline. After all, I'm here to interview for a movie.

Dino De Laurentiis single-handedly created the postwar film industry in his native Italy. Among the many movies he produced over the years were Fellini's *La Strada*, *Three Days of the Condor*, *Serpico*, and *King Kong*. He is interested in me for the lead role in his latest epic, the long-awaited adaptation of Frank Herbert's *Dune*. It is, by far, the most talked about movie of the year. It will also be the most expensive. Mr. De Laurentiis is building a brand-new studio from scratch just to shoot it.

After a good wait in the sweltering living room, I am called
to a dark, paneled study, not unlike the one at the beginning of
*The Godfather*. All that's missing is a wedding outside. Mr. De
Laurentiis sits at a desk, reading some sort of voluminous docu-
ment, while a casting director throws me softball questions meant
to show the great man my charisma and personality. A number
of Italian businessmen watch and listen closely.

Figuring (correctly) that he might be interested in what fellow
Italian Francis Ford Coppola has been up to on *The Outsiders*, I
show him a cast photo I've brought along. I want him to see me "in
character" as a sneak preview, as the film hasn't been released yet.

For the first time since I entered the room, De Laurentiis looks
up from his reading. He considers the group shot of the Greasers
and raises a hand, stopping my conversation with the casting
director midsentence.

They then begin an animated conversation in Italian and soon
the business guys join in as well. Mr. De Laurentiis is getting very
excited, looking at me almost for the first time, nodding to me as
he also looks back at the photo. Soon everyone is nodding and
looking at the eight-by-ten. Dino is excitedly tapping his finger on
the picture and now, at last, a word I can understand: "Star! Star!
Star!" he exclaims as he points at the cast photo. I lean over the
desk and realize he is pointing at Matt Dillon.

In spite of the Italians' enthusiasm for Matt, somehow I end
up with the offer to star in *Dune*. This is the exact kind of film
that takes an actor to the next level. Huge leading-man part, giant
budget, international appeal, and a built-in fan base for a book
people have been trying to shoot for years.

But there are two problems: There is no finished script and
Dino is demanding a commitment for three sequels.

It's hard to imagine now, as you look at films today, but there
was a time when no self-respecting actor would *dream* of making
a sequel. It was gauche, it was so shamelessly commercial, that it

simply *wasn't done.* (And don't give me the *Godfather II* example. That was an anomaly.) You didn't see *Heaven Can Wait 2* or *An Officer and a Gentleman: Boot Camp, Tootsie Too,* or *Four Days of the Condor!*

Eventually the stigma would be scrubbed away by corporate pressure, bottom-line-minded studio presidents, producers needing to keep the lights on, and stars tired of turning down cash while waiting for artistic parts that never come. But as I discuss the offer for *Dune* and its three sequels on the phone with my agents, it is a real issue. I table this discussion and turn to the problem of the nonexistent shooting script. While not uncommon, it's never a great sign.

My agents tell me that I can approve it before I show up for work. I won't have *official* approval, but "they'll work with me." Again, not a great sign, but I'm inclined to roll the dice. The upside on a movie like this is just too big.

"I just want to circle back to the sequel commitment clause," says one of my agents. "You will be committing to potentially doing all three *Dune* movies at their option."

"I've only read the first two books," I say. "Anyone read the third?"

"I have," says one of the agents.

"What do I do in it?" I ask.

"You become a sandworm."

"I'm sorry?"

"You become a sandworm. A big one. About three hundred feet long."

"I . . . I . . . I'm a *worm* in the second sequel?" I ask.

"Not all of you, just your head," says my agent evenly.

"It's a long, wormlike body, I do think it calls for three hundred feet, but it is only your head that would be seen, on top of the body. A worm-head, for lack of a better description."

There is a long silence.

"Not a huge commitment when you really think about it," adds another agent helpfully.

"Um, guys, I'm gonna have to get back to you," I say, hanging up.

As I will do for years whenever it's crunch time and I need to make a tough call, I take a long walk to think. I agonize over the decision. But I just can't get the image of my face on a giant tapeworm out of my head. I know the Italians are the world's masters of style, but I doubt even they could pull this off. I pass.

*Dune* ends up being an embarrassing debacle for all concerned. In spite of all the money and hype pumped into the movie, it died a horrible death. Had I done it, though, I guess I wouldn't have had to worry about the sequels.

❖

At home, my relationship with my family is in a strange, transitional phase. I'm earning a living and supporting myself but still living with the family. I'm changing by the day, growing more independent, branching out, and leading a life that includes them less and less. Steve has now turned part of our house into an office, where he sees his psychiatric patients on the weekends. There's nothing like being told to "be quiet" as an odd lot of troubled adults file through your home to make a teen boy want to flee. Mom is more reclusive than ever and when she is out from behind her closed bedroom door, she is likely to be fighting with Steve. It's an uncomfortable, sad, tense vibe, palpable enough to affect me, but not enough to prevent me from doing what I do best in these situations, which is to tune out. I love my mother but I have no idea what she needs and don't have the tools to find out.

I still go for my summer visits to see my family in Ohio. Chad and I sleep until noon, wander downtown to have lunch with Dad in his twenty-fifth-floor corner office, and spend the rest of the day playing endless rounds of tennis and draining every bottle of

Little Kings Cream Ale we can find. My father remains the most vigorous, vivacious, tough, and charismatic man in my life. Our grueling matches on the dark clay of the Hollinger Tennis Club are fueled by love, pride, and competitive rivalry. I learn of sportsmanship (and sometimes lack thereof), focus, and intensity. My dad is a former teaching pro and I rarely get more than a game or two off of him. In fact, I will not beat him until I am forty years old. At the time, he had recently survived lymphoma, and I was happy to show him no mercy. Neither of us would have it any other way.

But there are many other lessons that teenage boys need to learn. And most of these can't be taught over pizza at midnight or on the tennis court. I only know this now because I see it with my own teen sons. They don't really listen to speeches or talks. They absorb incrementally, through hours and hours of observation. The sad truth about divorce is that it's hard to teach your kids about life unless you are living life with them: eating together, doing homework, watching Little League, driving them around endlessly, being bored with nothing to do, letting them listen while you do business, while you negotiate love and the frustrations and complications and rewards of living day in and out with your wife. Through this, they see how adults handle responsibility, honesty, commitment, jealousy, anger, professional pressures, and social interactions. Kids learn from whoever is around them the most. Especially boys. In spite of our separation, I took those valuable lessons from Dad and also the ones that I could from my increasingly checked-out mom. But I was facing bigger stakes by the day in work, and in every area of my young adult life. And as I had done so many times before, I looked inward and formulated my own ethos as best I could. Like with so much in my life, I was making it up as I went along.

❖

Paul Newman is wearing his Chiefs hockey jersey from *Slap Shot* as he ushers me into his office. If I had to choose the ultimate person to work with (and emulate in every way), it would be this man with the famous lavender eyes now sitting cross-legged on the floor.

"Have a seat, kid," he says, as if he's talking to the Sundance Kid. I sit on the floor with him and we begin my audition for the movie he is directing called *Harry & Son*. I try to push away any thought about the possibility of being Newman's kid on-screen. *That* would be beyond belief. But other than meeting my lifelong idol, the rest is uneventful. I get the impression I'm not what he's looking for (eventually he will cast Robby Benson) and we say our good-byes.

On my way out, I see Matt Dillon coming in. As ever, Matt doesn't seem to have a care in the world, as if he were just out running errands. I wish him luck as he heads to Paul's office. "Yeah, thanks, man," he says, closing the door.

In the lobby I'm hung up by the receptionist, who can't find any validation stickers for the parking garage. As I wait, Dillon comes out of his audition. I'm surprised at how fast it was.

"Geez, man! How'd it go in there?" I ask.

Matt looks at me a beat and lights a Marlboro Red. "I dunno, man. He told me I needed to read poetry!" he says, then throws his head back and lets out a vintage Dillon "Heh, heh, heh!" laugh. Looks like neither of the Outsiders will play one of Newman's own.

❖

One of the great things about show business is that Monday can be disappointing and Tuesday can be exhilarating. Momentum and fortunes change on a dime. (It's why addicts are often drawn to the business. They actually enjoy the rush of the roller coaster.) After whiffing on *Harry & Son*, I'm an inch from getting *Class*, in spite of changing my mind about which part to play. Although the lead part of Jonathan the Virgin is more coveted, I found it sort of dull. I asked the directors and producers to let me read for the other role of Skip, the wiseass preppy rich kid who befriends Jonathan, because I thought the part was more entertaining. This is an instinct I would always follow; the best part is not the biggest, it's the one that is the most memorable. Some of my favorite roles would end up not being leads but ones that I took because I felt like I could do something unique with the part, like in *Square Dance*, *Tommy Boy*, *Austin Powers: The Spy Who Shagged Me*, and *Thank You for Smoking*. Other times I would be offered the lead and choose a supporting part that I felt was more challenging or out of the box, like Nick the deaf-mute in Stephen King's *The Stand*. Years later, I would switch roles at the last second again on Curtis Hanson's *Bad Influence*.

But now I'm on location in Chicago where *Class* will be shot, for the last screen test for my part. My competition is an actor who is one of those guys who gets white-hot overnight and is in the mix on a number of big films. He has everyone in Hollywood talking, and I just hope he doesn't get this one. His name is Raphael Sbarge. We will go head to head in the ballroom of the Chicago Sheraton tomorrow at 9:30 sharp.

But there is a catch.

My agents want me to fly home to work out some details in my deal before I screen-test, so I go to the production office and ask the secretary to book my flight back to L.A.

"Hey! Hey!" a giant bald man is yelling at me through an open door of an office. "Get the fuck in here, kid," he says, waving.

I realize this is Martin Ransohoff, the producer of the movie and a big-time player with hits like *Silver Streak* and critical successes like *Catch-22* and *The Americanization of Emily*. He also reportedly once beat the shit out of Sam Peckinpah. He is the embodiment of old-school Hollywood, from the days before bloodless MBAs and comic-book nerds took the place of the men with big vision and bigger appetites, men who understood and appreciated the lost art of the Grand Gesture. Yeah, sure, Marty might let his nut sack dangle out of his robe as he takes a meeting outside by his pool, but at least he takes his meetings outside by his pool!

"What the fuck do you think you're doing, kid?"

"Um, my agents say I should come home while . . ." I manage to get out before being cut off.

"Fuck your agents!"

"Well, sir . . ."

"Your agents are going to agent you right out of this fucking movie. Close the door and sit down."

I do as I'm told.

Ransohoff has what looks to be about fifteen strands of hair on his otherwise totally bald head. These strands are swirled together on his crown, but now he is so agitated that he is pulling at the tuft, jerking it straight out in a jabbing motion, revealing it to be at least two and a half feet long.

"Your agents are idiots. Let me tell you how this goes. Tomorrow morning at nine thirty, unless a fucking 747 hits you on the head, you are going to get this part."

This is news to me; I thought I was in a real horse race and that the screen test was a huge deal. "But what about the screen test? What about Raphael Sbarge?"

"Fuck Raphael Sbarge. There is only one way in this entire fucking universe that fucking Raphael Sbarge will *ever* play this part. And that is if you are so fucking stupid that you blow it all at the very last second by flying back to L.A. 'cause your ignorant asshole agents can't close your deal over a lousy couple of grand a week! You gonna give this part to Raphael Sbarge over a couple of grand a week?"

"No."

"I didn't think so! You are a smart kid. I'll see you tomorrow. Now get out of my fucking office."

It was sound advice. I got the part, as he promised, and I don't even remember the screen test.

I had hoped my pal Emilio would play opposite me in *Class*, but it was not to be. Instead, a kid from New York named Andrew McCarthy accompanied a friend to *his* audition for a small role in the film. While the friend read, a casting director asked Andrew if he could take a Polaroid of him while he waited. "Would you want to possibly be in movies? Maybe you could get a walk-on?"

"I don't see why not," Andrew told him as he took the Polaroid.

A month later, Andrew is starring in the movie. He never told me what happened to his friend.

Andrew and I are well cast, in that we are very different. He is aloof and observing—Holden Caulfield come to life. Within ten minutes of meeting Andrew, I know he won't be putting on the headgear to spar with me in the hotel hallway.

He does, however, convince me to accompany him on a pilgrimage all over Chicago to find sensory-deprivation tanks.

It's late in the evening the night before the first day of photography.

"Hey, Bob"—to this day he is the only human to ever call me that—"I think I found two tanks in the classifieds. Let's go." I was a huge fan of the recent movie *Altered States*, where William Hurt reverts to being some sort of ape-creature after spending time in a deprivation tank. I'm curious to see what might happen to me.

I don't know much about Chicago and its various neighborhoods but I am well versed in its music, so when we pull up to a tenement on the South Side of town, I know we are in way over our heads. Looking around at the devastated buildings and deserted streets, I don't really need Jim Croce's song "Leroy Brown" to know this *is* the baddest part of town.

We knock on a buckled door. A gentleman in a kufi leads us down into his darkened basement without saying one word to us. I am petrified. I'm reminded of John Wayne Gacy and his Chicago-area basement. If this guy pulls out a clown suit, I'm outta here. Andrew and I are shown two black, coffinlike, fiberglass enclosed tubes. The guy in the kufi opens them up. The smell of salt is enough to make my eyes burn instantly.

"Twenty-five dollars for half an hour. Fifty dollars for an hour."

"We'll take an hour," says Andrew, stripping down.

I climb into the tank naked. The water is at body temperature, with tremendous salinity to make you float effortlessly. Eventually, encased in the darkness, you forget you are in water at all. You feel nothing, no water, no light; you are suspended as if in the void.

I hear a terrible hammering. I realize it's my heartbeat. How long have I been in this thing? I wonder. I lay there stiff as a board, waiting for the kufi man to suddenly whip the lid off and stab me with a carving knife. I begin to have random thoughts as I panic in the claustrophobic darkness. What is *in* this water anyway? Does anyone know where we are? Do *we* know where we are? Would Raphael Sbarge be as scared as I am? Did Andrew quietly leave me here and go back to the hotel, where he's listening to Bob Dylan and playing his bongos? What if I'm locked in this tank or this basement? Why did Bill Hurt turn into an ape in this thing, anyway? Will my ape be as badass as his ape if the same thing happens to me? Why did I agree to do this in the first place?

I'm snapped to my senses by someone opening my lid. It's Andrew, already dressed, and still in human form.

"C'mon, Bob. Time to go home."

In the end, the only earth-shattering experience I got from

my time in the deprivation tank was a vicious ear infection. No wonder they never really caught on.

❖

The making of *Class* is a markedly different experience from that of *The Outsiders*. There is no gang of like-minded guys to keep one another company and keep one another's spirits up. At least Reid Rondell, my stuntman from *The Outsiders*, is brought in to double me and to stage the big fight that ends the movie. I do manage to spend time with Cruise, who is shooting *Risky Business* in town (the night I visit, they are filming the iconic Porsche-going-into-Lake-Michigan scene), but since both of us are so busy, it isn't the same. Also, Tom has a new perspective on his acting style, telling me, "I want to spend time hanging with you but Joel [his character] doesn't."

As Thanksgiving rolls around, I spend my first major holiday away from home. This doesn't help my loneliness but it does introduce me to another facet of the path I have chosen: You are going to miss a lot in life that most people take for granted. If you are not vigilant, that list can include holidays, birthdays, births, deaths, funerals, graduations, parent-teacher conferences, first steps, first words, school plays, trick-or-treating, Little League games, and just about every other moment that makes life worth living. Sure, there is an obvious trade-off with some of the great perks of success, but you can't build a life on a backstage pass. Or free swag at Sundance.

I join my director, Lewis John Carlino, for Thanksgiving dinner at the home of a powerful and well-to-do Chicago family. They are gracious hosts, welcoming us into their massive home overlooking Lake Michigan. Immediately my attention is drawn to a stunning blonde standing among the other guests. Her looks are arresting for sure, but what really makes her stand out is the fairy-princess costume she is wearing—complete with wings and a wand. I ask Lewis who she is. It turns out she is the nineteen-year-old daughter of our hosts, and I will be seated next to her.

At dinner I make small talk with the fairy princess, who, it turns out, has done some acting and is thinking of moving from Chicago to L.A. Again, I think of my girlfriend at home, but I haven't seen her in weeks. She is staying with her family in L.A. and is still not allowed to travel to be with me on location. Under the circumstances of my life, I have no business having a girlfriend at all, but I don't have the maturity to know it or the guts to call it off.

By 4:30 in the morning the fairy princess and I find ourselves in deep conversation at an all-night diner. I am deeply infatuated with her, but she informs me that she is a virgin and is saving herself for Jackson Browne, whom she has never met. A Jackson Browne fan myself, I swallow my disappointment, tell her she's chosen well, and wish her Godspeed. Soon it is so late that we are both falling asleep in our food. I walk her to a taxi and say goodbye. "Daryl Hannah," I tell her, "you are amazing."

❖

After having worked almost exclusively with actors of my age and experience level, on *Class* I worked for the first time with stars. Jacqueline Bisset was at the time a worldwide sex icon and respected actress to boot (a rare combo), and Cliff Robertson was an Academy Award–winning star, as well as a producer for his film *Charly*, which I had loved as a little boy back in Ohio. Jackie and Cliff played my mom and dad, and many years later this combo remains the best set of on-screen parents I ever had.

Here's what they taught me about working with stars: They know what the fuck they are doing. They have been there, done that, heard every line of bullshit imaginable, been hustled in every fashion, worked with lesser lights who had the ability to bring them down, had all the marbles hoisted onto their backs, then hauled the movies up the cliffs of adversity themselves to where public opinion and the gatekeepers of the industry stood waiting in judgment, ready to blame them exclusively in failure. Most stars are great-looking on the outside but tough as shit on the inside. They have to be. When you hear a star is "difficult" or a "diva" or "demanding," there are a few possible scenarios. The least likely is that you are dealing with someone who is still fairly new to the game and scared to death to have become so famous so fast, so they act out. They may also have a drug or alcohol issue and are making people's lives miserable as a result. The most likely, however, is that he or she has been surrounded by people who don't give a shit about the project at hand, and whose sole creative agenda is to cover their asses and save a nickel whenever possible. The star is the only one with the power to stand in the way of mediocrity and expedience, and often when they do, they are scapegoated.

Also know this: After years of working with, or getting to know, actors like Jodie Foster, Tom Hanks, Tom Cruise, Brad Pitt, Mike Myers, Jennifer Garner, Sally Field, George Clooney, and many others, I can tell you that stars are almost always the most gracious people on set. It's part of the job and they know it. You don't survive to become a star if you have a bad attitude.

Another thing I first observed on *Class* was the phenomenon of raw talent and star potential. In the movie, there was this gang of guys who were peripheral characters. To save money, local Chicago kids were cast and they all did fine. Except for one. He came from a large family with a history of acting locally—his dad played a priest in our movie. He was a nice-looking kid with big, soulful eyes, and was precocious and savvy in a way the others weren't. And every time he had a line, no matter how inconsequential, he drilled it. He had a unique sense of humor and an uncanny knack for ad-libbing terrific dialogue. Wisely, our director began to incorporate his contributions, and John Cusack's part expanded dramatically from its original, almost walk-on status to that of a memorable one. It was obvious that he was going to have a real future in Hollywood, if he wanted one.

*Class* wrapped in the late fall of 1982 and I flew home to Malibu. In the space of nine adrenaline-filled months, I had gone from having no career at all to starring in three movies (one for television) back to back. Every now and then I found a moment to think about what it all meant. Was this all a fluke or the beginning of something real? What would happen when all these movies, all in postproduction, were finally released? What would my life become? These are obviously "first world" problems but still, the level of psychic and emotional stress, particularly for an eighteen-year-old, is not to be underestimated.

Having been away from home for such a long time also put a new twist on all my friendships. I still had my group of friends from school, but more and more, the time away and the one-of-a-kind experiences were conspiring to set us apart. Once again, I was feeling different and having to work hard to fit in.

❖

*The Outsiders* is scheduled for a big Christmas release. All the actors have been spending hours in the "looping" stage (rerecording or adding dialogue as needed), trying to make the release date. None of us has seen any of the movie, so we love having a sneak peek at these tiny moments from a few scenes. Francis has the best sound department in the world, many of whom worked on the legendary sound design on *Apocalypse Now*. They are patient and great teachers and I learn everything I can from them. Looping, or ADR as they call it today, is an art. Most actors hate it, few are good at it, but early on I was taught its value and worked hard to be good at it. Today, whenever I get a compliment in postproduction about my looping ability, I thank Francis's team of experts.

The movie looks amazing. It's shot in CinemaScope and looks as big and full of dramatic grandeur as *Gone with the Wind*, which Francis modeled it after. I want to see more, we all do, but until Christmas we must make do with these little teases. Somehow Emilio has gotten word that the very first coming attractions, or trailer, for *The Outsiders* is playing in front of a movie called *Spacehunter: Adventures in the Forbidden Zone*, with Peter Strauss and an unknown fifteen-year-old girl named Molly Ringwald. We are all dying to see it, and so Emil, Cruise, and I pile into a car and drive to the only theater we can find that's playing it. We end up thirty miles away, in Marina Del Rey. There are only about fifteen people in the theater. *The Outsiders* trailer comes on, and it's like watching our future flash before our eyes. When it's over, you can hear the fifteen people murmuring. On the drive back to the Sheens' house we are ecstatic.

But within days comes ominous news. *The Outsiders* release will be delayed from Christmas 1982 to the following spring. I am devastated. I want so badly to see the result of all the hard work. I also know that until everyone else sees it, my career (and life) will be in a holding pattern. I am too green in the ways of the business to understand that when a big movie moves off a Christmas release date, it's a sign of trouble. In retrospect, I should have picked up that something wasn't right. Tommy Howell is working so much on the postproduction that he is completely AWOL from any kind of socializing with us. Emilio also spends weeks doing and redoing lines for different versions of the same scenes. For some reason I'm not needed in this latest frenetic wave of work.

As the weeks drag on, and I wait for the release of *The Outsiders*, I spend hours in the looping stage on *Class*. There's a lot of confusion over what the movie should be: a raunchy sex comedy like the recent hit *Porky's*; a smart, subversive teen version of *The Graduate* (my vote, not that anyone cares); or a thoughtful,

angst-filled meditation on coming-of-age à la *Catcher in the Rye*.
The studio and Ransohoff want *Porky's*, McCarthy and the director want Salinger. As always in Hollywood when there are competing visions and no one powerful and creative enough to unite
them all, you get them all. The result is usually an uneven, tone-
less mess. The comedy isn't always funny, the drama isn't always
dramatic, and sometimes it's funny when you want it to be dramatic and vice versa. But, if you are lucky and you have some
good people involved, enough of the movie works anyway. When
they threaten to change the title to *Beginner's Luck*, I know the
*Porky's* camp is winning. All I can do is work hard and hope for
the best.

These kinds of struggles are what bond people in the business
together. It's why actors marry other actors and why sometimes
they form cliques. Unless you have a personal experience or stake
in the making of a movie, it's hard to understand why someone's
going nuclear when his or her movie's title is changed. So, I com-
miserate with Emilio, Howell, and Cruise. They, in turn, talk to
additional pals they have worked with, like Sean Penn and Tim
Hutton. We are one another's support and sounding board. We
aren't looking to form some sort of "actors club" (Brat Pack, anyone?) or to be cool, we just want to be around people who are
dealing with the same new, mysterious, frustrating issues.

As the release date for *The Outsiders* grows imminent, a group
of actors is flown up to screen the movie for the school in central
California that petitioned Francis to make it. I'm disappointed
that I wasn't invited, but I figure that there probably wasn't enough
room on the plane Warner's rented. Besides, I'm set to see it the
following week.

The next Tuesday, I'm standing in a tiny, claustrophobic hallway outside a screening room at Universal Studios. Only a few
people are gathered in the hall. This is an extremely select, pri-

vate advance screening. I don't think I've ever been more excited or more nervous. I see the cinematographer Steve Burum.

"This movie's gonna make a hundred million dollars," he says to no one in particular, staring at his feet.

I'm let into the screening room and settle into a midrow seat in the back. Even though there are maybe twenty other people in the theater, I want to be alone. It's an old, run-down room, but as the lights go down and the first elements of sound come up, I know the equipment is state of the art. Stevie Wonder begins to sing "Stay Gold" and the *Gone with the Wind*–style credits begin. I see my name. It's listed under the heading "The Greasers." I read the list—Tommy, Patrick, Emil, Ralph, Matt, Tom—and I'm so proud of them. After the hair-raising auditions, the intense shoot, the extended delay of our big debuts, the point of the whole exercise is finally unspooling, with an opening credit sequence of amazing emotion and grandeur. In an instant you know there's *never* been a movie for teens like this. Maybe Steve Burum is right. Maybe *The Outsiders* will live up to and surpass all expectations.

The first scene begins.

There must be a problem in the projection booth. Instead of opening with the first scene in the script, the movie has jumped almost ten scenes, to a big close-up of Matt Dillon getting ready to walk to the drive-in. I wait for the movie to stop and return to the beginning—the whole first fifteen minutes with the introductions to all the Greasers as we rescue Pony from the Socs (and I do my Starsky and Hutch move over their car), and the scene where Pony and I talk in bed about Mom and Dad and why we are orphans, and the other great scenes from the book that we had worked so hard on.

Soon I realize this isn't like my misadventure back at the Malibu Cinema. These movie reels are exactly as the filmmakers want them. This is the final version of *The Outsiders*.

I feel like I might vomit. Most of the scenes of the Curtis brothers are just *not in the movie.* Is this a joke? Can this be happening? It's like being invited to a big party in my honor that's thrown by a favorite uncle, showing up in my best clothes, seeing all my friends inside, and the uncle appears to say, "What are *you* doing here? This is our party." I am completely blindsided with humiliation.

The movie continues. I don't even have a close-up until almost the halfway mark. The character of Sodapop, so essential to S. E. Hinton's book, has been so excised from the movie that the filmmakers are forced to loop a terrible exposition line on the back of a girl's head in an attempt to explain who my character is, since all of his introduction is now gone. "Oh, your brother is Sodapop. He's the dreamy one who works at the D.X., right?"

I try to calm myself and enjoy the amazing scenes that weren't cut out: the rumble; the beautiful scenes with Tommy and Ralph; Emilio's ad-libbed laugh lines. But it's hard. At least I will finish strong with my big breakdown scene in the park. After all the screen testing of that speech and the struggle to get it right when we shot it, it *couldn't* be cut because it not only ends the movie, it sums up the entire relationship of the three central characters, the Curtis brothers.

On-screen, Matt Dillon is dying after ad-libbing the line "You'll never take me alive." (I remember shooting this scene, watching Matt bleeding to death on the street. It was a cold night and Matt was sent to his trailer. As I did my close-up I was looking at a sandbag lying on the ground.) I sit up in my seat. Tommy and I really went to the well together on this one; I can't wait to see it pay off. Matt's death scene ends. They cut away. Here comes the biggest sequence of my career . . . but instead, the end credits roll. The movie is over. The sequence is gone. The climax of the book is out as though it never existed.

The lights come up. I'm dazed. My entire story line was cut

from *The Outsiders*, easily ten scenes and twenty minutes of screen time. Now I know why I wasn't invited to the screening at the school. I try to look unaffected and gather my composure as I blink in the light of the emptying screening room. Later I sit in my car and wonder: Why didn't anyone tell me? I drive home in a fog. All I can think is that I must have been terrible in those scenes, and no one wanted to say anything so they just took them out.

In my driveway, I sit in my car for a long while, trying to figure it all out.

My disillusionment and disappointment are so complete that I know then and there that I will never truly get over it. And I won't—at least not until I find myself in another small screening room, this time in Australia, almost twenty-five years later.

❖

*The Outsiders* opened on March 25, 1983. I went with Tommy Howell and stood in the back of the massive Mann Theatre in Westwood Village near UCLA. This was the prime movie theater in all of L.A., maybe the world. It was packed; there were even people sitting in the aisles—illegally. That the movie bore no resemblance to the book made no difference to the masses of girls who screamed from the first frame of the film to the last. There may not have been much (if any) of my acting left, but the filmmakers made certain to keep the scene where I came out of the shower, barely concealing myself with a towel.

As the movie ended, people noticed Tommy and me and a mob rushed us. Security guards were called in as we were pinned into a corner. It was even more intense outside in the street. There was a line of people around the block for the next showing and they, too, had heard we were in the theater and pounced on us as we tried to run to our car. Girls grabbed our clothes and screamed as they pulled at our hair. We dove into Tommy's truck, driving away in a frenzy.

It was official. We were young movie stars.

*The Outsiders* didn't make a hundred million dollars. It did something even more spectacular. It launched all of us into the zeitgeist. Almost immediately, each of us was rewarded with a big film role. *The Outsiders* was not just the first great teen ensemble, but it also created a group of male stars who would dominate the next generation of movies.

❖

In 1983 Timothy Hutton is the only guy around our age who already has an Academy Award. He is the top dog—and for a good reason. But now I hear he has pulled out of what was to be his next movie, *The Hotel New Hampshire*, based on the best-selling book by John Irving. Irving's last film adaptation, *The World According to Garp*, was a critical and box-office success, so *New Hampshire* has a big profile from the start. Now that Hutton is gone, everyone is scrambling to get the coveted lead role of John, the book's narrator.

Like Coppola, the film's director, Tony Richardson, is an Academy Award winner, as well as a revered leader of the new wave of English cinema. Tony's film *The Charge of the Light Brigade* was one of the most important British films ever made, and with *Tom Jones* he won his Oscar for best director. He is a rebel (like his ex-wife, Vanessa Redgrave, who is the mother of his lovely daughters Natasha and Joely) and one of the more eccentric directors still valued within the growing commercialization of the studio system.

I hike up the long driveway to a large home with a breathtaking view over the Sunset Strip. A staffer lets me in the front door for my first meeting with my prospective director at his home high in the Hollywood Hills.

"Come in, come in. I'm in the living room," a strange, wonderful voice calls out, the sort of voice you could never forget.

I follow the voice and as I round a corner and enter a two-story living room, a large parrot swoops through the air and attaches itself to my face. Blood erupts through its beak as I try to fight the thing off. It's squawking and flapping, beating me in the head with its wings. I grab the bird by its neck and pry it off of me. It flies up into the rafters, where I see it gather with a number of other birds, all clearly let wild in the house.

I don't think I'll make a very good impression with blood running down my face and I don't want Tony to know I almost broke the neck of one of his prized pets.

"Um, I'll be right there!" I call as I scurry to the kitchen to clean off my wound. After a moment, I enter the den, where Tony is sitting, working on the script.

"Hello, Rob. What's wrong with your face?" he asks as we shake hands.

"Bar fight," I say, and he laughs.

We spend the next hour talking about the movie. He tells me he has cast Jodie Foster as the heroine, and the iconic sex symbol and current It girl European actress Nastassja Kinski as the troubled romantic interest who wears nothing but a bear suit in the movie (only John Irving could come up with this). Beau Bridges will play the patriarch. We talk about the challenges of portraying a character who will age a decade in the movie and about the themes the story deals with, many of them controversial, including incest and rape. Tony tells me that he wants to make a sweeping epic about an eccentric American family, and to pull it off he will need the right actor to anchor the movie.

I realize I am listening to an iconoclastic visionary trying to see his way clear to making a studio movie into a grand, yet accessible, art film. But he reminds me of Coppola and I'm honored to be in the running for a challenging role in a movie of such big themes.

"When do you think you'll start reading actors for the part of John?" I ask.

"I won't," he says.

"Oh, really?" I reply, trying to hide my surprise. After the gauntlet of *The Outsiders*, it seems inconceivable to me that a director would have no auditions at all.

"There's no need to," he continues.

"Why not?" I ask.

"Because I've found who I want," he says, eyes twinkling mischievously. "It's you."

It was the first—and last—time a director had the vision and the guts to give me a role in the room. He didn't consult with producers, agents, or the studio. He just did it. We started shooting in Montreal, Canada, three weeks later.

❖

Sitting in the lobby of the Manor Le Moyne in Montreal, my latest home away from home, waiting to meet Jodie Foster, I'm really nervous. I'm a huge fan. (Forget the landmark *Taxi Driver*, how about *Bugsy Malone!*) I think she's beautiful, *know* she's smart (she has made headlines as the first star to take a break from Hollywood to conquer the Ivy League), and am unsure how to handle all of the controversy that surrounds her. Ever since John Hinckley shot President Reagan, trying to impress her, she has been under unrelenting scrutiny. Some asshole nobody kook looking to gain the spotlight violated her private life and in the process almost ruined it. At the time, I couldn't possibly imagine what that must be like.

Jodie turns out to be the great joy of *The Hotel New Hampshire*. We connect immediately. We are both child actors in transitional phases of our lives and careers, share similar working styles (no drama, no nonsense), and have loving, smart, and very complicated mothers. Shooting the movie will be the beginning of a long friendship during which I will watch her grow into her potential, despite the adversity. Jodie Foster should be any actor's role model. She is certainly mine. Many years later, my personal life would painfully and very publicly implode. Of all the many people I had known or worked with over the years, there was only one who took the time to write a note of support: Jodie.

The atmosphere on a movie is often dictated by its subject matter and, if the director has a strong vision, his personal worldview. *New Hampshire* was awash in familial deep-bonding and bed hopping that would make a Feydeau farce seem tame. The major underlying theme of the book is painful and sometimes complicated sexual awakening, and Tony Richardson created an atmosphere of exploratory, innocent permissiveness that resulted in something like a free-love commune. The backstage sexual energy would then be captured in our work on-screen. Coppola wanted to toughen his cast; Richardson wanted to break down conventional relationships.

One evening, after a long, emotional day of shooting, Nastassja Kinski stops me in the hotel lobby.

"Rob, how about you and me tonight? Dinner?" she says, fixing me with a laser stare, her massive eyes glowing. I've not really had much interaction with her even though the film is halfway complete, because in truth, I find her intimidating. *Time* magazine has just placed her on its cover as "The World's Most Beautiful Woman." I'm barely nineteen years old and have no experience with a woman of her beauty, sexuality, fame, and angst-filled charisma.

"Um, dinner? With me?" The minute I say it, I know I've revealed myself as the acting nerd from Dayton, Ohio, and not as a newly minted movie star. Nastassja gives me a look that says, Helloooo? Do I need to spell it out? and replies, "Yes. *Tonight*."

"Oh, yeah! Sure! No problem. Sounds good," I answer, trying to sound casual. She gives me a full-lipped, pouty smile and walks off.

Holy smokes! What just happened? Obviously, I know where

my duty lies in this situation, but YIKES! This is the woman whose dark, erotic (and nude) performance in *Cat People* had me playing the cassette of the theme song over and over. Also, anyone who could wrap herself in a python (in her famous poster) has got to be a force to be reckoned with. This is going to be some evening.

And so began a wonderful, adventurous, and intense on-set relationship. We practically created our own world, working on an emotionally demanding and ambitious film all day, then retreating to each other at night. Clearly it also meant the end of my already hot-and-cold long-distance romance with Melissa. And although we would be in each other's lives off and on for some time, it would never be the same.

*The Hotel New Hampshire* remains among the most emotionally intense location experiences of my career, second only to *The Outsiders*. The film itself, however, was crushed at the box office by a little movie called *Splash*, starring my fairy princess, Daryl Hannah. Looking at *New Hampshire* today, I can't imagine that any current studio would green-light it, in spite of the book's best-seller status. It's not a movie for a mass audience. Its quirky, provocative plot, which spins toward the two leads committing incest, would relegate it to low-budget, independent-movie status, at best. As for the finished product, it's a heroically flawed movie, reaching for something great and sometimes coming very, very close. It attempts too much and also accomplishes much. I'm very proud of it. I wish more people had seen it.

## CHAPTER 13

Back in L.A. after months of shooting on location in Montreal, I'm emotionally hungover. I gave my all in my performance, fell in love (literally) with my New Hampshire family, and now we've scattered back to our individual lives. It's over. Just like that. I'm still only nineteen years old and the end of every movie feels like a breakup. I cover my malaise by looking for fun and adventure wherever I can find it, most often on nights out with the boys. Since *The Outsiders*, this has been a habit and now it's accelerating.

With most of my friends away at college, I return to the sanctuary of the Sheens' Gilligan's Island–like pool. Emilio and I continue where we left off—hard-core workouts, tons of reading and auditioning, doing postproduction on the various movies we've wrapped, and trying always to improve our standing and our ability as young actors. By this time, both our little brothers have thrown their hats into the ring as well, so they aren't busting our balls anymore. Tom Cruise is also around, and he and I are awaiting the release of *Class* and *Risky Business*, respectively. I've seen *Risky Business* and know that the first-time writer/director has created something original and very stylish. But I'm not sure anyone is prepared for how huge it would be or the velocity at which it would send Tom into orbit. I'm hoping that with *Class* I can have similar success.

Then I pick up a copy of *Newsweek* and read the review of *Class*. A quick glance at the table of contents sets the stage— "Film Preview: *Class*—A Vile Concoction, page 98." The critique itself has the single best and most prominent use of the word "debacle" that I will ever read. I have to laugh, it is so brutal. I'm relieved that the reviewer left the actors fairly unscathed, and truth be told, the many competing chefs *had* created a concoction. It's clear *Class* is not going to be my *Risky Business*.

Many people still buy into the idea that actors can control and plan their careers. This is, to put it plainly, bullshit. Sure, if you are a directing auteur like Spielberg or Cameron, you can control everything you do, but an actor? C'mon. Even the biggest star is at the mercy of the material offered to him. You hope and pray you have a good part, then you hope and pray the rest of the script is equally good, then you hit your knees and beg other people who you think are talented to join you, then you cross your fingers that they don't hack it up, phone it in, or fall down on the job. After the movie is done, you say the rosary, read the Torah, and otherwise try to ward off the bad editors, meddling studios, terrible ad campaigns, horrible release dates, unforeseen snowstorms, and critics lying in wait. If you are lucky enough to successfully navigate all of these variables, then maybe, just maybe, you will be rewarded and the audience will show up and give you a hit. All any actor can really do is take the best material available at any given time, do good work, and hope for lightning to strike.

After the release of *Class*, I begin a pattern that will take me through the rest of the decade, shooting two movies a year on location and trying to catch up on life (and my sleep!) in the few months in between. It's a nomadic, transitory existence, punctuated by hotel rooms and brief, heated relationships. I have very little contact with anyone not involved in the world of filmmaking. My dream of a legitimate career in movies has been achieved, but there is no real sense of victory. I'm too busy trying to build on this momentum to take stock of what's happened so far, or how I feel about it.

❖

New York City is a magnet. I return again and again, using American Airlines Flight 21 like a luxurious shuttle. These were the days when you knew you would find someone interesting on the plane, when flying was fun and not something to be dreaded. With a hiatus between movies and a growing new circle of industry pals to see, I'm back in Gotham. I do have one small piece of business to attend to, and it will put me face-to-face with one of the more memorable icons of the twentieth century.

Andy Warhol wore a wig, right? The great man has passed and there is no longer need for discretion on this account, correct? Whether he did or he didn't, to my unsophisticated eye at the time, the hair, the '50s beatnik glasses, the black uniform, and the skin like tracing paper—they added up to an unforgettable impression. Surely there isn't anyone reading this who can't picture him clearly in their mind's eye, the rare art-world superstar who himself would have a lasting personal image. I first meet Warhol in an unadorned, nondescript warehouse. In the '80s, if it didn't happen in a crappy warehouse, it wasn't cool.

Andy has a camera team recording as he interviews me for

his underground cable-access TV show, which is a mixture of Manhattan celebrity avant-garde art and unapologetic commercialism that only Warhol could create. Think *Wayne's World* for people who smoke clove cigarettes. I am not a student of the contemporary art scene, but I am curious to see what a noted cultural genius like Andy Warhol will want to talk about.

"What's it like to be famous?" Andy asks. His voice is actually even more striking than his look, if that's possible—an odd mix of a sly, singsong whine and a sexed-up, ironic Liberace. All of his follow-up questions are in the same vein: queries on "celebrity," the definition of "beauty," and the world of "movie stars," a term he loved. I do my best to sound like I know what I'm talking about, and soon it's over.

On my way out he stops me. "I want you to meet Cornelia [Corneeeeeeelia]," he says. I know he is referring to Cornelia Guest, the eighteen-year-old blue-blood heiress, "debutante of the decade" and all-around Manhattan It girl. I've seen her picture in the papers and think she's cute.

"Sure, that'd be nice."

"We will pick you up and go to Diana's concert tomorrow," he says, referring to Diana Ross's free concert in Central Park. We make a plan to meet.

Andy, Cornelia, Diana. It's a very different crowd from my pals back on Point Dume. This is the fastest of the fast, intriguing and achieving and in the spotlight at the center of the contemporary cultural stage.

There are one hundred thousand people crammed into the meadow in Central Park. Dark, ominous clouds threaten on the horizon. Diana Ross insists on doing the show despite alerts for deadly lightning strikes. Before the dangerous weather and torrents of rain force her to stop, she will give what is today considered a historic performance. Sitting in the wings, Cornelia, Andy, and I know we are seeing something extraordinary.

As the giant storm breaks, the masses run for cover. One hundred thousand people trying to get out of the park on a good day would be pandemonium; with lightning crackling and thunder crashing, it is dangerous chaos.

The three of us navigate the panicked throngs, wading through ankle-deep mud, and hiding as gangs of hoods exploit the confusion to rip jewelry off the soaked, defenseless concertgoers.

We take shelter at Café Central, just off Central Park on the Upper West Side. Known as the launching point for any legit night on the town, at this midday hour it is deserted and we take a table at the window to watch the scene outside.

The bar is famous for its kamikaze, mixed until recently by Bruce Willis, who has just left his position running the best bar in Manhattan to try his hand at acting. Turns out, he is pretty good at that as well.

"Let's play a game!" suggests Andy, with little-boy enthusiasm.

He clears the flatware on the paper tablecloth and grabs a bunch of crayons at the center of the table.

"I want everyone to draw their best version of a pussy," he says mischievously. "Don't let anyone look at it until we are all finished."

If nothing else, I feel this exercise will provide a good source of conversation with Cornelia, who I've been trying to chat up, without gaining much traction. She grabs a crayon and starts drawing furiously, as does Andy. I cover my part of the tablecloth so they can't watch and begin my artwork. I make a calculated call to go hyperrealistic. I begin to work on an almost gynecological rendition of a vagina, a subject I am having more and more experience with these days. The three of us work in concentrated silence. Soon we are all done.

"Okay, show yours, Cornelia," orders Andy, and she presents a fairly demure-looking pussy of the Patrick Nagel school. I go next, unveiling my hypergyno masterwork. With a flourish and a cackle, Andy Warhol reveals his sketch. It's a rudimentary stick figure version of a cat.

"Now *that's* a pussy!" he says.

Later we all sign our names below our work at Andy's instruction, because "that's what artists do."

Youthful pride and a desire to seem cool prevented me from taking Andy's drawing as we left. This glamorous world was new to me and I didn't want anyone to know how unsure I felt in it. Only now do I see how often this held me back, kept me from making real connections and, more specifically, a signed original Warhol!

Years later, after Andy's death, *The Warhol Diaries* was published. I was happy to see that our day together had made its way into his amazing journal of an extraordinary life.

❖

In the fall of 1983 I arrive in London to shoot a movie called *Oxford Blues*. It's the first script to come my way that will give me the true lead, complete with first billing—a big step in a young actor's career. The film deals with a cocky American who has a crush on a European princess and schemes to meet her. I suggest we try to get Princess Stephanie of Monaco for the role. It would require little acting on her part, or mine either, since she's a real princess and I have a crush on her from afar. Inquiries are made. There is no response.

The shoot is entirely on location in Oxford, England. I've never been to Europe, and I have a horrible time with jet lag in the first few weeks. On a weekend trip to London, the city is paralyzed when an IRA bomb detonates in front of Harrods department store at the start of the Christmas shopping season, killing a number of innocent shoppers. I'm getting to see the world from beyond the traditional American perspective, and some of the things I'm seeing are troubling. But some are thrilling.

I become close with the young producer of the film, an Englishman named Cassian Elwes. One weekend he invites me to his family's country estate, Runnymede House. Jet lag once again has me awake at sunrise, so I'm killing time by walking in his enormous backyard, or "garden," as he calls it. I come upon a giant elm tree and underneath it is a massive rock, about the size of a dining room table. It's covered with leaves, but my eye catches something beneath the debris. I clear away the dirt, leaves, and cobwebs to reveal a metal plaque, its lettering worn by time and weather. I climb up onto the rock to read it. It says, "On this site the Magna Carta was signed by King John in 1215." My on-set love affair in England was not with a costar, but with the country itself—the history at your fingertips, the traditions that are still embraced and revered, and the cleverness of her people. I was smitten and still am.

With *Oxford Blues* complete, I fly to New York City to do publicity for the opening of *The Hotel New Hampshire*. For the press tour of *Class* a few months earlier, Andrew McCarthy and I did a sort of two-man bus-and-truck tour of the country, appearing on local morning news and talk shows, staying in giant suites, and getting to know various locals somewhat intimately. It was an adventure in room service and benign debauchery. Believe me, after you do your tenth morning show where they want you to cook an omelet while asking you what Jacqueline Bisset is like, you're looking to blow off some steam. (This publicity road show is so gruelingly banal that for the movie the studio released before *Class*, all the actors refused to do it. The studio was forced to send a *parrot* that appeared in the movie instead.)

But this trip to New York holds more promise. I land at JFK and get into a limousine for the ride to the hotel (this being back in the day when actors didn't insist on street-cred SUVs or enviro-cred Priuses). Then I'm off to meet Jodie Foster and her roommate at Yale, Jon Hutman (later to be the production designer on

*The West Wing*), and their group of friends. We are to rendezvous at a new underground club called Area.

There is an absolute mob standing in the bitter cold outside a nondescript metal door to a ramshackle building in an obscure location in downtown Manhattan. Although I still have a decent share of my privacy intact, most people under the age of twenty-five, particularly girls, know who I am, so there is a commotion as the bouncers help me navigate inside to find my friends. I haven't been to many clubs (I'm still two years away from drinking age), so I feel the kind of exuberant, giddy excitement of possibility that the occasion calls for. As I enter the club and pass the live performance art of a fully naked woman sleeping, I am unaware that this place, at this moment, is the living embodiment of the innocent excess of the '80s. Every era has its high-water mark—that one irreproducible moment so full of promise that people can spend their entire lives trying to recapture it. For the go-go 1980s big-city club scene, it all crystallized on this night in a Manhattan warehouse. Soon enough, we would learn that cocaine was bad for us and so was conspicuous consumption. We would hear of a new disease called AIDS. But these game changers were unimaginable this night and the club is filled with a level of energy and abandon that might never be seen again. Depeche Mode is blasting as bodies move. The new young voices in literature, Jay McInerney and Bret Easton Ellis, icons like Andy Warhol, important actors like Robert De Niro and Jack Nicholson all hold court, and music stars like the Go-Gos drop by to flirt and mingle. Sitting with the lovely and hilarious Jodie, I am exactly where I want to be, surrounded by this incredible group of creative talent at the top of their game.

"Jodie, I went to the men's room and there were *girls* in there!" I say, never having seen anything like it. "I mean, how can a guy pee with a girl smoking a cigarette next to him?!"

I leave at sunrise. In a few hours I'll have rounds of interviews and it will be a struggle to stay awake and focused. Something has occurred to me: With every increasing encroachment of my privacy, with each additional loss of the ability to lead a normal life, to cover my deep discomfort, I will compensate by enjoying the fun that comes with it. And all these years later, looking back, I'm glad I did it. Because for a while, it worked.

For *Hotel New Hampshire*, I'm sitting for an interview with *People* magazine for what is to be my first major exposure in mainstream media. (Today, a hot nineteen-year-old would likely be put on the cover, but this was still a time when that distinction was reserved for those who had a track record of actual achievement. Coverage by the legit press was an honor bestowed on accomplished, "real" stars only, like Redford, Newman, Beatty, Fonda.) After the interview is over I feel an unnameable unease, which will only increase after the photo shoot. I have a vague notion that I'm doing something wrong, but I can't put my finger on what it is. The press I'm getting is good on one level—it's putting my name out there and is, in and of itself, an indication of my growing profile in Hollywood. But there is a slight air of condescension and a lack of seriousness in the coverage. I'm hoping that people want to know who I really am and what I'm about, but I'm not getting those kinds of questions.

In hindsight, I know why. First and foremost was the way I looked. There is just no way anyone is likely to take a nineteen-year-old boy as pretty as I was seriously. Even I wouldn't. I look at myself in those early movies and pictures and am stunned by the disconnect between how I felt on the inside and what I looked like on the outside. People looked at me and made a judgment. It's the way of the world. I do it, too, sometimes.

The other reason that my early press had a lack of seriousness was that, as a good midwestern son and people pleaser, I wanted to be liked and (as I was in school) be a "pleasure to have in class." The world "no" was not in my vocabulary in spite of my sometimes feeling like I should say it. So, as a result, I posed for photos that I shouldn't have (I remember letting one photographer paint Brooke Shields–like eyebrows on me) and answered questions that would've made de Tocqueville seem like a lightweight. If they asked it, I answered it. No one close to me had the wisdom, experience, or instinct to guide me or play bad cop when needed. And it is *always* needed if you want to last. The survivors either naturally have that tough, uncompromising side, develop it later, as I thankfully did, or hire or marry someone who has it.

But however confusing my relationship with my nascent public image might have been, it would become more complicated with time.

❖

Even as a young actor, I knew that any time I could work with an important director, I should jump at the chance. So in early 1989, when Roman Polanski wants me to meet with him in Paris, I immediately hop on a plane.

I'm picked up at Charles de Gaulle Airport in a torrential downpour. My driver is cursing in French slang that I can't understand in spite of studying AP French in school. I read Camus's *The Stranger* entirely in the language but have no idea what this guy is yelling about. The only words I recognize are "rain," "strike," and "fuckers." Ahead, the Champs-Élysées is barricaded by protesting farmers who have covered the famed avenue with rotting produce. In spite of the stench, my first view of the Arc de Triomphe brings tears to my eyes.

Roman Polanski has summoned me to Paris to screen-test for *Pirates*, a movie he's making with Jack Nicholson, which will reunite the two men who made *Chinatown*, considered by many to be the greatest movie of the modern era, behind *Citizen Kane*. If I get the role, I will play a young man kidnapped by Nicholson and indentured into a life of high-seas plunder. It is a huge-budget movie and a rare opportunity to work with two living legends at the top of their powers.

I'm dropped off at a studio on the outskirts of the city. Roman greets me as I exit the cab.

"Welcome to Paris."

He is small, hard with muscles, and immediately exudes charisma and charm that could knock out an elephant.

"Shall we get you ready, no?" he asks.

My character is a shipwreck survivor, so he wants me clinging to the mast, dressed in tatters. His crew puts me in a glorified loincloth and leads me to a small, rudimentary set of a masted ship.

I've always been an instinctual actor. From the start, I've believed that confidence in your own instinct trumps the ponderous and often pretentious preparation that is sometimes more lauded because it sounds sexier, more "intense." That day, my instinct tells me to break out a full French accent, even though it has never been discussed. It's a risk, I go for it, and Polanski seems pleased.

I am a little thrown, however, by the great director's shooting style. He pushes the big Arriflex camera right up into my face, maybe six inches in front of me. The wide lens smashed in tight was a technique I hadn't encountered, and not many use it today.

Jack Nicholson is not there to do the scene with me. I figure he's in L.A., probably watching the Lakers. Instead, I work with a sweet and well-meaning Frenchman who, even if he were scientifically engineered, could not have been less like the actor he was filling in for. After a while, we take a break as a local gypsy attempts to sell the crew his hoard of leather goods.

"He comes to all my sets," Roman says warmly. "Good jackets, no?"

Soon we have completed the scene and I'm shuttled back to

my hotel, just off the Champs-Élysées. I am wired from the shoot and bursting to explore this city I've studied and admired for years. But it's freezing and rain is still coming down in sheets. I make the best of it by wandering around the hotel, a European classic, complete with the kind of grille-gated elevator that characters in thrillers get murdered in.

As I wander the halls, a door opens and a bleary-eyed man looks out. I recognize him at once as Bill Murray, one of my favorite actors.

"I thought I heard room service," he says.

"Sorry. I hope I didn't disturb you."

"Oh. You're American!"

"Yes," I say.

"Good. These frogs are driving me crazy. Wanna watch some golf?"

I spend the next few hours learning the finer points of the game from Carl the groundskeeper from *Caddyshack*. I want to tell him that on *The Outsiders* we had *Caddyshack*-watching parties at least once a week, but something tells me I shouldn't. I explain that I'm here for a screen test for Polanski's *Pirates* movie. He tells me he is working on his first serious role, *The Razor's Edge*. We talk for hours and he's funny as hell. What a great surprise to meet a hero under these strange circumstances. Soon I have to meet Roman for dinner and we say our goodbyes.

"Thanks for letting me hang out," I say as we shake hands.

"Thanks for not stealing my wallet. Oh, and good luck on that pirate thing."

We go to a restaurant called Pacific Palisades and are surrounded by American girls—so much for experiencing foreign culture. There must be fifteen models, all stunning, at our long table in the back of the room. Roman sits at the head, and a few men whom I don't know are mixed among our group. Roman has taken good care of me, placing me between a fantastic redhead and a breathtaking blonde. I spend most of the dinner like a spectator in a tennis match with my head on a swivel. Both girls are funny, nice, and interested. As the dinner winds down, Roman motions for me to come talk to him.

"Thank you so much for this dinner. This place is amazing," I say.

"Ah. It is nothing. We will do many like this during the movie," he says. My heart leaps and I wonder, does this mean I have the part?

"Sure, that would be great," I reply, trying not to seem as excited as I feel.

For a moment we both stand there, watching the scene before us. The wine has been great, the women are pretty, and possibly a great movie is in the offing. What could be better?

"May I give you some advice," says Roman, placing a hand on my shoulder.

"Um. Sure. What's up?" I ask.

Roman gestures to my two beautiful tablemates and says, "You better make up your mind or you will end up jerking off."

I take the master's advice and spend my first night in the City of Lights in a romantic, impulsive, and too-brief encounter that probably wouldn't have happened but for Roman. Thank you, Mr. Polanski. Viva la France.

I awaken at dawn for the early flight back to Los Angeles. I kiss the sleeping redhead good-bye and slip quietly out of the room. Closing the door, I trip on something at my feet. It is a beautiful leather-bound book. I open it to find it's a first edition of *The Complete History of Pirates*. I look closer and see there is an inscription. It reads:

To Rob—

All the best on your movie.

Your pal,

Bill Murray

✧

One of the more bizarre rituals in Hollywood is the process of anointing "The Next Big Thing." In an industry that thrives on young blood, it's a science that seems to become more inexact with every passing year. (Although the high watermark was probably in the late '90s when *Vanity Fair* put an actress on its cover who had never starred in a movie.) It's always been a subjective process; the industry gatekeepers and tastemakers have to put the touch on you before you've accomplished anything substantial. They go on a series of criteria: publicity, reputation, previous work (although this can easily be ignored), spin from agents, jive from managers, pressure from publicists, and sometimes talent. Age makes an impact and looks are critical. Romantic leads need to look the part, which is to say they must be sexy, but not sexual. Serious actors should look like they are from the mean streets of the eastern cities or the Australian outback. Comedy stars need to be asexual—an exact ringer for the guy who fixes your dryer and absolutely, positively not a threat to turn your girlfriend's head.

Obviously there are exceptions to this formula, but they are rare. And when it does happen, it's in spite of the system, not because of it. It also goes without saying that The Next Big Thing can also be a flash in the pan, given that a new one is crowned about every six months (dictated by TV's pilot season or the movies' summer and Christmas release dates). The good news is: that's a lot of slots; the bad news is: there's gonna be some newbie busting your rice bowl every six months.

With the reaction to *The Outsiders,* the release of *Class,* and the pedigree of a project like *The Hotel New Hampshire,* I find myself in the heady, pressure-filled bull's-eye of the star-making machine.

I am either offered parts or in "conversations" on most movies. But on the other hand, I am not even considered for certain others because I have already been discovered. And the bigger the director, the less likely they are to use another big director's find.

Polanski has offered me the part in *Pirates* and now I have to wait for him to finalize the movie's funding. This goes on for months and eventually Jack Nicholson tires of the process and drops out. I continue to wait but I start to hedge my bets by looking at other projects.

So, while the director of *Chinatown* hopes I stay patient, I am hounded by the director of *Hot Dog . . . The Movie*, who wants me to do *his* new film. It's a movie about the rugged, cutthroat world of junior ice hockey, called *Youngblood*. Despite my love of sports, I have no real connection to hockey, so I pass on the film. Also, ideally I'd like to continue to work with directors with more experience.

There are exceptions, of course, because you never know who will become a great director. I meet with John Hughes for *The Breakfast Club*, but he wants to make his own discovery of an "unknown." So the fantastic part of John Bender goes to newcomer Judd Nelson. When Emilio gets a role in the movie, I decide that I need to choose a movie of my own. It's time to get off the sidelines; careers lose momentum in an instant. And momentum is everything.

Every once in a while I read a script that I know is going to be a hit. *Top Gun, Jerry Maguire, The West Wing*. But the very first one I came across was a script called *Footloose*.

Joe Tremaine runs one of the leading dance studios in Los Angeles. I'm in the back row of one of his beginning classes, brushing up on my old moves from the days of John Kenley and Peanut Butter and Jelly. *Footloose*'s director, Herbert Ross, has given strict instructions that I come ready to bust a move for his screen tests. The lead in the movie is a star-making part and everyone wants it. I'm going to have to will my way through this dance audition/screen test somehow and then hope my acting can do the rest. But here in the stifling, crowded dance studio, I see that I'm never gonna be John Travolta. But I'm not one to give up—you never know what's in the cards.

The movie's producers are Craig Zadan and Neil Meron. They are lobbying for me to get the part and coaching me through the process. In spite of my low-level dance skills, as I walk onto the soundstage at Paramount Studios, I know I have a shot. Herb Ross addresses the assembled group of actors. There are a couple guys I recognize, but no one famous. I take that as a good sign.

"Hello, fellas," he says, looking a little like Roy Scheider as Bob Fosse. "We will be learning a full routine today to 'Rockin' the Paradise' by Styx. You have an hour to learn the steps, then we will do the number and make our cuts."

Wow. This is just like *A Chorus Line*, I think. All around me people are doing intense stretches and otherwise warming up their "instruments." I figure I ought to do the same, so I do some calisthenics I remember from my fifth-grade soccer team. The choreographer goes through the routine and I actually follow along pretty well. My time at Joe Tremaine's dance studio is paying off.

Eventually the director returns, followed by the producers and a phalanx of studio executives, all in Armani power suits. They sit in a line of folding chairs facing us. We shuffle in place nervously.

The choreographer counts off "One, two, three!" and the speakers blast the opening bars of the song. All twenty of us go into the routine. I know better than to think—that would just mess me up—so I trust instead and . . . holy shit, it's working! Out of the corner of my eye, I see one guy stumble. Another loses his place completely. But I can also see that some of these guys are smokin' it.

The routine ends with a big running dive to the knees and a stage slide across the floor. I decide I'll make up with enthusiasm what I lack in technique. The big finish approaches. I explode into a sprint, leap as high as I possibly can, and come down on my knees hard, skidding a good ten feet across the floor. There is a grotesque *pop* that can be heard over the music, and my right knee explodes in pain. Within seconds it is the size of a butterball turkey. I look up at the director and black out.

I didn't get the part in *Footloose*. I *did* get a torn meniscus and an assurance that they weren't going to cast an actor anyway; they'll go with a pro dancer. I get driven home to rehab my knee. A week later, they hire Kevin Bacon, an actor.

Meanwhile, back on the continent, Roman Polanski still isn't ready. He has recast Jack Nicholson's part of Captain Red with Walter Matthau. Talk about a different way to go! While I'm a fan of Mr. Matthau, I'm having a hard time envisioning him as a dangerous, daring swashbuckler. But I'm sure the legendary Polanski sees something I don't, so I remain patient.

Meanwhile, MGM, the studio that is making the hockey movie, is relentlessly trying to get me on board. And when a big studio pulls out the guns for a charm offensive, it's hard not to be swayed. I reread the script, looking for something I can bring to the role, and begin a series of talks with the young director, Peter Markle. Turns out he played junior hockey and knows the world inside out. His passion gets me interested.

Almost eight weeks after my screen test in Paris, I take the bull by the horns and call Polanski myself. If he personally tells me to hang tough, I will. I leave a message at his home. After waiting another two weeks with no return phone call, I say yes to *Youngblood* and good-bye to *Pirates*.

Roman would eventually make the movie with Walter Matthau. An unknown French actor who looked exactly like me would play my part. It would be neither Mr. Polanski's nor Mr. Matthau's high-water mark—*Pirates* would sink without a trace. So much for career planning.

With principal photography six weeks away, it's time to tackle the single biggest challenge of making *Youngblood*: I can't skate. I mean, not even a little bit. There is talk of wheeling me around the ice on a platform and only shooting me from the knees up, but I veto it. I remember the Ron Howard motorcycle disaster too well. I will instead embark on an intense six-week training regimen. The studio hires a power-skating coach and a hockey coach. A physical trainer is given the challenge of adding fifteen pounds to my still-scrawny teen frame. The crash course will be so intense that I am relocated to a small apartment a block from the rink where I will train. This is my daily schedule:

| | |
|---|---|
| 7:30 A.M. | — breakfast |
| 8:00 A.M.–10:00 A.M. | — power-skating lesson |
| 10:00 A.M.–10:30 A.M. | — meal |
| 10:30 A.M.–12:30 P.M. | — weight training and cardio |
| 12:30 P.M.–1:45 P.M. | — lunch |
| 2:00 P.M.–4:00 P.M. | — hockey training |
| 4:00 P.M.–5:00 P.M. | — big afternoon meal |
| 6:00 P.M.–7:30 P.M. | — hockey scrimmage |
| 8:00 P.M. | — late meal |

It's a brutal, physically painful ordeal. But after six weeks of it, I'm bigger and stronger, and can skate like the wind. The *Youngblood* preparation program got me hooked on physical challenges, adrenaline sports, and daily training, all of which have been a big part of my life ever since. Every movie gives you a gift. This was *Youngblood*'s.

I keep hearing about another movie in the casting stage that's getting a lot of attention, *St. Elmo's Fire*. I'm already in preproduction on *Youngblood* and exhausted by its rigors, so I haven't really tracked this script as it became a hot commodity among other young actors. And suddenly, young actors are everywhere.

Studios are filling their pipelines with material by and for people under twenty-five like never before. They've seen enough promise in the performances of *Taps, The Outsiders, Caddyshack, Risky Business,* and *Fast Times at Ridgemont High*. It seems like there are new opportunities and new actors appearing daily. In this Wild West gold rush, even industry insiders can't keep track of what's what or who's who. This youth movement is so conspicuous, it's begging for a "catchall" label or category to describe all these new faces making their mark.

Columbia, the studio making *St. Elmo's Fire,* wants me in the movie. The director and producers, for whatever reason, do not. My agents convince me to read the script and I immediately fall in love with the part of Billy Hicks, the lovable, debauched, sax-playing ladies' man. The studio brass twists the director's arm and he agrees to meet me as a courtesy. But he has made it clear that I'm not "right" for the part of Billy, though he *might* consider me for the square, rigid yuppie, Alex. Coming off the movie *D.C. Cab*, starring Mr. T, he sees this as an opportunity to step up his game, so he's being very protective of his vision.

A meeting is scheduled quickly, before I leave for location for *Youngblood*. I know the director's feelings about me playing Billy and I have no interest in the other role, so I hatch a plan.

I meet the director, Joel Schumacher, on a late spring afternoon. I've been out on the town the night before and am feeling pretty shot. I make no attempt to hide it. In fact, I bring a six-pack of Corona with me to the meeting. Mr. Schumacher clearly thinks I'm not wild or dangerous enough to play this part. I'm going to show him otherwise.

The sun is blinding as I blink through watery eyes. I'm looking for Building 125 on the Columbia lot. The guard at the gate has been less than helpful.

"Follow the blue line to the red line. Make two rights. Then follow the blue line again until you get to the western back lot.

Then go to the water tower, where you will pick up the *dotted* green line to its intersection with the yellow line that wraps around the commissary. Your meeting will be on the left."

After a few steps, I'm lost. I look for someone to help me and see an extraordinary sight. It's a girl in a see-through sundress, backlit, revealing a gorgeous body. She has long, light brown hair that she has tied up and over (completely covering) a straw cowboy hat. It's a look I've never seen before or since. She is standing about twenty yards away, looking right at me. We lock eyes. Before I can ask her for help with directions, she steps between buildings and is gone.

Eventually I find Joel Schumacher's office. I'm very punctual by habit but this time I'm glad I'm late; it will have the desired effect. I wander in, holding my six-pack. Joel is a stylish, funny, smart, and sometimes bitchy man who dresses like a Ralph Lauren model. We hit it off at once. He is bemused as I pound a beer and regale him with semiaccurate stories of wild nights on the town. I know he is looking for recklessness and a big sense of fun in this character, so I give it to him. At all costs, I don't want him to think of me for the yuppie, square role.

Soon, the beer is taking effect.

"Joel, I'm sorry. I need to use the men's room."

"Just use the one here in my office. I have to step out for a phone call, anyway."

Joel goes to make his call and as I'm getting some relief from pounding my Coronas, suddenly the door to the bathroom opens.

"Oh, hi," says the beautiful girl in the sundress.

"Um. Hi," I say, stunned,

"Joel told me to come on in. I didn't know anyone was in here. Sorry," she says, without seeming sorry at all. She smiles winningly. And then, in a one-in-a-million voice: "I'm Demi."

With that, she and I were off to the races. Demi Moore at nineteen was a study in charisma and raw talent—a wild child with bona fides. It was obvious she was perfect to play the sexy, troubled, and magnetic Jules. She and I sat on Joel's couch, talking like we'd known each other forever. Joel said very little; he was assessing whether we would make a good on-screen couple.

I think Demi and I wondered the same thing, and so after the meeting adjourned, we spent the next few weeks trying to figure it out ourselves. Between the *Youngblood* workouts in the daytime and hanging out with Demi in the evenings, I was burning the candle at both ends.

Whether Joel Schumacher cast me of his own volition or was forced to by the studio is open to debate (I think he was forced), but one way or another, I got the role I wanted in *St. Elmo's Fire* a week before I left to shoot *Youngblood*. For the first time, I was starring in two movies back-to-back, and my agents were looking for a third. I could feel the expectations and the pressure build around me. Part of me loved it; part of me was scared. Within my family, I had also taken on a new role. With the money I'd made so far, I bought my family a house. A home owner at twenty—this was an irrevocable step into responsibility and adulthood. It also changed the balance of power in our family. As Cyndi Lauper was singing at the time, "Money changes everything," whether you want to admit it or not.

The public attention had been getting progressively more out of hand and now was just unmanageable. It was not unusual to be mangled at an airport by Argentinean schoolgirls on holiday or followed on roads and highways by coeds, secretaries on lunch break, or moms from the carpool. Sometimes this adoration was nice and human, with a real connection and feedback, and it gave me a rush. Sometimes there was no interest in me as a person (let alone as an actor) whatsoever. It was as if people were on a big-game safari and had stumbled across a living Bigfoot and just wanted a hair sample and a smiling photo. These encounters left me feeling like I was living in a zoo, but I denied myself the realization that it bothered me. After all, who the hell was I to look askance at such good fortune?

One day I picked up a copy of *USA Today*. On the front page was one of their famous (and hilariously banal) pie charts that are meant to present a daily snapshot of America. On that day the title was "Who We Love." According to the graph, 10 percent of America loved Simon Le Bon, 28 percent loved Tom Cruise, and 68 percent of America loved me. Now even I couldn't deny it. I was The Next Big Thing.

I should have been elated. From as far back as the hours spent at the Dayton Playhouse, my driving goal was to have an acting career. I had worked hard, taken advantage of luck and opportunity when it came my way, and succeeded beyond anything I would have thought possible. But satisfaction often took a backseat to an unnameable sense of unease and low-grade melancholy. These feelings weren't always there, and when they did bubble up, I was able to quiet them by throwing myself into work or play with a vengeance. But late at night, or anytime I was left alone with myself, doubt, fear, and unease would rock me oh so gently, subtly, and quietly, like a baby in a bassinet. Never enough to raise an alarm, yet always enough to remind me it was there. Someday I would need to get to the bottom of it. But not yet.

## CHAPTER 14

Patrick Swayze and I reunite for *Youngblood* and I am once again enthralled by his mastery of anything physical. While I had to work hard to look good on my skates, he seemed to be a natural from the start. But by the first day of shooting, we both look like we've been skating forever.

The producers need to fill the large arena where we are shooting with a crowd, so they invite fans to come see us in the flesh. Swayze and I take bets on how many would show. I think maybe five hundred; he thinks more like a thousand. When two thousand people show up, some carrying handmade signs and all going crazy, we can't believe it.

"Hey, little brother," says Swayze, "looks like we're hot shit!"

He skates out to a giant roar and cross-steps like Wayne Gretzky into the corners.

I skate out to an ovation and fall on my ass.

Swayze is a relentless spirit. He never sleeps, works out like an animal, and writes and records music on a portable studio he has set up in his hotel room. He has written a song for *Youngblood* called "She's Like the Wind," and he lobbies 24/7 to get it into the film. Everyone "yes's" him to death, hoping he'll forget about it and get back to acting. Eventually he *will* get the song into one of his movies—it will be a breakout smash for *Dirty Dancing*.

As the shoot grinds on, I am often in full hockey gear in my trailer with a saxophone around my neck. It's not a good look, but lunchtime is the only moment I have free to prep for *St. Elmo's Fire*, which will shoot as soon as I wrap.

By the time I'm done with eight weeks of fourteen-hour days on or around the ice, I swear I will never lace up a pair of skates again. And while it's definitely been a rush to have fans surrounding my trailer and milling in the hotel lobby, I'm relieved to return to the other half of my life at home in Malibu, with my family.

The property I bought has a guesthouse for me that I have designed to my specifications. It's about what you would expect from a twenty-year-old in 1984. Modern, stark, with lots of glass—picture a set from *Miami Vice*. Even though my family is living on the same one-acre lot, it's the first place I can call my own. I barely have time to acclimate before I'm off to Washington, D.C.

⬧

In the classic film *The Exorcist* the priest, now inhabited by the demon, throws himself down a long, foreboding stairway somewhere in Georgetown. After a long night of "research" for *St. Elmo's Fire* (it's about a bar after all), I find myself with Emilio and Judd Nelson at the top of these stairs, peering into the darkness below.

"This is pretty freaky," I offer, as we try not to tumble to the bottom in our present condition. Judd breaks into a perfect Linda Blair and recites some of the movie's more memorable lines involving hell, mothers, and fellatio.

We are a week into shooting and I've never had more fun in my life. Once again I'm working with Ally Sheedy and Emilio. Judd is new in my life and I discover that he is whip smart and hilarious. It's my second movie with Andrew McCarthy. I adore the wildly talented Mare Winningham and envy Emilio's on-screen romance with the stunning Andie MacDowell. Demi and I connect so well on-screen that I don't mind when she jumps ship and switches to a more serious relationship with Emilio. It's one big, fun, wild, talented bunch—a sort of "pack," if you will.

I have a theory that sometimes an actor gets a character that they love so much that they can't let go. They lose themselves in the exciting, or possibly frightening, challenges the role offers. Directors, producers, and even studio executives egg you on, thrilled that you are inhabiting the role so well. All your needs are catered to; your only responsibility is to deliver this character to the screen. You get swept up in the moment, and if the right part comes to you at the right time, you stop playing the role and start living it. It becomes your persona.

I sink my teeth into Billy Hicks, the lady-killing rockin'-and-rollin' funmeister, and never look back. For so many years I was the nerd, the last picked for sports teams, the acting freak, the one who couldn't get the girls' attention. Now I have the part of the guy I could never be, no matter how hard I tried, and people love me in it. So I run with it. For a long time.

❖

My return from shooting *St. Elmo's Fire* is met with sad, tragic news. During the filming of a stunt for the TV show *Airwolf,* a helicopter has gone down. On board was my friend and stunt double, Reid Rondell. He would not survive. I mourn the loss of a friend and colleague and am reminded that although accidents are rare, filmmaking can be dangerous. This is also the week the space shuttle *Challenger* explodes. Along with the rest of the country, I grieve for the brave crew and their families. I am moved by President Reagan's beautiful and soaring eulogy, which included the beautiful lines of poetry: "They . . . 'slipped the surly bonds of Earth' to 'touch the face of God.'" It is stunning oratory and I look up the White House speechwriter who crafted it. Her name is Peggy Noonan, and I make a note to follow her and the other West Wing speechwriters in the future.

Having spent the last six months starring in two movies back to back, I am ready to have some serious fun. A phone call from Emilio provides a perfect excuse.

For weeks, Emilio has been trailed by a reporter from *New York* magazine, who is doing a cover story on him as the youngest writer, director, and star to make a movie since Orson Welles (it's true, you can look it up). He's been swamped in postproduction, in editing rooms, and in marketing meetings on his movie *Wisdom*. (In hindsight, I could have used a little wisdom myself when I agreed to join him and the reporter for an off-the-record dinner). Emilio is worried that the reporter has only seen his serious, hardworking side and is eager to show him that he can have fun as well. He also wants to take him out for a night on the town as a thank-you for all the hours spent on the profile.

A spur-of-the-moment dinner party is put together at our favorite hangout, the Hard Rock Cafe. Our gang from *St. Elmo's Fire* is invited and we are all still in some way living our characters' relationships. Judd Nelson joins me, and a number of fun girls are invited, in case the writer is single. When we take our usual booth at the Hard Rock, the place is pretty chaotic. It's full of buzzed kids our age, all looking to have a good time. Sexual possibilities are everywhere; there is food for days and more kamikazes than the emperor's fleet at Midway. The reporter, a balding, skinny guy who made no real impression on anyone, eats and drinks with us like it's his last night before the electric chair. Emilio, always generous, picks up the very large tab. The writer hugs us all good-bye and thanks us as he hops into his cab. Judd, Emilio, and I watch him go.

"Thanks, guys. I think that went really well," says Emilio happily.

A few weeks later, the writer drops his story about Emilio as an auteur. Instead, he writes a sneak-attack, mean-spirited hatchet job about our dinner in his honor. *New York* magazine runs it on its cover with a studio photo from the soon-to-be-released *St. Elmo's Fire.* The headline: "Hollywood's Brat Pack."

According to the reporter, what he observed during our dinner wasn't the exuberant camaraderie of peers or a celebratory thank-you for him, but the obnoxious exploits of a "pack" of interchangeable, pampered, spoiled, vacuous, attention-seeking actors who were long on ambition and fame but short on talent or humanity. As he drank our booze, ate our food, and chatted up the girls at the table, he gave us no indication that he held us in such condescending, low regard.

The "Brat Pack" article was an instant classic. In one cover story, an entire generation of actors, many of whom weren't even present, were branded with an image conjured up to sell magazines. Some of these actors would never escape this perception or the moniker. The story primed the pump of an inevitable media backlash against the industry's growing obsession with youth. Other reporters duly took their cues from the story, and overnight every profile had whiffs of the article's passive-aggressive vitriol. So, when *St. Elmo's Fire* opened shortly thereafter, the critics were ready to hate it. And they did.

But audiences don't care about *New York* magazine and most don't read reviews. *St. Elmo's Fire* opened to big box office and was the must-see date-night movie of the summer. Its soundtrack was inescapable for weeks, went to number one on the charts, and became a romantic classic that people are "married and buried to" to this day.

The film captured an idealized yet believable world where friends were everything and you faced an uncertain adult life together. The character of Billy Hicks stood out in a cast of compelling characters, and the poster of me with my saxophone sold out its run and could be found in bedrooms and dorm rooms around the world. When I went to a Halloween party and saw guys dressed as me from *St. Elmo's Fire*, I knew that the movie had hit the zeitgeist bull's-eye.

My instinct on which part to play proved correct. Billy was just the right mix of sex, trouble, humor, and empathy to be the role that I'm asked about and identified with more than any other (with the exception of Sam Seaborn on *The West Wing*). The lovable rake became a large part of my persona and I embraced it, on all levels. Having spent quite enough time sitting in the nerd area of the quad, I was ready for this seismic change.

And the "Brat Pack"? Although the term spent at least a decade as a vague pejorative in the press, interestingly, a lot of the public saw it as something cool. To them it was just their version of the Rat Pack: a group of people whose movies they dug and who seemed to have fun making them. Nothing more, nothing less. Of the many great attributes fans have, my personal favorite is their ability to see through salesmanship, cynicism, and bullshit.

But for the actors *in* the Brat Pack, this new scrutiny, the minimizing and condescending lumping together of very different talents and personalities, took a toll. It was the end of the carefree, innocent nights on the town together, and the end of a number of friendships. Some never got over their resentment and some never had the chance to work their way to being identified with other, perhaps more iconic, projects and roles.

And while the writer acted like a scumbag, he did coin a great phrase. And so today, I own it. I'm proud to have been a leader of the "Pack." Twenty-five years after the summer of *St. Elmo's Fire*, there are rereleases, TV specials, and anniversary articles. It's always an honor to be part of something that stands the test of time.

And to the writer, if you are still around somewhere and read this and want to apologize, I am open to sitting down to dinner. But this time, you can pay.

✦

From the time I was a young kid, politics were exciting to me. Back in Dayton, Ohio, in the years when I was being shuttled to play practice in my stepdad's VW, I would listen to him bitch about Richard Nixon and follow the Watergate hearings he was listening to on the radio. I punched in numbers at the phone bank to roll calls for Senator Howard Metzenbaum and sold Kool-Aid for McGovern, whom I snuck under a barricade to meet. It was in the waning hours of the '72 campaign, at a large rally on the courthouse steps. I slid up through his security detail and tugged on his raincoat.

"I hope you win," I said.

"Me too," said McGovern.

Now, years later, the Hollywood political machine has taken note of my expanding public profile. My early acting heroes had almost always been activists (Newman, Beatty, Redford), and so when the call comes to join Jane Fonda for a "coffee and a discussion at her home," I am excited to go. Not only am I predisposed to take an interest, but also Hollywood activism seems like an esteemed tradition.

I park on a busy residential street in Santa Monica, looking for Jane Fonda's address. I'm surprised she doesn't live in Bel Air or Beverly Hills, hidden away behind big gates like the other stars. But then again, there is no one quite like her. She starred in some of my favorite movies. *The Electric Horseman*, *The China Syndrome*, and *9 to 5* on their own would today be considered an entire career of achievement. But this wouldn't include her debut, *They Shoot Horses, Don't They?*, or her Oscar-nominated turn in *The Morning After*. She has an important production company. She is suddenly making millions of dollars with her workout tapes. Before anyone in Hollywood was entrepreneurial or smart enough to think of "branding" themselves, there was Jane in her leg warmers.

I walk through a small security gate right off the sidewalk and step up to a comfortable home surrounded by tall hedges. I'm let inside and find a place in the corner of the living room, which is packed with various industry types. I see Meg Ryan, whom I know from her work with Tom Cruise in *Top Gun*. I see Stephen Stills from Crosby, Stills, Nash & Young. There is that great-looking guy I've been seeing at auditions named Alec Baldwin. I also recognize the producers from *Footloose* and a few others.

As we all mingle, Jane descends the staircase, passing a giant Warhol portrait of herself. She greets us and introduces her husband, Tom Hayden, an extremely smart and intense guy in the fashion of an über-left-wing Dustin Hoffman. Soon he will become the first person I know to drive an electric car.

Jane and Tom lead a lively and passionate discussion that is as far-ranging as it is partisan. There is talk of the grave threat of the nuclear-power industry ("the China Syndrome"), the impending, desperate need to disarm the military, and various paths toward a cleaner environment. Tom Hayden knows his way around fiery rhetoric and Jane Fonda is Jane Fonda for a reason; so when they finish, we are a whipped-up mob ready to storm the Bastille for any cause they want. I leave impressed with them both, Tom for his big brain and Jane for her passion and beauty. I have always had a crush on her and now it is off the scale.

Hollywood was (and is) a one-party town. Tom and Jane's unique, well-oiled indoctrination machine operated with total air superiority, there being absolutely no opposing viewpoint (let alone megastar mouthpiece) anywhere within the industry. They had the monopoly on the newly budding nexus between politics and show business, and with their intellect and charisma, and I was thrilled to be included. As I said good-bye, Jane put her hand on my shoulder and fixed me with those icy blue eyes.

"Thanks for coming. There's so much to be done together."

❖

Lack of privacy is the expected, if complicated, collateral damage of any career that takes off. As I navigate through the insanity, I am taken by surprise at what a burden it is on my family.

My brothers now have complete strangers in their faces, probing their business for good and ill. For every beach bunny who now chats them up, there's someone else who is looking to use them to get to me, or as a message board for me. "Tell your brother he's soooo hot," or "Tell your brother he's a fag."

My grandparents, square Republicans living in the tiny town of Sidney, Ohio, awaken one night to find three teenage girls standing over their bed. "Is Rob Lowe here?" they ask—why they think I would be in my grandparents' bed under any circumstances is just one of the oddities of the evening. Turns out the girls had broken into the house. This being the polite and nonconfrontational Midwest, no police are called and no parents either. Grandma makes them some coffee to sober them up and off they go.

Within a few weeks there is a "Goldilocks" incident at my new bachelor pad in Malibu. I am on the road somewhere when my mom and Steve hear the laughter of girls in the middle of the night and investigate to find two girls who have broken into my house and are fast asleep in my bed. They are also wearing my underwear.

And so it goes. My dad takes to unplugging the phone at night to avoid the incessant "Is Rob Lowe there?" calls. He now spends an inordinate amount of time at the law practice fending off inquiries from everyone from the *National Enquirer* to families of girls who want me to show up at their prom.

It only gets worse when I come home to visit. We spend a lot of time being chased by caravans of cars and roving packs of fans. We are careful not to eat in front of the plateglass window at our favorite diner, because the crowd could accidentally break through as they press against the glass. On a few occasions I have to leave via the rear exit and be taken home lying down in the back of a police car.

One summer Chad brings his best pal, Charlie Sheen, to Indiana, where we water-ski. The paper puts long-lens surveillance-type photos of us on the front page with copy stating that we've been "sighted in the area," like convicts on the run or perhaps a group of Sasquatches.

Slowly we all begin to adjust to this level of scrutiny. For me, it just becomes a fact of life—neither good nor bad, because it's almost always both. And as long as the upside is that my career continues to thrive, it's a small price to pay.

⌘

*Sexual Perversity in Chicago* is the best script I have yet read. Based on the classic play by the great David Mamet, it's funny, moving, and romantic. For a while Jonathan Demme was going to direct, and my *Footloose* rival, Kevin Bacon, was going to star, but now the project is free and clear and the studio brings it to me.

Ed Zwick, a new young director, is now at the helm; this will be his film debut. Together, he and I begin searching for the three other main characters to round out this Chicago-based snapshot of sex, love, and commitment.

I am at my happiest moment of the decade. I am working on a major commercial movie that's about something meaningful, is brilliantly written, and will demand a big-time romantic lead performance to carry it off. The role I will play of Danny is an Everyman, emblematic of any era: trying to rise at work, but stifled; wanting to break out on his own, but afraid; comforted by a best friend who he may have outgrown; and suddenly challenged by a one-night stand who he may love. The themes of the movie speak to me in a way that my other roles did not. Like my character, I, too, am beginning to feel that there may be more to life than tortured, on-again, off-again relationships on the one hand and commitment-free girl-chasing on the other. Danny's journey will be a personal one for me as well.

But first, we need a girl. A girl who can stop traffic and break your heart while she's doing it. This is a love story of the simplest, and therefore highest, order. Naturally we see every actress imaginable for the part of the sexy, smart, and practical Debbie.

I read with and then screen-test with all the actresses— Rebecca De Mornay, Mariel Hemingway, even my own on-again, off-again girlfriend, Melissa Gilbert. We see unknowns. We see them all.

Finally, it comes down to Mariel Hemingway, hot off of working with the master Bob Fosse and the great Robert Towne, and an unknown redhead named Melissa Leo.

I like them both. Mariel is awkward and sweet, with the vulnerability that made her so stunning in Woody Allen's *Manhattan* still intact. She also towers over me, which I think is a cool and funny sight. Melissa Leo is totally different—wild and tough, she exudes an overt sexiness and a take-no-shit attitude. But I can't get the studio to back her. She's too much of an unknown and, in their eyes, not a traditional beauty. (So she would miss this opportunity to break out and would for years work steadily and under the radar. And today, some twenty-plus years later, she is finally being acclaimed for her great work in movies like *Frozen River* and *The Fighter*. As the saying goes, "Don't leave before the miracle.")

The director, Ed Zwick, wants to cast my old pal Demi Moore. I am against it. I feel the idea has already been played out with the success of *St. Elmo's Fire*. But Demi tests with me and when we watch the footage, it's hard to argue with the chemistry. Demi will play Debbie and she will kill.

Elizabeth Perkins gives the single best audition I have ever seen before or since. She will play Debbie's smart-ass friend, Joan. Jim Belushi originated the role of Danny's chauvinist, know-it-all best friend, Bernie, years before, back in Chicago. Although we read a multitude of "comedy" actors, including the notoriously hilarious David Caruso (I kid you not), Jim's name had not been taken seriously. I think it was one of the producers who had been with *Sexual Perversity* since it was a play who insisted we meet Jim. So we did.

And that was that. There was no one else on the planet to compare.

In my opinion, Jim, Demi, and Elizabeth would never be better than they were in the newly named *About Last Night*. (The entertainment culture was still genteel enough then that the words "Sexual" and "Perversity" were banned in many publications.) Jim was the definitive comic embodiment of the male id run rampant, Elizabeth the brittle, yet empathetic, bitch on wheels for the ages, and Demi proved to be the best choice possible. Our personal history, and our mutual fondness for each other, were the basis for an honest and raw exploration of themes that we were both trying to understand. What is love? What is the value of sex?

How do you find the courage for commitment? How do you know when it all comes together?

The shoot was emotional, tough, but exhilarating. The flak-suit sequence at the beginning of the movie is classic Mamet, requiring verbal precision that had not been required of me before. I found I loved the challenge and that I had a facility for the timing and type of dialogue that values specificity of language. Years later I would recognize the same requirements when I read *The West Wing*. Ed Zwick proved just the right master of tone for a movie that still makes me laugh and moves me today. It is my best work of this period of my life and a film that still has the power to make you laugh, swoon, and cry. Today, *About Last Night* is considered a classic. I'd put it up against any "date night" movie ever made.

It was around this time that I finally saw a movie about another romantic commitment-phobe, *Shampoo*, starring Warren Beatty. Between my journey playing Danny and seeing Warren isolated and devastated by his inability to recognize and embrace love, I began to question my own romantic relationships. Watching the ending of *Shampoo* was like being shown a possible preview of my own life. Without some major changes, I could be just like Warren's character—drowning in fun and attention but devoid of love, alone on Christmas Eve.

But in the meantime, there was too much action available to this twenty-one-year-old male, so in spite of a new, quiet voice telling me where it could all lead, I was nowhere near ready to listen. Crank up the music!

❖

The one-two punch of *St. Elmo's Fire* and *About Last Night* has put me in the sweet spot of industry success, fan appreciation, and press coverage. But I know I need to use these hits to raise myself to the next level. Tom Cruise has been doing this beauti-fully and shows no signs of stopping. He has gone from the youthful appeal of *Risky Business* and *Top Gun* to working with Martin Scorsese and Paul Newman. He has transitioned, truly, into adult-themed films, in which he can work for the rest of his life. So I read tons of scripts a week, and at the mercy of the mate-rial available, I try to find ways to manage the stress of waiting for the Next Right Script.

In the meantime, I make a small, independent movie that will be one of the first films to premiere at Robert Redford's fledgling film festival, Sundance. I play a developmentally challenged, and eventually suicidal, white-trash Texan. *Square Dance* also stars the great Jason Robards and Jane Alexander, but the film's calling card is the lead-role debut of Winona Ryder. My poor, confused Rory is unaware that his love for Noni's Gemma is doomed from the start. I am playing completely against my It-guy persona and will eventually receive some of the best reviews of my career and a Golden Globe nomination for best supporting actor.

I also use my downtime to travel to Massachusetts to do Che-khov's *Three Sisters* at the prestigious Williamstown Theatre Festi-val. I will play Tuzenbach, the tragic lover, in a cast that includes theater heavyweights like Daniel Davis, Kate Burton, Roberta Maxwell, Stephen Collins, Amy Irving, and an actor who has always intrigued me, Christopher Walken.

The heat is unrelenting. It's 102 degrees inside of Chris Walken's black Cadillac. For some reason there is no air-conditioning. He also likes the windows rolled up. We are cruising the small town of Williamstown, looking for a place to eat and maybe drink.

It is the end of the first day's rehearsal. I've thrown myself into this high-powered production to hone my stage chops. I don't want to be one of the many movie stars who can't hack it when it matters the most. It's important to know you can make it all hap-pen live, every night, without multiple takes and good editors propping you up. I've sort of forced myself onto Chris, knowing that with his level of talent, mystery, and, let's face it, weirdness, if I didn't befriend him stat, I might get too freaked out to ever do it.

So we bake in his Caddy.

"I saw. Your name. It's good. It was on a list. Of the cast. I'm . . . glad it *was* you. I wasn't sure. If it was true," says Chris, scanning the street.

"I don't. Drink anymore. I would eat a donut," he says, spying a coffee shop and pulling over.

We are quite a sight getting out of this giant hearse among the summer tourists on the main drag. Within seconds people are milling around us and we have to abort our plans. People pound on the Caddy as we drive off.

"Girls were screaming. Zoweeeee!" he says, and giggles like a kid.

Chris and I become unlikely buddies during our *Three Sisters* run. He is unexpectedly sweet, with an odd yet vaguely self-aware sense of humor. He is also brilliantly unpredictable on-stage, which makes him one of the most riveting actors in contemporary theater.

One night, in front of a full house, he walks to the apron of the stage, turns his back on the audience, and plays an entire speech directly to me in a voice so conversational that old ladies start yelling from the back row.

Another time, our director, the esteemed Nikos Psacharopoulos, asks Chris to stop directing his dialogue to the audience, and not to look into the seats during important scenes. But Chris is having none of Nikos's requests.

"Why *wouldn't* I look at them? I know they are there. They know I'm here. It would be rude to ignore them!"

Getting nowhere, Nikos moves on to a complicated and boring lecture on the severity of the angle of the "raked" stage we are using. He goes on at length about sight lines and safety issues and the angle of the slope. Finally, Chris has had enough. "Oh. And don't bring your bowling ball onstage. It will roll into the front row!" he says, cackling like a maniac.

I love and admire Chris, who is not who most people think him to be. From him I learn the value of avoiding conventional interpretations of material whenever possible and to be funny whenever possible—even if some people don't get it.

That the Oscar winner for *The Deer Hunter* is also a comic genius will take our pigeonholing industry almost three decades to figure out. I knew it in one ride in a Cadillac.

I once saw Chris appear with Diane Ladd in a reading of the sappy warhorse *Love Letters*. A more unlikely bit of casting I can't imagine and Chris did not disappoint. Backstage I asked him how much rehearsal time was required.

"None."

"What? What do you mean 'none'? You never rehearsed this play?" I ask, incredulous.

"They're letters. I wouldn't know what's in them," he said, picking his teeth distractedly.

Genius.

rtistically pumped from these last two projects, I settled into a dizzying late summer. *About Last Night* was
still rolling at the box office and my romantic-leading-
man status was in full flower. I was pulled in seventeen different
directions from all areas of my life, everyone wanting something.
Oftentimes it was great. "Do you want to go backstage and meet
Bruce Springsteen?" "Do you want to host MTV's live New
Year's Eve?" "Will you visit the kids of Children's Hospital?" But
a lot of the time it was people who I didn't have any connection
to, wanting something for nothing, looking to hitch a ride. The
audacity and chutzpah was, and continues to be, shocking.

For instance, my grandfather and grandmother were major
presences in my life, whom I loved deeply. When Grandma died, I
was back in Ohio at her bedside, holding her hand. Eventually, I

was done crying and they began to prepare her to be taken away. Reaching over my grandma's body, a nurse handed me a pen and said, "I hope you don't mind, but could I have your autograph?"

This kind of thing happened all the time. And here's the problem. I was (and still am) aware of the good fortune that hard work has brought me. I don't want to seem ungrateful. I also genuinely like people. I want to get to know them in a real way. I am bummed out at the concept that someone just wants a scribble from you, when it's clear they've never seen your work, they just know you're "famous."

I began to feel a counterintuitive, melancholy loneliness and even low-grade anger at these moments. I didn't like the way it made me feel when a passing car full of teenage girls screeched to a halt, emptying the crazed occupants, who bull-rushed me, pointing, screaming, and laughing. Years later, someone will call this phenomenon "objectification." Then, I didn't really know that I was being treated like an object. I did, however, begin to treat some people the way they treated me.

❖

Apparently, the drinking water in California is very, very bad. Additionally, known carcinogens are being routinely put into the water table, our food supply, you name it. And when you really think about it, there's only one place to turn in such circumstances. Stars! Lots and lots of stars!

It's Jane Fonda calling to ask me to join her on a campaign to pass Prop 65, the Safe Drinking Water and Toxic Enforcement Act. The producers of *Footloose* want to put together a USO-style, celebrity-filled bus tour to barnstorm around the state, talking about cancer and water. Clearly, this will have more impact than my Kool-Aid stand for McGovern. I tell Jane to count me in.

The bus is set to leave at 7:00 a.m., an hour I simply don't see unless I'm being paid. The night before, I am at frenemy Michael

J. Fox's house for the kickoff party, this being our attempt to settle a fairly friendly but simmering rivalry. A few months before, I was ringside at the Marvin Hagler–John "the Beast" Mugabi match and had a run-in with Michael, whom I had never met.

"Hey, Lowe."

"Oh, hi. Nice to meet you."

"Yeah. Um, where the hell was *my* invitation?"

"Your invitation? Invitation to what?"

"To join the Brat Pack. I guess it was just lost in the mail."

I looked at him closely, to see if he was kidding.

"Ah, well, fuck it. I got my own thing goin' now anyway. The Snack Pack!" he said, turning back to the fight, with a twinkle in his eye.

Eventually we spent the postfight debating whose movie themes were better: "Man in Motion" vs. "The Power of Love." We were both big fans of beverages and so we started buying each other drinks and talking crazy, good-natured, competitive smack.

"Hey, Teen Wolf, what time is it?" I asked.

"Screw off! You've made seven movies. My last one [*Back to the Future*] made more than all of yours *combined*!"

And on and on.

At one point, we were seriously contemplating our chances of sucker punching Sugar Ray Leonard, who seemed small to us. Thankfully, even we knew that it would be suicide and that Ray is one of the nicest guys ever. "Can you imagine if we did it, though?" Fox said, and we both fell about the room, laughing like idiots.

The party at Mike's house is much the same, with tremendous ball busting on both sides and an acknowledged mutual affection. Around 4:30 a.m., I can take no more of Mike's beloved dog's attention, so in spite of a free, live living-room performance by Tom Petty's lead guitarist, Mike Campbell, I beg off to bed. I stumble to an out-of-the-way guest room and am unconscious in seconds. Even the commotion of a large object leaping onto the bed doesn't stir me; I figure I'll let Mike's dog sleep where he wants. Soon the room is absolutely freezing and I'm glad to have the warmth to snuggle with. Mr. Michael J. Fox may be making a fortune in movies, but I can tell you what he's not spending money on: his heating bill!

"What the hell is going on?" asks Mike's assistant at first light, rousing me from my cozy confines. I'm still feeling the effects from last night and I try to open my eyes.

"Oh, sorry. I let the dog sleep with me."

She stares at me with a look that distinctly says, Oh, now I've heard *everything*.

I look next to me to discover Mike is in the bed, not the dog. I leap out of bed.

"Jesus Christ!" I say with a start.

"Shuuuut up. Tiiirred," says Mike, just like my teenage sons do today. "Get out of my bed," he adds.

I decide it's not worth trying to explain and stagger out to the kitchen. Please, Lord, let Marty McFly at least have some coffee in this crazy house.

Eventually Mike and I pile into a rented Greyhound bus for the two-day road trip. Our itinerary has us stopping for big rallies in Santa Barbara, San Luis Obispo, the farms of Salinas Valley, Berkeley, and finally a giant gathering at the historic Fairmont Hotel in San Francisco, where Jefferson Starship will perform.

On the bus, I see many familiar faces. Obviously, Jane and Tom are there, along with Whoopi Goldberg, Morgan Fairchild, Ed Begley Jr., Daphne Zuniga, Peter Fonda, Stephen Stills, Ed Asner, Mike Farrell, and others.

There's lots of political shoptalk and everyone is raring to spread the message of voting for the initiative, which the ag industry and chemical companies are spending heavily to combat. In fact, they are outspending us by many millions. But we have the one thing they don't: the power of celebrity.

Ensconced in the back of the hot, stuffy bus, Mike and I are like geckos in a terrarium. Still very much playing the bad boy from *St. Elmo's Fire*, I open the emergency hatch on the roof for some fresh air and a better view. Soon Mike and I are sticking our heads out like a pair of Labradors as the bus flies up Highway 101.

"Do you hear that?" I scream at Mike over the howling wind in my face.

"Whaaat?"

"I hear a siren!" I say, and sure enough, highway patrol is screaming up behind us.

"Oh shit! I think he's after us!" yells Mike.

We both duck back inside and close the hatch.

There is a commotion in the aisles, as it becomes clear that we are indeed being pulled over. This ought to be good. Knowing full well that I could still probably explode a Breathalyzer, I'm glad I'm not driving.

The driver pulls the Greyhound bus to the shoulder. The cop asks him to step outside. If this becomes a strip-search situation, I'm quite sure there are some folks on the bus who will have an issue. Peter Fonda shakes his head.

"Wow, man. Busted by the heat before we even get started."

"Maybe he's been paid by Dow Chemical to stop us," someone adds.

Now the driver comes back on board.

"The officer wants everyone off the bus."

This is quickly becoming the kind of situation that generates headlines you don't want.

"I'll go first," says Jane, exiting.

"I got your back, sister," says Whoopi, right behind her.

And so we all disembark, piling out one after another after another like a celebrity clown car. By the time Michael J. Fox and I file past the cop, he is in a starstruck daze, looking at us all lined up on the side of the highway in the middle of central California farmlands.

"Whoa. Wh . . . what are *you* guys doing here?" he asks.

Jane takes charge, telling him our mission and giving the poor man both barrels of her A-list movie-star charm.

"I see," says the cop, flummoxed. "I pulled you over because you were speeding and I saw people trying to escape via the roof."

"That was me, Officer. I was actually trying to close the broken hatch with Mr. Michael J. Fox here," I say, gesturing to Mike, who is trying to be invisible.

Now the guy really loses it.

"I just saw *Back to the Future!*" he gushes.

Mike elbows me. "I'm sure *St. Elmo's Fire* was sold out," he says under his breath.

Soon we are all posing for photos with our new friend from the California Highway Patrol.

"My sergeant will never believe this!" he says as he gets a good-bye hug from Whoopi Goldberg. "You all slow down now. And good luck on Prop 65. You got my vote."

We file back into the bus and roll out. They say politics is retail. We just made our first sale.

We roll into the towns and hold our rallies. The crowds are massive and vocal. Sometimes Mike and I have to retreat back to our perch on the roof of the bus to get out of the frenzy. These communities are a million light-years away from the Hollywood universe and they've never seen this kind of celebrity activism before. And in spite of the several unintentionally comic moments (like sitcom stars telling lifelong farmers how to grow "safer" crops), it feels good to be in service of a cause greater than my own self-interests, a cause that adds some substance and humanity to my increasingly rarefied existence. I enjoy the moments when I can connect with people in their world and on terms that are related to their own lives.

Soon enough I will have more perspective on the complicated relationship between Hollywood activism and its effectiveness, as well as its true intentions, but for now it gives me a much-needed way to channel all this personal attention into something I hope is meaningful.

The Safe Drinking Water and Toxic Enforcement Act will pass with a huge margin, despite being massively outspent by the opposition. Its success will usher in the ballot-initiative-movement phenomenon that is now out of control in California. (One would hope the government wouldn't need its citizens to take matters into their own hands; making laws is their job—they should be better at it.) Today it is a crime to knowingly expose the public to carcinogens in the workplace or in the public food or water supply, without notification. You can still see our Prop 65 notices of such dangers posted in public spaces throughout California.

❖

The cliffs are windswept and brutally tall. The beach before them is so wide, it's clear that there was nowhere to hide. The young men who were shot dead here would've been exactly my age, dying alone and unprotected, giving "the last full measure of devotion," in the lonely, cold mist of an early June morning.

I am standing at the German gun emplacements of Pointe du Hoc, where so many fell. On my left there is the beautiful and appalling field of crosses and Stars of David for the heroes whom, until today, I had never seriously considered. Brokaw would eventually write his book and Spielberg would one day make his movie, but in the early fall of 1986, nothing has prepared me for the emotion of this great battlefield on France's Normandy coast.

I've come to nearby Deauville for its film festival, to promote the European release of *About Last Night*. Ed Zwick and Jim Belushi are back at the hotel. I've come on a whim to see the sights with a new friend who has led me to this desolate overlook.

Glenn Souham's security company is handling our needs while in France, and he and I have become friendly during the dull black-tie dinners and long press junkets. Glenn is Franco-American, tall, sandy haired, and athletic, from a renowned family whose war exploits earned them an emblazonment on the Arc de Triomphe. After walking me through a tutorial of the events of D-Day, he leaves me alone to take it all in.

I'm twenty-two years old. I've never known for want. There's always been food on the table and the sweet smell of possibility, of a horizon free of impediment. I had opportunity, worked hard, and made my dreams come true. Here's a guy on a plaque, eighteen years old, from Iowa. Another is twenty-two and from a town in northern Michigan. A door lowered; they ran into raging fire; if they lived they tried to climb those terrible cliffs, hand over hand, wide open to the barrages from above. If they got there, some fought, some charged into the maw of the .50 cals, anything to silence the howling guns, to save their brothers and achieve the objective. To do the job. To save our country. All the training, all the planning, all the money, all the strategy, finally and simply came down to that. When the door was lowered, could the twenty-two-year-old from Michigan step out and face the job at hand?

A stiff wind is blowing off the English Channel and it's making my eyes water. Glenn stands back with the big, black Mercedes and the chauffeur. There's another black-tie dinner and it's a long drive back to the resort. I need to get going. People have paid money to see me, to meet me, and to congratulate me on the achievement of the film. I walk back to the car, past the graves and the flags, past the boys from the United States who never came home. I hop in the back, shut the door, and drive away.

The dinner is held in an ornate seventeenth-century ballroom. There are beautiful women. There's a lot of wine. But I'm quiet.

Someone asks me if I have something on my mind. I say no, but I do. It's a twenty-two-year-old marine from a town in northern Michigan.

✥

*About Last Night* is well received at both the Deauville and Venice film festivals. Sex, love, and commitment are story lines that travel well.

At one of the hotels on my press tour I stop by the magazine shop with my new pal Glenn.

"Rob, I noticed you looking at Princess Stephanie of Monaco on the cover of *Vogue*."

"Yeah, I think she's beautiful! It's a great cover shot of her."

"Have you ever met her?"

"No. Never. *Oxford Blues* was sort of based on her and we asked if she wanted to try acting. I'm actually hosting a charity event for the Princess Grace Foundation in a few months just to meet her," I say. It's true. The chance to finally meet Princess Stephanie is the only reason I agreed to host the event, to be held later in the year in Dallas, Texas.

"My company provides security for the Grimaldi royal family. Would you like me to introduce you?"

"Sure."

"I will inquire then."

Within a few days, Glenn has the go-ahead. Now we are back in Paris, and I say good-bye to the *About Last Night* gang.

"I'm going to stick around, have some fun," I explain.

"Whaddya got, a hot date?" jokes Belushi.

"Maybe," I say with a smile, and we hug.

"Don't do anything I wouldn't do," says Belushi.

I never told Jim that I had met his brother so many years ago and that when I did, his one piece of advice was "Stay out of the clubs." Now I was about to begin a whirlwind romance that would end with me never wanting to see another club as long as I lived.

The doorman at my hotel is grim-faced when I return. "I'm sorry, monsieur. You cannot go outside, there has been another bomb."

I try to sneak a peek but can see nothing; in the distance, sirens howl. This is the third blast in the last week and Paris is becoming increasingly and rightfully paranoid. It is at the point where it would surprise no one if the Eiffel Tower were blown up.

I look across the lobby and see Irwin and Margo Winkler, parents of a friend of mine. Irwin produced *Rocky* and many other great movies. They invite me to see a "very rough cut" of Irwin's latest movie the next day. Figuring that during a siege there's not much else to be done, I say yes.

The next afternoon I'm sitting down with the Winklers in a private screening room. I don't know what movie this is or what it's about. The lights go down. I'm about to have the greatest movie-watching experience of my life.

The print is indeed rough. There are no titles; in fact, it jumps awkwardly into the first scene. I can hear poor temp sound. Two men are driving a '70s-era car. Robert De Niro and Joe Pesci. Cool! I loved them in *Raging Bull*. They banter. They are menacing and somehow funny at the same time. They pull the car over, go to the back, and open the trunk. There's a man inside, bloody, begging for his life. They look at each other, pull a gun, and shoot him in the face. Freeze frame.

*Goodfellas*, even without dissolves or color correction, and with missing scenes, blew my doors off. The seven-minute, uninterrupted tracking shot through the Copacabana alone was groundbreaking. (Years later, we would do similar elaborate tracking shots in *The West Wing*.) But when Scorsese threw down "Layla" on top of the sequence, when they find all the dead bodies, I knew I was seeing the future template of storytelling. And, indeed, now every TV show has to have a classic song punctuating a big scene in a dramatic, counterintuitive way.

The lights come up and even Irwin, I think, is stunned.

"Maybe this will work after all. Who knows?" he says, looking dazed.

Outside the screening room there is chaos. Cars are careening around and sirens once again fill the air. It's another bombing and panic is building. Suddenly Glenn appears out of nowhere.

"Get in my car *now*! All of you," he orders.

We pile into his Mercedes. He places a blue police siren on the roof and pulls the car up onto the sidewalk. Then he guns it.

No one speaks.

After a hair-raising ride, he drops us back at the hotel.

"You'll be safe here. If you ever get into trouble in Paris, the George V is the safest hotel to be in." I want to ask why and how he knows this, but I don't. The Winklers gratefully say good-bye and make their way into the lobby.

"Oh, and I will come for you tomorrow to meet the princess. Call me at this number at noon," he says, looking for a piece of paper to write on. He pulls a card from his wallet and scribbles the number.

"Don't worry. It's safe now," he says as he drives off.

Walking away, I look at the card. On it is the cell number he's written, but embossed on the card itself are three words in familiar, official font that make my breath catch: The White House.

Who the hell *is* this guy?

High noon finds me in the Mercedes headed for Trocadero, across the Seine from the Eiffel Tower. Glenn is running through the protocol for meeting the princess. Being a true-blue American, I am feeling our hallmark mixture of romantic fascination and eye-rolling impatience.

"If it's a formal setting, she is to be addressed as Her Serene

Highness. If members of the palace are present, the protocol will be stricter. You will be presented to her, and then you may introduce yourself. At that time, she can respond."

He pulls to the curb, without warning. "We must change cars now. Quickly," he instructs, and we hustle to another waiting sedan. Now we reverse direction. Glenn casually eyes the rearview mirror.

"Okay. We are a go."

"Nice car," I say, looking at a strange grouping of multiple cell phones (this in an era when they were huge and built into the dashboard).

"Why do you have so many phones?" I ask.

"They are for different purposes," he answers mildly.

I wait for further explanations, but get none.

"You gave me a White House card yesterday—where did you get it?"

"Oh, sorry, I ran out of my own cards."

Again I wait for more, but there's nothing.

This time I press.

"So, you just happen to have official White House business cards? You have a siren that lets you drive on sidewalks and multiple secret phones in your cars? What exactly is the deal?"

Glenn drives for a couple of blocks as if forming an answer that will have the proper combination of authenticity and casual, friendly subterfuge. Finally he answers.

"I have many different areas in my life. I am in different countries; I help many kinds of people. I get to see many, many things. Things you would never imagine."

"Do you work for the French government?" I ask.

"No."

"Do you work for the White House?"

"No, but obviously they know me and I know them."

Before I can continue to pry, we have pulled inside a grand apartment building on a gorgeous residential avenue.

"We are here."

Glenn rings the doorbell on a beautiful mahogany entry and we wait. I don't know what the official purpose of this meeting is, have no idea what she's been told about me or why she's agreed to meet me. I assume there will be a discussion about our cohosting the upcoming charity event. As footsteps come up behind the door, I have one last thought before it opens: I hope Glenn didn't tell anyone I have a crush on this girl.

With the entire preamble about protocol, I expected a palace representative to greet us. But the door opens to reveal a surprisingly soft and vulnerable-looking version of the Princess Stephanie from the cover of *Vogue*. This in-the-flesh incarnation is also *much* prettier, with a delicate quality that is clearly lost in pictures. Her eyes are an intriguing mix of twinkling mischief and deep and profound sadness. They may be the bluest eyes I have ever seen. I know at once, I'm hooked.

"Hi, I'm Stephanie." Her voice is scratchy and low, but with a crystal finish. "Come on in."

We do. Stephanie is barefoot, wearing jeans and a white T-shirt. She leads us into a large living room where an exotic-looking Mauritian girl is watching TV and eating potato chips.

"This is my roommate. Would you like something to eat?" she says, gesturing to a platter of hors d'oeuvres.

Glenn takes this moment to excuse himself; clearly this is no formal meeting. It's more like walking into a blue-blood heiress's apartment and hanging with her and her pal.

The three of us sit and chat. No one brings up the charity, and in fact, no one talks of why we have gotten together at all. It's as if she's been expecting me to come, like a friend she hadn't seen in a while.

I watch her as we talk. She's funny (an absolute necessity for me) and she stretches like a cat. Her roommate doesn't say much, which is just as well. Stephanie and I chat about nothing in particular; it's easy and relaxed. I agree to go to a dinner with a group she is putting together.

By the time the entrées arrive, she is sitting on my lap. By dessert, neither of us is interested in anything other than getting the hell out of there and back to her apartment. Only later will I realize what a "closer" Her Serene Highness is, when I discover that between courses she excuses herself to call the butler at the apartment to pack up the current boyfriend's clothes and remove them before we return from dinner. It really is a wonder what can be done with the proper foresight and staffing.

If I feel a little thrown by the velocity and heat from the first meeting, I don't let it slow me down. The next morning, I check out of my hotel and move in.

I become so immersed in the princess's hermetically sealed exotic lifestyle that I might as well be in the Witness Protection Program. In Paris, our days begin at noon at the earliest, then possibly we do some official business, running around the city exploring and shopping, then drinks back at the apartment, dinner at nine or ten at night with a group that is never less than eight, enough vodka and tonics to float the battleship *Bismarck*, then dancing at the nightclubs till four or five in the morning.

My dad, whenever he got frustrated by disinterest in the grunt work of daily life, used to always say, "You better become either a movie star or a prince." Who knows, maybe I'll go two for two.

"How did your family come to rule Monaco?" I ask Stephanie one day. It seems like something I should know.

"Hundreds of years ago, my family and some others knocked

on the village gates dressed as monks. When they were let inside, they killed who they had to and took over. We've been there ever since," she answers, sipping her vodka tonic.

After a few weeks I am getting restless in Paris. Although Stephanie is working on a recording career, there is a profound lack of work ethic in her circle. And while I can party and drink with the best of them, even I need a day off from time to time. Not an option with this group. So I begin waking up before Stephanie and working out with Glenn, who is a champion martial artist.

"Rob, if they were to rip my heart out, I would still walk; if they were to tear me open, I would keep coming. If they pull my insides out, I will still be crawling," says Glenn one day, apropos of nothing.

"Is that what they teach you in martial arts?" I ask.

"No. It's just who I am."

"Okaaaay," I say, not sure of his point. "Good to know."

With consecutive hit films behind me, I'm getting antsy to go home and take care of business. (The life of idle leisure is proving to be more taxing than I thought it would be.) My agents are putting together my next movie, and with my new profile as a romantic leading man, it has a lot riding on it. I tell Stephanie, who understands. She will come to L.A. in the next few weeks for a meeting on a record deal. I begin to pack my things.

I come across a magazine under a stack in Stephanie's closet. It's French, from six months ago, and I'm on the cover.

"Look what I found!" I say to her. She blushes.

"I put it away when I finally met you. I kept it on my nightstand for months," she says.

❖

Glenn drives me to the airport. I've had to leave on even shorter notice to make a meeting, but all flights are full. Glenn, however, always keeps two seats reserved on every Concord flight out of France. I use one to go home. But now the autoroute is in total gridlock. There is no way I'll make the flight. Glenn wheels the car onto the side of the road, hits the blue siren, and drives the entire way on the shoulder of the freeway. Every once in a while we clip a car's side-view mirror and it shatters with a bang. Glenn is unfazed.

As we pull up to de Gaulle, I am overwhelmed by a sense of finality. A very romantic, chaotic, exotic, bomb-filled month or so is coming to an end. In a life of extraordinary moments, even I know this one was remarkable.

"Good-bye, Glenn. I can't thank you enough for all your help. For taking such good care of me, and for the fun and friendship."

"And for Stephanie?" he smiles.

"Glenn, I've been around you almost every day for weeks and I've never heard you even attempt a joke. Until now."

"I am learning from you. I want to have more fun in my life. I admire your ability to do that," he says, looking almost wistful.

"Well, I admire you, too. Even if I don't know what the fuck you're really up to!"

He smiles and looks down. I head for the gorgeous needle-nose jet glinting in the morning sun.

I have my lunch meeting at the Russian Tea Room in Manhattan, fly home, and eat dinner alone at McDonald's in Malibu. I am transitioning back to reality.

Back in Paris, Glenn goes to the gym after dropping me at the airport, and then heads home. Getting out of the Mercedes in front of his house, he is shot multiple times in the chest, by three masked gunmen. He collapses onto the hood of the car. Hearing shots, his girlfriend comes out of the house, calling his name. When he hears her voice, Glenn forces himself to rise and button up his jacket, sparing her the sight of his wounds, which he knows are grave.

"I've been shot; I need to go to the hospital. We won't be able to wait for an ambulance."

He gives directions as she drives. He crosses his legs to hide the blood pooling in his seat. He is white and consciousness is fading. The ride takes fifteen minutes.

"I think the back entry will be quicker at this hour," he calculates.

Somehow he walks unaided into the ER. The staff take one look at him and rush to help.

"I have five wounds. I believe they are 9 mm," he tells them before passing out.

Glenn dies on the operating table.

His girlfriend tells me the story, in a matter-of-fact delivery. She is obviously in deep shock. I am sitting among my luggage at my house; the phone was ringing as I walked in the door from McDonald's. I try to offer any comfort I can, but I, too, am devastated. I may not know who Glenn worked for or who had him murdered, but I do know that it was likely a pro from the highest levels. Which means it was well planned; which means they waited for the right moment; which means they waited until the moment I was gone.

I was later told that Glenn was honored by both the French and the American governments for heroic service. President Reagan had a small private ceremony at the White House and wrote a lovely letter of condolence to Glenn's father. Neither of these ceremonies, nor the assassination itself, was covered in the press in much detail. Glenn Souham's killing remains unsolved.

❖

Fans breaking into my house to steal underwear. Princesses. Professional hits in broad daylight. My life is becoming unreal, even to me. And in spite of a (very) small inner voice warning me that this kind of chaos is not a good thing, I don't know how to stop it.

Long, eventful careers, by definition, have cycles. Cycles are almost impossible to identify until you are well into their sequence. In retrospect, Glenn's death would be the first movement of a cycle in which I would be put in the wrong place at the wrong time and with people whose agendas conflicted with mine. Or to put it simply: Now would begin a period when I couldn't catch a break. Sometimes it would be completely my fault. Sometimes it wouldn't.

My relationship with Stephanie is the first casualty of this undercurrent of conflict. While our life in Paris was a magical escape from reality, life in America is unrelenting reality. My mother, now deep into her illness, has a psychotic break after going off the drug Halcion, cold turkey. Steve, who has been prescribing medications for her, wants her committed; she wants him investigated for overmedication and attempted poisoning. This, as I bring the princess home to meet them.

As Stephanie sits waiting in the living room, my mom has me cornered in the bedroom, forcing me to examine various used wads of Kleenex she believes have been shaped by Steve into voodoo dolls in an attempt to "intimidate" her into silence about his "poisoning."

I should have sent the princess packing, called the family into a room, and gotten to the bottom of all the insanity. Shamefully, I did not. My conflict/stress/reality-avoidance mechanism, engaged so long ago in that hot Dayton lumberyard, had now grown into a monster.

Stephanie and I flee back to a "safe house" where we are encamped, trailed by rabid paparazzi. There is a large bounty for the first photos of us together, but so far we have managed to stay under wraps.

Finally, it is time for us to fly to Dallas, Texas, for our cohosting duties. The Princess Grace Foundation raises money to support young, fledgling artists, wherever they may be. The

annual ball is always long on both Hollywood and actual royalty. Tonight's black-tie event is packed; Frank Sinatra will perform.

In the VIP area, I lock eyes with the chairman of the board.
Never known as a people person, Ol' Blue Eyes is under siege at
the moment; Kitty Kelley's eviscerating bio has just come out. As
Sinatra makes a beeline for me, I'm anxious. He marches right
up, inches from my face, which he grabs with both hands. He
leans in close, looking intensely into my eyes. He then slaps me
upside the head, hand. "My grandkids *love* ya!" he says, and walks
off.

Stephanie, in the month I was in Paris, never introduced me
to her father, Prince Rainier. I thought it odd that she wouldn't
want him to meet her new boyfriend. Now I'm hosting an event
for his charity, he's standing ten feet away from me, and I still
haven't been introduced. He's glancing at me from time to time,
but it's clear he has no intention of saying hello, much less thanking me for the two days of press and fund-raising I'm doing on
his behalf. My American anti-caste-system inclinations begin to
stir. I look over at him. He turns away.

Finally, I walk to him and offer my hand. The prince is doing
that thing one does of concentrating really hard on a bullshit story
someone is telling, hoping to avoid any interlopers. No luck this
time.

"Excuse me, sir," I say, as his group stares, openmouthed.
"I'm Rob Lowe, I'm hosting this event and dating your daughter.
Welcome to the United States."

Later in the evening I find my old friend Cary Grant.

"Young maaaaaan!" he calls. "Congratulations on all of your
success. I'm sooo proud of you."

It's a nice full circle from his early, kind words so many years
ago. We talk for a while and he moves on. Within months he
will be gone, the greatest movie star who ever lived. I know his

amazing body of work well by now and take solace that I will have more to remember him by than soap on a rope.

Stephanie and I are now over the buzz of our initial meeting, and it's becoming clear that the mutual infatuation has been sated. We both know it's time to move on.

Near the end of the evening I look to the head table. It's late and the men have congregated together, as have the women, who are off somewhere. I see Gregory Peck, Robert Wagner, Cary Grant, and Prince Rainier and approach the group.

"Excuse me. I just wanted to say good-bye and thank you for letting me be a part of a wonderful evening."

Rainier grunts and nods, the rest offer warm good-byes and I head out.

Then, when I am almost out of earshot I hear my future *Austin Powers* costar Robert Wagner say: "Ya know, guys, I think that kid's banged every one of our daughters."

❖

Peter Bogdanovich made *The Last Picture Show*, *Paper Moon*, and *What's Up, Doc?* consecutively, in the early seventies, in what was probably the greatest back-to-back-to-back achievement of any director. Each movie is a classic and, for my money, two of them are perfect (*The Last Picture Show* and *Paper Moon*). Now, after an extended banishment, he is back in Hollywood's good graces due to his newest hit, *Mask*, for which Cher was nominated for an Oscar.

I screen-tested for *Mask* and lost the part to Eric Stoltz. Bogdanovich had me put a stocking over my face with eye holes cut out, to simulate the "mask" that the actor would wear. But he told me, "Your eyes are too identifiable, too unique." And that was that.

But now he is directing a romantic comedy, and I've chosen it as my follow-up to *About Last Night*. I loved what Bogdanovich did with Ryan O'Neal and I'm hoping he still has the mojo to do the same with me. And looking at *Mask*, it seems like a good bet.

But from day one my instincts scream to me that there are serious problems. For the slightly older female lead, names like Michelle Pfeiffer, Jodie Foster, and Melanie Griffith are discussed. But Peter is adamant that he be allowed to cast Colleen Camp, a good friend of his, with whom he's worked before. I like Colleen, but I know this type of movie needs star power. Still, I defer to my director, who, after all, has made some of the best movies in the genre.

Peter also wants to rewrite the script from page one. The script was good enough to get us all to want to do it in the first place, so I'm worried about changing it. Even when Bogdanovich adds a major new character for his girlfriend to play (in spite of her having never acted before) and creates another role for his estate manager, I say nothing. Maybe these changes will elevate the movie to *What's Up, Doc?* But inside, I suspect otherwise. Rather than blow the movie apart, which confronting Bogdanovich most certainly would have done, I drink almost every day after work to quiet my conscience.

Any one of these conceptual changes *alone* should have been sufficient grounds to depart immediately over "creative differences," but I had no leadership in my life. (My agents also represented Bogdanovich and they weren't going to rock the boat.) And I was an inveterate people pleaser who had very few personal boundaries. Plus, I loved Peter. He is one of the most well-read men I have ever met and among the most charismatic. He could lead you anywhere and you would follow, happy to be in his entertaining, insightful company. But every artist can chase his own vision into a blind alley. And on *Illegally Yours*, he did just that.

After seeing the final cut, the studio let it sit in the can as unreleasable. Eventually, it came out in a few cities to scathing reviews. The original writers took their names off of it. But stars have no such luxury, no way to avoid the fallout, and that is one of the reasons they get, and deserve, the big bucks.

My agents and I were smart enough to go directly to another movie to minimize the damage to my leading-man momentum. And this time, the movie would turn out pretty well.

*Masquerade* is a sexual thriller out of the Patricia Highsmith mold. Morally ambivalent in tone, it is a dark, sexy, and sophisticated movie that gives me my first antihero role. Meg Tilly is terrific as the vulnerable heiress I seduce, and Kim Cattrall is perfect as my bored, sexually predatory mistress. Directed by Bob Swaim, a hot director who has recently swept the French Oscars, it also reunites me with Oscar-winning cinematographer David Watkin. With Oscar-winning composer John Barry on board, the filmmaking is state of the art.

Until this movie, I've been relegated to fairly pedestrian locations. Tulsa. Chicago. St. Augustine, Florida. But *Masquerade* shoots entirely in the Hamptons and I fall in love with the low-key, old-money style and lazily debauched nightlife.

Charlie Sheen is also in the Hamptons, shooting *Wall Street* with Oliver Stone and Michael Douglas. It's a good combination for fun and we make the most of our surroundings. Charlie and I compete to see who can play harder, then show up to work and still kick ass. Verdict: Sheen by a nose.

By the end of the *Masquerade* shoot, I'm raw and ragged. I've done two films with no break at all. In both I was in every scene, working thirteen-hour-plus days from February to July. *Masquerade* was a grind for all concerned. On the last day the writer says to me, "If this fucking movie doesn't work, I'm quitting for television."

The movie bombed. It was stylish and sexy (maybe too much so), and I still like it very much. But the studio releasing it was being sold and was in chaos. I also heard that the studio president's wife hated "all that sex" in the movie. At any rate, my stock took another hit and it would be my last starring role in a studio movie for years. *Masquerade*'s writer kept his promise and quit for TV. A half billion dollars later, I am happy to have driven Dick Wolf, the creator of the *Law & Order* franchise, out of the movies to greener pastures.

CHAPTER 16

With the disappointing performance of these last two movies, the rocket ride suddenly and dramatically slows. The heady and exhilarating g-forces that have buffeted, stimulated, and medicated me for years have quieted and I look to fill the void.

I've thrown myself into politics. In the middle of a thirteen-state tour, I find myself in Minnesota, about to do an early-morning live TV interview for presidential candidate Michael Dukakis.

I've been traveling with and for the Massachusetts governor off and on for the last eight weeks. I've come to love the unique blend of backbreaking campaigning and passionate policy strategy by day and hard-charging nightlife when the day is done.

The staff, the advance team, and the traveling press corps can be like a band of marauders in the name of "The Great American Experiment." And while today's road adventures pale in comparison to campaigns of yesteryear, there are still enough of the old-guard hacks around to keep the dream alive.

We've all come out for a freewheeling convention where Jesse Jackson stole the show with his classic "Keep Hope Alive" speech and almost-spoiler candidacy. There is also tremendous drama surrounding the choice for vice president. Will it be Jackson? Will it be the young buck Al Gore? Will it be an unknown? Unlike today's long-form infomercial conventions, where everything is carefully scripted and nothing left to chance, the Atlanta convention of 1988 was probably the last of its kind in that there was some actual chaos and drama.

Downtown one night I was standing with a group from our delegation at the doors of a nightclub. The doorman was hassling me hard for an ID, which I had left in my jacket in the car.

"Dude, you need proper ID to get in. No one under twenty-one allowed," said the guy.

"But, you know it's me, right?"

"Yeah."

"And you know I'm over twenty-one?"

"Sorry, need your ID. No exceptions."

Geez, these guys are like the Gestapo! I cursed as I schlepped back to find my jacket.

Finally in the club, I was approached by two girls who wanted me to join them back at their place. This being most twenty-four-year-old guys' dream scenario, I suggested we reconvene at my suite. Having just received the third degree from the doorman, it never occurred to me that there could be anyone in the club who wasn't of age.

As the three of us left, I had no idea that this romp would set in motion events that would ultimately, through a painful, long, and circuitous path, lead me to greater happiness and fulfillment than I could have ever hoped for.

And now, sitting for my morning-show interview in Minnesota, I feel the unmistakable saltiness that is the precursor to a live on-air vomit. As they count down to air, I quickly grab a wastepaper basket and hide it at my feet.

"Three, two . . . Goood morning, Minneapolis! Today we are talking to Rob Lowe, who's in the Land of Lakes for Michael Dukakis! Good to see you, Rob. How ya doing?"

I vomit into my shoes. The food on the road and the grueling after-hours' agenda is taking its toll in every way possible. I try for moderation, but my whole life, I've only known one gear: full speed ahead. Outrun loneliness, outrun feeling "different," and outrun the shock that dreams coming true don't change your feelings. And like anything with the accelerator stuck, I am bound to crash. But not quite yet.

Although it's probably just a coincidence, after I'm done in Minnesota, Dukakis goes up three points, statewide.

Back on the campaigning plane, or "Sky Pig," as it was called, I witness something that no one should see. Walking to the front compartment, I see the would-be commander in chief having his makeup applied. It is like stumbling into a hot-dog factory: You like hot dogs, you know terrible deeds go into making them, but nothing prepares you when you actually see it. A lot of male candidates wear makeup these days, but that doesn't make it right; it really should be a Screen Actors Guild union violation.

I like the governor and his family a lot. Like an unfortunately large number of would-be leaders I have known, Mike Dukakis is much more engaging in private. However, his running mate, the legendary Texas senator Lloyd Bentsen, turns out to be the *real* star of the ticket. He and I travel throughout Texas together and he is mobbed like Mick Jagger wherever he goes. Even hot young coeds lose their minds for the seventy-year-old senator. He is brave and romantic; every time we fly, he reaches out to hold his wife B.A.'s hand. They have survived two plane crashes together and they still keep going. One night, at some terrible Motel 6, I'm with the traveling staff, watching him debate Dan Quayle. "You're no Jack Kennedy" remains one of my favorite moments in television history.

The last presidential debate took place in Pauley Pavilion at UCLA. Sitting with the high command, we all know it's over for our guy after the very first question. Bernard Shaw of CNN opens the debate with:

"Governor, if Kitty Dukakis were raped and murdered, would you favor an irrevocable death penalty for the killer?"

There are gasps at the question's premise and audacity. Then, you can feel the silence filling the room like methane. With the right answer from the candidate, it will explode and everyone knows it. Dukakis whiffs.

Instead of saying, "Well, first of all, I'm offended by your premise," or coming up with a forceful rejoinder to Shaw's provocative bushwack, he's lethargic and passionless about his wife being raped and murdered. If he had said, "As you know, Bernie, I am against the death penalty in all circumstances. That said, if someone were to harm my wife, you'd probably get to use it on me," the guy might've been president on the women's vote alone!

Back at the scene of the crime, I address the fourteen thousand people packed into the historic UCLA arena. It is less than twelve hours away from the polls opening on election eve, and the place is rocking. Even in a campaign that is clearly behind, in the last moments everyone believes (or at least hopes) that a miracle is at hand. When Dukakis takes the stage, there is a last gasp of optimism.

Later, flying down the entirely closed 405 freeway, I get my first taste of the majesty (and convenience) of life at the threshold of the presidency. The armored limo, the decoy, the war wagon, the staff cars, the follow vans, the press vans, the ambulance, and the phalanx of thirty motorcycle cops providing red-light running escort and protection. The trip from UCLA to LAX should take twenty minutes on a good day. We are on the plane in twelve.

At 3:45 a.m. we land in an Iowa cornfield. Temporary floodlights illuminate the large crowd that has assembled at this ungodly hour to offer support at this final campaign stop.

As the governor speaks for the last time, I see frost on the cornhusks, vapor rising off the crowd as people listen in the cold. I watch a man raise his small son up onto his shoulders and I remember scurrying under a barricade to meet George McGovern so many years ago. Now I'm grateful to have been able to experience firsthand the emotional, bunker-mentality altruism that marks all campaigns. On my left, I see one of Dukakis's inner circle, a large, tough Boston Irish Catholic. He is wiping away tears.

We land in Boston before sunrise on election eve. I go to the hotel to make live, drive-time radio pitches to get out the vote. By midafternoon I'm with the rest of the campaign at headquarters for the potential victory rally.

If anyone has ever wondered what comedian Al Franken did to earn a seat in the Senate, they obviously were not among the thousand people watching the results come in at Dukakis campaign headquarters. Franken, saddled with the single worst job on the planet, works relentlessly, alone on the ballroom stage, to keep up the room's fading spirits. But the crowd can read the writing on the wall, and in the hour and a half Al vamps, he gets maybe three laughs. The Democrats should have given him a Purple Heart; instead, years later, they brought him to D.C.

Michael Dukakis is a profoundly decent, earnest man. He is a personification of the possibilities open to the families of immigrants to our great country. I admire him very much. Now he is onstage, humbled and gracious in a crushing, decisive loss. I'm standing in the wings just offstage. After today, it will be time to go back to other pursuits, but nothing will offer the same satisfaction as trying to help change the country, even in a peripheral role.

Dukakis is wrapping up his concession. The crowd is on its feet; there hasn't been this much emotion in this campaign in months. Michael waves a final farewell and the room explodes. He stands there, taking it in. He's not an emotional man, but it almost looks like there are tears in his eyes. A final wave and he walks offstage. He stops when he sees me and offers his hand. "Thanks, Rob. I'm sorry I let you down." And I can see that this time, indeed, the emotion is real.

❖

Months have gone by with no decent movie offers. There are always bad ones, however, like the offer to shoot a sex-filled romantic comedy in Italy, for which I would be paid a fortune and given a Ferrari, or the half million dollars for ten days' work, to do a remake of *Heidi* (Charlie Sheen would do it instead). The poor performance of my last two movies has put me in a predicament: too famous to be new and not enough box-office mojo to get the big movies, at least not at the moment. Anyone can run a career when the going is good. But it's in the down times, the quiet times, that long-term careers are really made. You need to find ways to stay in the conversation, to be current and to reinvent yourself.

It sounded like a good idea at the time. Would I like to participate in the opening of the 1988 Academy Awards? Without hesitation, I said yes. Mistakenly, I take this as an honor, if not a duty. After all, I'm from Ohio; if someone asks you nicely, you do it. Particularly if it's the Academy of Motion Picture Arts and Sciences!

I'm invited to the home of the man who will be producing the broadcast, veteran Hollywood showman/producer Allan Carr, who has made some very big movies, including one of my all-time favorites, *Grease*. He also, however, produced a movie version of *Sgt. Pepper's* without the Beatles and wore a caftan. In retrospect, perhaps I should have known better.

The pitch is simple, an elaborate musical number in the style of the famed Copacabana will open the show. A who's who of old-time Hollywood stars will participate, including the biggest box-office queen of her era, Snow White. The gag will be that her date stands her up and I will gallantly come to her rescue. We will then sing a silly, fun duet to the tune of Ike and Tina Turner's "Proud Mary." Did I mention that no one was on drugs when they came up with this idea?

The great Marvin Hamlisch will be in charge of the music, and other numbers will feature members of "young Hollywood," like Patrick Dempsey and Christian Slater, tap-dancing and swinging around on ropes. Figuring that the plan is to add fun and levity to Oscar night, I sign on as well.

Every star can make a bad movie or TV show. If you are lucky, you may get to stay in the business long enough to make several. But very few get to participate in a train wreck in front of a billion people.

There are ominous signs from the beginning. During rehearsals it becomes clear that some of the older Hollywood legends cannot walk unassisted. So the grand procession is scrapped and they are placed at tables where all they have to do is wave. Snow White is played by a sweet but inexperienced actress with a very high falsetto. The plan is for her to walk the audience and sing to Meryl Streep, Jack Nicholson, and others. However, when the big night arrives and she is faced with the living, breathing, actual stars, her voice jumps up two more octaves to a tonal range that could bust a dog's eardrum (to make matters worse, it will later be discovered that Allan Carr and the Academy have forgotten to get clearance from Disney to use Snow White in the first place). By the time I make my entrance, live, in front of a billion people, she has that thousand-yard stare common to all performers who are going into the tank. We've all been there, I know the look. I look deep into her eyes, trying to get her to focus on me and steady her nerves. We start our bit together and it seems to be going well.

Then, out of the corner of my eye, I see the great director Barry Levinson in the middle of the audience. He has made *Diner*. He has made *The Natural* and is about to win two hundred Oscars tonight for his new movie, *Rain Man*. There is nobody hotter or more important on the planet. I see him very clearly now. His mouth is agape. He almost looks ashen. He turns to his date, his face a mask of shock and disgust. Even in the middle of singing a duet I can very clearly read his lips as he says, "What the fuck is *this*?" Bravely, I soldier on. I tell myself, who cares what he thinks—he's just an acclaimed artistic-genius writer and director about to be anointed King of Hollywood, you can't please everybody.

I leave the stage, not having a real sense of how it went over, Levinson's reaction notwithstanding. I make my way to the greenroom, deserted at this early part of the show except for an elderly lady with flame-red hair. She is sitting in a corner alone.

"Young man," she says. "I had no idea you were such a good singer. Please come sit with me."

I realize it is Lucille Ball. I go and sit with her and she takes my hand and holds it tightly. She says nothing now, but doesn't let go, and together we watch the broadcast play out on a monitor. After a while she lets go of my hand and asks if I can find her some aspirin.

"My goddamned head is killing me, sweetheart."

I get Lucy some Tylenol and she kisses me on the cheek. I

watch as she goes on to receive her Lifetime Achievement Award to a standing ovation. Within weeks she will pass away.

Every year people debate what's wrong with the Academy Awards; why are they always so long, so boring, or just plain terrible? Why are viewers so uninterested? I have my theories, but of these two things I am certain. First: Don't ever try to take the piss out of the Oscars. The ceremony is not merely escapist fare for the average American; it is of cancer-curing importance, an evening of the highest seriousness, to be revered at all costs. I hadn't realized that. As my teenage sons would say, "My bad." And second: When Lucille Ball likes what you do, it's hard to give a shit about anyone else.

❖

I have just finished remodeling my new house in the Hollywood Hills. It's a quintessential Rat Pack–era bachelor's pad, chosen by me for its view, privacy, and proximity to the Hard Rock Cafe, the latter criterion most revealing of my current state of mind.

I'm becoming increasingly isolated. I rarely see my family, and I don't know how to deal with my mother's unraveling marriage or her deteriorating health. I can't escape into work, as my Oscar disaster hasn't done my career momentum any favors. So in this period of malaise, I look to boost my spirits where I can.

I now am on a feel-good treadmill. Long weekends of adventure and imbibing, weekly *Monday Night Football* get-togethers with the boys, which inevitably lead to Tuesday morning sunrises. Romantically, I am all over the map; I date a group of girls who are beautiful and fun-loving and whom I promise nothing. If they would like more of a commitment from me, they aren't letting me know.

That said, I'm also capable of pushing the boundaries of dating technology. I've taken to using MTV as a sort of home-shopping network, and it's not beneath me to call up to get the contacts on the sexy dancer in the latest Sting video. I find C-SPAN to be useful in this regard as well. Seeing Oliver North's secretary, Fawn Hall, being sworn in during Iran-Contra, I make a note to track her down. Later I will take her to Jack Lemmon's Lifetime Achievement Award dinner at the American Film Institute. Future costar Sally Field will give me a Barry Levinsonesque "Whaaaat the fuuuuck" as I breeze by her table with the striking blue-eyed strawberry blonde from the Pentagon.

Like for Warren Beatty in *Shampoo*, whose active love life made him feel "like [he] was going to live forever," spinning the many plates of my relationships makes me feel engaged and alive. New infatuations give me a rush that my career can no longer provide. I even live up on Mulholland, where Beatty's character lives at the end of the movie, when he finds himself with nothing to show for his years of skirt chasing.

And, indeed, as my twenty-fifth birthday approaches, I am feeling pretty empty. Sitting with family and friends at the back room at Mateo's, I feel like I'm turning thirty, or even forty. Not one part of me feels like someone in his midtwenties; I've been grinding so long and have traveled so far and seen so much that I've doubled the standard emotional mileage. I'm way past warranty.

But if one or two drinks make me feel better, then clearly three or four will *really* do the trick, so I take my medicine well. And why not? Last time I checked it's still the '80's, right?

❖

Finally, a great script comes my way. *Bad Influence* was submitted to producer Steve Tisch by a new young writer as a writing sample. Tisch, showing the kind of wherewithal that would one day make him the only man with both an Oscar and a Super Bowl trophy, says let's make *this* script. We bring on newcomer Curtis Hanson to direct, and, like Ed Zwick before him, he is launched to the A list and films like *L.A. Confidential* and *8 Mile*.

*Bad Influence* is a Faustian story of a meek, regular Joe seduced by a charismatic and possibly dangerous stranger into a life of excitement and sex. Way ahead of its time, David Koepp's screenplay is a marvel of tension, erotic atmosphere, dark humor, and vengeance fulfillment. I originally want to play the more traditional role of the average Joe, but Koepp takes me to lunch and begs me to play the dark and charming sociopath Alex. (Koepp is smart and the movie's artistic success will also supercharge his career. He will write *Carlito's Way* for Al Pacino and a little movie called *Jurassic Park* as his next projects.) By the time coffee arrives, I've switched parts and James Spader will eventually play the other.

Curtis Hanson is also a fantastic writer and one of his best additions to the script is the use of a videotape to "bring down" my character. Personal video recorders are the new big thing and entire movies are being made about the phenomenon. In fact, we cast Spader after seeing a rough cut of *Sex, Lies, and Videotape*. During the hilarious and harrowing set piece in the middle of *Bad Influence*, Spader tells my character that his greatest wish is to get out of his impending engagement. So my character, Alex, secretly videotapes him having sex with a girl he provides and shows it as a "special presentation" at his fiancée's holiday party. Wish granted.

Personal videotaping had rarely been employed as a "gotcha" device in movies, and *Bad Influence* used it perfectly. I related to it as well, since I had been videotaping almost anything that seemed even remotely interesting to me.

Rehearsals are held in a big church just off Highland Avenue in the heart of Hollywood. Just before lunch one day, I'm asked to meet and approve my makeup artist for the film. A production assistant brings her in.

I can't believe what I'm seeing. Striding toward me on outrageously long legs is a sexy and big-spirited blonde girl, with whom I'd had a blind date years before. It had ended in a sort of confused muddle; both of us were dealing with breakups, and although we hit it off like gangbusters, neither was in any position to make more of a go of it. I vaguely remember her telling me that she was a makeup artist and not taking her seriously. She was far too cute, young, and fun; she hardly fit the middle-aged, union crew members mold I had grown used to.

"Hi, Sheryl," I say, surprised.

"Hey, Rob, good to see you again," she says, and I'm struck once again by her big, blue eyes. We make small talk. We've both seen each other around the circuit we travel in, and we have many people in common. Eventually, we sit at a long foldout table in the middle of the old church meeting hall to talk about the job at hand.

"What do you want to do with this character?" she asks. "How do you want him to look? 'Cause I have a couple of thoughts."

At this point in my life I've done countless movies and many hours of television, and have worked with many makeup artists, some the best in the business. But not once has one asked me how my character should look. I sit in their chair and they do whatever they do and that is that. I have a thought: This girl *sees* me differently.

And she is different, too. Different from all the other girls in my orbit. As we work together I realize that she is an artist of the face. Later, when she becomes the first choice of every big leading man, including Al Pacino, Alec Baldwin, and Harrison Ford, I will know why. Not only is she great to be around (and let's face it, beautiful) but she knows her shit *cold*. Go look at Al Pacino in *Glengarry Glen Ross* and you'll see what she's capable of.

My character in the film is extremely debauched. He has no boundaries and knows no responsibilities or consequences. I'm digging deep into this world, living this character almost constantly in my own, much less malignant version. And I'm rewarded at every turn, because the performance and the movie are turning out so well.

But when Tom Brokaw leads the evening news with my personal videotape exploit from back in Atlanta, I know I've got a problem. When he's done with me and the *second* story is Tiananmen Square, the first democratic uprising and potential revolution in the six-thousand-year history of China, I know it's a doozy.

Sometimes being a trailblazer is overrated. If the Kim Kardashians and Colin Farrells and all the like had let their video oeuvre out into the zeitgeist before me, mine may have been met with a mere titillated shrug. But in 1989 it wasn't yet common, or even possible, for young couples to "sext" and Skype each other with nude tapes and photos. Today, there are people who think nothing of taking a naked pic and sending it to their sweetheart. And for some, having a sex tape is something to aspire to; they are even created for the express purpose of publicity, money, or career advancement. Not so, back in the day.

As I (and a lot of people) struggled to figure out how I stupidly put myself into this videotape mess, I was approached by no less of an authority on sexual mores than Mr. Hugh Hefner. "You had to do it," he said. "The technology existed!"

The unrelenting media scrutiny and fallout from the videotape debacle will overshadow *Bad Influence* completely. Although very well reviewed, the press coverage is mostly about what an idiot I am, and the movie suffers at the box office as a result. The director gets hot from it, James Spader gets hot from it. For me, it's another movie that doesn't perform. That it was released by a tiny independent studio didn't help matters, but in the end, even a major studio probably couldn't have overcome the unfortunate nexus of "life imitates art" that I'd created. Depressed and under siege, I stay at home and self-medicate. I make sure that the fun is always on call to keep me from thinking too hard about my bad decisions and the circumstances of my life. I welcome the support of my family and friends, and after years of work and hundreds of miles traveled for so many liberal Democratic candidates and causes, I wait to hear from my many friends in that world. The calls never come.

✢

On a more positive note, to help promote the movie, I am asked to host *Saturday Night Live* for the first time.

Walking into studio 8H, I feel like I've conquered show business. Forget my current, stalled movie momentum and role as a public piñata. I'm hosting *Saturday* Fucking *Night Live*, a show I've worshipped since its first year on the air back in 1975! Even in my increasingly jaded disillusionment, this opportunity makes me giddy as a kid as I walk the halls of my heroes.

My agents and other advisors beg me not to do the show. Historically, it has been the unmasking of many a star as an unfunny stiff, so they don't want to take any chances. But I'm a gamer, always the guy to take my shots. Sometimes it blows up in my face (Snow White) but sometimes it can lead to a whole new world.

"Do you want me to write you a 'Wayne's World' sketch or a 'Sprockets'?" asks Mike Myers, one of the few cast members who writes.

It's about midnight on Wednesday and I'm in his tiny cubbyhole office. I choose "Sprockets." I love his character of Dieter, the unisexual, avant-garde German talk-show host with the masturbating monkey. I have no desire to do a "Wayne's World," a concept I don't get at all, although I've not seen many sketches.

Mike goes to work, typing underneath a giant poster for the movie *Halloween* that reads, "The Curse of Michael Myers!" This would be the beginning of my part in a number of classic projects made with the magic of Mike Myers and the *SNL* pedigree.

The show will be a huge hit. At one point I play the then massively popular talk-show host Arsenio Hall (complete with giant, fake fingers) and the next day *USA Today* writes about it. No one has seen me like this and suddenly I'm on the radar of Lorne Michaels, who has created more legends in comedy than anyone ever has or will. He is the most important and influential tastemaker and gatekeeper in the comedy universe.

As the famous *SNL* closing theme plays that night, I am elated, having gotten away with what all my advisors had thought so dangerous. I hug my cast mates: Dana Carvey, Adam Sandler, Chris Rock, David Spade, Phil Hartman, and Mike. Lorne chose them from nowhere and now they are the 1927 Yankees. Murderers row. I went to bat with them on live television and in the process discovered that I liked hitting a major-league fastball.

✦

I'm asked to promote *Bad Influence* in Australia with a major press tour followed by a vacation of my choosing as compensation. I can bring one friend. This is going to be a luxurious, exotic trip of a lifetime (I've chosen Fiji as the vacation) and I want to bring the right companion. I run a mental checklist of my guy pals as well as some of the girls I'm seeing. Do I go with a lover or with a friend? Then I realize, I have one person in my life who is both.

We bonded deeply during the shooting of *Bad Influence*. I was impressed with her artistry and prodigious work ethic. I was happy to be included in the many adventures she concocted for the large group of friends who orbited her. Her advice in my time of chaos was unique and practical, not the airy-fairy navel-gazing or the by-the-book, play-it-safe strategy I encountered elsewhere. When she came by to see me, she sometimes cooked (a total shocker for a beautiful girl in L.A.) and organized my coffee-table books. Eventually, we were lovers, but each of us was well-known to be "tough to catch." Sheryl Berkoff came to Australia with me and this set in motion a series of events that would unfold rapidly and change my life forever.

Australia is a blur. I've brought along a number of pain pills for my old *Footloose* knee injury and I gobble them like Sweet Tarts. Sheryl, who is the most even-keeled girl I've met when it comes to partying, spends most of the time making sure I don't wander off with the more dangerous members of the band INXS. In spite of her attempts to keep the craziness to a dull roar, I leave Down Under with a big tattoo and a series of press appearances, neither of which I have any memory of participating in.

By the time we reach Turtle Island in Fiji, I'm out of pills and feeling more present. Sheryl lends me books to read (Richard Bach's *Illusions*) and new music to listen to (Sinead O'Connor). There are only twelve other couples on this tiny, romantic tropical paradise where they filmed *Blue Lagoon*. I haven't had this kind of escape from L.A. or the concerns of my life and career in years, if ever. And I've never been with such an easy companion. I begin to feel the lift of the hazy, heavy fog of career, pressure, partying, and self-obsession. In fact, on my first day on the island I have an epiphany.

Sheryl and I are being led along a jungle trail, overgrown with palms, ferns, and bamboo, as the Fijian tribesman shows us to our quarters. Rounding a giant, vine-encrusted tree stump, we come to a small, thatched-roof bungalow.

"This will be your home," says the tribesman, with a beautiful smile, making his exit.

But something has caught my eye. It is a small wooden sign, placed on the front door and hand-carved by the locals. Branded into the wood and then hand-painted, it says: ROB + SHERYL.

I'm flooded with emotion that I cannot name. My eyes blink back tears. I feel lonely and comforted all at once. At the sight of the fairly innocuous sign, I feel an overwhelming sense of occasion, like someone has put my future in writing and I am witness.

And irrationally I know that we will be *together*, Sheryl + Rob, and the years unfold before me. Ebbing up from my unconscious and unnamed fantasies, a road is opening and a world is forming and it is full of love and marriage and children and joy and fear and wonder. It is a crystalline vision of our potential lives together. Rob + Sheryl.

But I shake it off. This is ridiculous! What is this, a bad movie on the Hallmark Channel? This type of life is the *last* thing I'm looking for. I order up some kava, the local root that makes you buzzed, and try to push my vision out of my thoughts. But in the days on Turtle Island, watching Sheryl run along the azure water and lying with her head on my leg under the blazing nebula, I can't stop thinking about the little wooden sign on our bungalow door.

By the time the helicopter arrives to fly us off the island, I've given in to my growing affection for Sheryl. The time away from my normal life has cleared my head enough for me to listen to that tiny voice cued by the sign and to acknowledge that even I may be worthy of something more, something real, something with no agenda, that doesn't live in total, slavish service to career, public perception, family turmoil, or the pursuit of a good time. I tell Sheryl I love her.

"I love you, too," she says, and in her remarkable blue eyes I see the full range of response.

We climb into the waiting chopper, its rotors blasting sand into the lagoon. We lift off, hover for a moment, then head into the rising sun. We are moving quickly. Sheryl and I have a long journey ahead.

CHAPTER 17

I t takes less than twenty-four hours back in L.A. for me to
destroy this relationship that, away from the chaos of my life, I
had wanted so much. Away from the pressures and temptations
of my everyday existence, I was a different person. Someone who
wanted to slow down, someone who wanted some consistency
and commitment. And finally, I'd found the right person, Sheryl,
with whom I could attempt to fashion this new life.

But back in my bachelor pad in the Hollywood Hills, this
vision is immediately fogged by fear and force of habit. I am frozen and unable to see a way off the merry-go-round.

As usual, a night out with the boys leads to tequila and a
party. Properly anesthetized for a night among the throngs, I
look for the cutest girl I can find. Sheryl, ever the career girl, is
asleep at home, leaving early in the morning for yet another

movie on location. I'm drunk and back at my place with a total stranger.

At about midnight Sheryl calls to check in on me (I was supposed to have called earlier). She hears a girl's laugh in the background. I try to play it off but she knows what's going on.

"This isn't a good idea," she says.

"What do you mean?"

"You and I. We should just be friends."

"No. I'm sorry. I want to be with you. Really! I . . ."

"Rob, stop. Listen to me. We've always been friends above all else. Let's not ruin that. You should go do what you need to do, be with who you want. But I can't be your girlfriend."

She's not angry. I can't even tell if she's sad. It is actually the worst possible scenario because she just seems *done.*

"Good-bye, Rob. Let's talk when I get back from location."

She hangs up.

I hold the phone in my hand. I stare out the big plate-glass windows and see the girl, illuminated by the lights of the cityscape. She is backlit and it is dark, but it looks like she is naked, swaying gently to the sounds of Robbie Robertson coming over the outdoor speakers. She is beautiful, for sure, and she beckons me with a mischievous smile and a bottle of Cuervo.

"How do you feeeeel?" she yells, and I hear it muffled through the glass window.

"I feel nothing," I answer, even though I know she can't hear me.

⚜

"Rob! Rob! Pick up, it's your mother!" It's a few hours later and I'm standing over my answering machine with its seventy-three unanswered messages. "Rob, please. Are you there?" begs my mother, clearly in a panic. But I am too fucked-up to pick up the phone; there is no way I can face her in my condition.

"Your grandfather is in the hospital. He's had a massive heart attack."

I listen to my mom as she describes his critical condition and asks for my help. Still, I do nothing. I stare at the answering machine, frozen, until my mother hangs up.

As shame and guilt begin to penetrate my altered state, I begin to hatch a plan of attack.

*I need to chug the last of the tequila*, I tell myself. *So I can get to sleep, so I can wake up ASAP and deal with this.*

This insane logic holds right up until I catch a glance of myself in the bathroom mirror. Then, very slowly, I turn and face myself full-on. I'm so hammered that I can barely stand. The girl I love has just left me, because I can't keep my word and I have no integrity. My grandfather is dying. My mother is in crisis, desperate for help and comfort, and I am cowering and hiding in shameful avoidance. I have arrived at the bottom.

Since I was a boy I've been running. Running to make my mark. Running to avoid reality. Running to avoid pain.

And now . . . a moment of clarity. I can run no longer.

I go into my bedroom, past the sleeping girl, and find my wallet. In it is a business card that I have carried for over a year. I find it and pull it out. It's from a drug-and-alcohol counselor named Betty Wyman. I take her card, head back to my office, and sit next to the phone. I hear the terrible chirping of the early-morning birds. I watch the cityscape, gray on the horizon as the sun begins to rise. A new day is beginning.

I make the call. It's May 10, 1990.

❖

There are many kinds of rehabs. You can pretty much get any setup that suits you. You've got your shaved-head cuckoo's nests and hard-core lockdowns, you've got your latte-sipping, horseback-ridin', yoga-centric country clubs. You've got your remote, spartan locations; you've got 'em smack-dab in L.A., convenient for visits from managers, agents, publicists, and dealers.

I'm on a plane headed to Arizona for a middle-of-the-road version. Betty Wyman, in her wisdom, got me the hell out of L.A. to a serious rehab, but well short of a lockdown. Less than forty-eight hours have passed since I called her, but Betty moved quickly when I said, "Help me. I want to stop. I'll do whatever you tell me to do." Now I sit, shaking with anxiety, next to her associate, Bob, who is escorting me to the monkey farm.

Bob is a former Hells Angel. He's tattooed head to toe, with a beard that makes him look like Charles Manson but a voice that sounds like Kermit the Frog.

"Let me tell you my story," says Bob, attempting to comfort my now crushing anxiety, and to bond us together.

"I first remember feeling different and scared and anxious when I was a little boy and my mom invited the mailman into our apartment. We found out later, but didn't know then, that she was a paranoid schizophrenic," he says in his sweet, Kermit-like sing-song. "Anyway, she stabbed the mailman to death, then cut up his body with a butcher knife. She made me lie down in our bathtub and placed his severed limbs on top of me. She told me that God would be angry but this would protect me." Bob takes a sip from his fifteenth cup of black coffee and continues. "Anyway, that was hard for me. And growing up after Mom was committed, I got into heroin and selling it. I went to prison. But when I got out, I got sober and have been now for seventeen years."

I try to conjure up an appropriate response to this story, but my instincts tell me that since there is no way to top it, I should just take it in. Bob smiles. "Don't you worry about a thing. You are right where you should be. Scared. Freaked out and shattered. Ain't nobody ever gotten sober who wasn't."

The rehab (I won't name it, to protect anonymity, and any names I use in this chapter have been changed) sits in the low foothills of glowing, red-rock mountains. There is nothing but saguaro cactus for miles. If I decide to flee, it will be a long walk to civilization.

But I won't flee. Bob will check me in and say good-bye, and I will begin one of the most exhilarating, liberating, and exciting four weeks of my life. Scary, yes, and filled with unspeakable emotional discomfort, but for me, it's unquantifiable relief that I am being shown a different way to live. I am so tired of the lying, my inability to keep my word, the bullshit relationships, the hangovers, the cover-ups, and the helplessness to stop doing the things I truly want to stop doing. I had long ago become a creation that was an amalgam of self-crafted persona built to succeed and public image made to be consumed, piled on top of a precarious shell of a little boy wanting to be loved. Finally, the whole thing has caved in around me, and I am *thrilled*. Now, just maybe, I could find out who I really am.

My roommate is a loud, snoring, middle-aged cross-dresser. I melt wax and put it into my ears to sleep at night. I'm gonna be here for thirty days, and I'm not gonna make it without sleep.

Unlike in some rehabs of today, there are very strict ground rules here. Whereas now a rehabbing starlet can check in and still swan around the Malibu Country Mart to get a frappuccino and a copy of *Us Weekly* to take to her mani-pedi before her photo shoot, we have no reading materials, TV, privileges to leave, or even caffeine. It's for serious folks only, the Harvard of treatment centers.

I am under the care of a hip, young counselor named Mike. And being hip is a big plus for me because my greatest fear is that being sober means being boring. And that, to me, would be worse than cirrhosis of the liver.

I am also worried about people finding out I am in rehab. When I share this with Mike he says, "You don't think people

*know* you party too much? You should *hope* they hear you're getting help!" But it proves to be a moot point as by the third day I
have to hide in the pool to escape the helicopters from the
*National Enquirer.* They tell me that there is a wonderful program that's helped millions get sober called Alcoholics Anony-
mous. I wouldn't know. My level of anonymity consists of being
on the *Enquirer* cover, dressed in my underwear (they used a
movie still), with a headline about rehab for sex addiction, which
in hindsight is an improvement from my last national media
exposure—at least this time I have underwear—but it pisses me
off because the sex addicts in the center have *much* more interesting stories and treatments than my group of drinkers did.

But my relationships with women (and every other relationship in my life) are a big part of the puzzle that was worked on
each day in therapy. I dig into my issues with my mother, her
illnesses, my father and abandonment, and my relationship with
being famous. I am surprised by what I learn about myself. I
assumed that since I love "the scene," I also love crowds and
people and small talk and the like. Free of alcohol, I learn that
while I do love people, I hate small talk, am bored by idle banter,
and am wildly uncomfortable in big rooms with people I don't
know. I want a real connection, not a surface one, and in its
absence, I will medicate my discomfort and boredom.

Like being in Fiji, being in treatment lets my real self emerge.
But first, it will have to gradually strangle the good-looking, successful, charming poster-boy pod person that stunted its growth
many years ago. There is a school of thought that believes your
emotional maturity is frozen at the exact age you become famous.
My experience tells me this is more true than not, and I got
famous as a teenager. So, if I want to be a fully functioning,
sober adult, I had better get busy.

Sheryl is the only person other than family I let visit me. And
showing her true colors, she works from 9:00 p.m. to 6:00 a.m.

on location in Seattle, drives an hour and a half, catches a plane, flies three and a half hours to see me for the one hour allotted on Thursdays, makes the return trip, and is back at work that same night.

I am never happier to see anyone than when I see her mane of blonde hair in the window of the arriving cab. We hold hands in the dayroom (anything else was grounds for expulsion) and walk along the trails through the enormous cactus.

"I'm proud of you. I love you," she says. And I feel better already.

Fridays are graduation days. I'm standing in the large circle we form to surround those who are leaving this cocoon to try their hand at a new life in the real world. Some won't make it ninety days; most won't make it beyond a few years. And for some, this is not their first time in treatment. Some come back again and again, more broken and yet more brave each time. It's painful to watch. I don't want to do this again. Not ever.

I know two things: I take direction for a living and I'm competitive. This gives me great advantage. If they tell me to stand on my head to stay sober, I'll do it. And I won't let anyone get the better of me while I try. So as I slowly gather my days free of alcohol or any mind-altering substance, I know that I won't give up my string of days, my time, for anyone or anything. I can be so extraordinarily self-centered, now I will try to use that for a greater good.

I would kill for a cup of coffee. I would drown puppies for a Big Mac. I would really also very much like to get laid. Forget not drinking for thirty days, how about not having sex! I mean, I hadn't gone thirty *hours* previously! And what would that be like stone-cold sober? Without even a glass of wine to loosen me up? Will I really *never* drink again? No toast on New Year's, no celebratory sip at my wedding (if I ever have one), no beer with the boys—if I ever father a boy? Not even a sip? Not ever?

After days and days of therapy, discussion groups, watching some very shattered people pull themselves together, tugging at the frayed strands of their lost lives, it is time to leave. I've been to "sober school" and as always was the first to sit in the front row, ready to learn. And I loved every inspiring, painful minute.

But now, as I stand in the good-bye circle, I'm filled with shaky apprehension. In three hours I will be back in L.A., in the bachelor pad, right back in the middle of life designed by a man I hope I no longer am.

But Sheryl will be with me. Over the four weeks of treatment I earned her trust and another chance for us to be together. I hug my counselor, Mike, good-bye. He looks me hard in the eye.

"Remember. You can be one of those celebrities who go in and out of rehab or you can just stay sober. It's completely up to you."

Sheryl and I slide into the cab for the ride to the airport and back to our lives. We pull onto the beautiful, winding desert road, the scenery extraordinary on all sides. I try to look ahead, to see where the road is leading, but I can't.

❖

The bomb shelter is about the size of a giant dining-room table. The Israelis packed into it speak no English and I can barely see them as the pill box's only illumination is a dull overhead light-bulb. The shelter sits two stories below a community park in a suburb about twenty-five minutes outside of Tel Aviv. I'm on location, making a new movie, but I need an AA meeting and this is the only one I can find. I have no idea what these guys are talking about as my Hebrew is limited, to say the least. But being with people, however different, who have the same disease and are filled with newfound grace is exactly what I need. After all, I'm only sixty days sober.

The movie I'm making is called *The Finest Hour*. The end

product won't be mine. In the early, heady, euphoric, I-don't-give-a-fuck, my-life's-been-saved days of my early recovery, I'm happy to let the chips fall where they may. I wanted to play this character, a tough Navy SEAL, and to experience that world.

I trained with the SEALs at BUD/S (Basic Underwater Demolition/SEAL) in Coronado (in fact, I broke a rib on the hellish obstacle course). I spent hours training underwater, learning to scuba dive, being thrown into the ocean with my hands and feet bound and trying to stay afloat, and practicing "ring pickups," in which a passing Zodiac yanks you out of the water as you swim to the surface. I became a marksman with an MP5 automatic and learned to hold my breath for two minutes and twenty seconds while swimming underwater. I did daily open-ocean swims in full fatigues and boots, and carrying a backpack. I had the time of my life.

But when Sheryl and I landed in Israel to shoot, it all went to hell. The film's producer was the notorious and infamous Menahem Golan. Known for making the occasional rare gem among a lifelong oeuvre of cheap schlok, Golan had recently been on a roll with his company, Cannon Films. He would now overpay to attract legit talent (Dustin Hoffman was doing a movie for Cannon until Golan took out an ad welcoming him to the "Cannon Family" before his deal was done, at which point Dusty bailed) and then make the films for as little money as possible. Hence, this movie about the American military was being shot in Israel.

We butted heads on day one. I had absorbed the pride and professionalism of the heroes I had trained with among the SEALs and wasn't going to let cost or expediency keep me from portraying them in the correct light. So when they didn't want to provide the authentic (and probably expensive) weapons that real SEALs carried, I balked. I finally had to purchase and ship the MP5s, rather than use the Israeli-made Galil, which would have made me a laughingstock among "the Teams."

In spite of the movie having a ton of action, as one would reasonably expect from a movie about underwater commandos, Mr. Golan did not want to pay for a stunt coordinator or stuntmen. Instead, some of the cast who had been SEALs worked with former Israeli commandos to set up and execute the stunts. Swelled with new, sober exuberance as well as a high level of testosterone from my intensive training, I thought, no problem, I'll just do my own stunts. It would almost cost me my life.

After my AA meeting, Sheryl is applying my camo makeup, which now, after weeks of wearing it, has made my skin painfully raw. "Be careful out there," she says as we are jostled by the heaving PT boat that serves as our shooting location.

We are miles off the coast of a horrible, bustling port on the Mediterranean Sea, somewhere near the city of Haifa, to shoot the climax of the movie. I will be hanging off the back of a burning, speeding patrol boat, being dragged facedown in the boat's wake, struggling to free my foot, which is tangled in a rope. As I struggle not to drown, I will reach up, hack myself free with my KA-BAR (knife), fall into the boat's massive wake at full speed, and be shot out through the foamy turbulence to safety. One of the former SEALs does a test run and it all goes to plan, so I take my place as cameras roll. I notice Sheryl has left her perch on the front deck; she doesn't want to watch.

I'm wearing a cable under my fatigues that attaches me to the racing, lurching boat. After I'm dragged for a few seconds, I will "cut" the rope, and the cable will release, throwing me into the wake.

Of course the Cannon budget prevents the use of nontoxic (but probably expensive) "bee" smoke, so rubber ties are burned instead, as smoke blankets the boat. Choking, I lower myself backwards and go headfirst into the wake. I'm submerged to the waist and buffeted so hard that the buttons on my top are immediately ripped off. I never hear them yell action.

I struggle to breathe and not dislocate an arm as I'm dragged at full speed. When the director has enough footage, he releases the cable. With a snap, I am violently sucked into the wake, tumbling head over heels, again and again, like being in a washing machine. Unlike during the test run, I'm *not* being spit out of the back; in fact, I'm now drowning for real.

I hear an awful thudding noise as I continue to tumble out of control. I realize it's the sound of my head hitting the hull of the boat. And now I can also begin to feel the sensation of being sucked underneath, toward its massive propellers. When I hear a muffled, high-pitched whir, I know I'm going in. I have a last thought: Maybe all this gear I'm wearing will give me some protection from the blades.

And then I'm hit. The force almost knocks me out with its violence. Everything goes black. When the cobwebs clear, I'm choking on seawater, floating behind the patrol boat, finally free of its prop wash. Seeing that I was headed to the propeller, one of the former SEALs had jumped into the wash, bear-hugging me in protection as we headed toward the blades. Miraculously, his added weight was enough to knock me out of the vortex.

After I'm hauled back onto the boat, Sheryl goes nuclear. "You are done shooting today. Fuck these assholes and their incompetence. I'm taking you home." The director wants no part of Sheryl and calls a wrap. I thank the SEAL for saving my life.

A few days later, I try to return the favor of gallantry on the set when the producers attempt to force a young actress to take off her top during a scene. It's totally uncalled for, completely gratuitous, and the girl is scared that if she doesn't show her tits, she'll be fired. I take her aside. "Put your top on, and keep it on. If anyone makes a peep, send 'em to me, tell 'em I said no one takes their clothes off on this movie." Soon Menahem Golan is storming around the set, but the scene is cut.

"Menahem, is everything okay?" I ask.

"No! Everything is terrible! I come to set to see nipple and I see *nothing*!"

It's no surprise to me when the underfunded *The Finest Hour* bombs. But I don't care. After spending my entire life single-mindedly drilling down for success as an actor, I'm less and less interested in the Hollywood program. With a new perspective from sobriety and a new, meaningful relationship, it's harder and harder to care about my latest review or box office. I want what I've never had. A normal life. And so, after spending the eighties working on a career, I will spend the nineties working on my life.

❖

Sheryl won't move in with me. She has a house of her own, works hard to pay for it, and values her independence. So we divide time between our places. I'm coming up on a year sober, after daily recovery meetings and once-a-week men's group-therapy sessions (which I love). I've never been happier, and when someone points out that "Sheryl is someone you want in your foxhole; she'd jump in front of a bus for you," the words hit a nerve. And so, on June 20, 1991, I ask her to marry me, parked up on Mulholland Drive, before the magnificent Los Angeles skyline. Sheryl says yes.

I knew my fiancée was a go-getter, but nothing prepared me for what happened next. Like for most guys, the mere act of proposing was a herculean feat that I thought would keep me in my gal's good graces for months, and maybe even years, to come. But no. Within twenty minutes of arriving home from Mulholland, Sheryl has gotten me to name a date—and the date is only one month away!

Her logic is this: If you are engaged, then it's just a sham unless you mean it. And if you mean it, you should have no issue with setting a date. Can't argue that. And the quick turnaround on the wedding day?

"Rob, if we wait, every Tom, Dick, and Harry will come out

of the woodwork to talk us out of it. The naysayers, the fearmongers. The press will weigh in, you name it, and everyone will want their two cents' worth. This is about *us*, no one else. What's the worst thing that can happen? If it doesn't work out? I'll always be your friend!" she says.

And so we make a secret plan. We will be married in four weeks on July 22 in an intimate and under-the-radar affair.

My mother goes ape. She has all kinds of ideas in her head about Sheryl's agenda, as do a number of my friends. (Twenty years of marriage and two almost grown sons later, I'm sad to say that these folks' concerns had more to do with their own agendas than my or Sheryl's well-being.) Although Mom will eventually calm down, Sheryl and I remove the "Does anyone object to this union?" portion of the vows, just in case of a mutiny.

We tell the thirty guests that they are going to a wedding-themed charity lunch, so they will dress appropriately, won't be thrown by the decor, and will have no idea what's happening until we lock the doors. Friends of ours have provided their beautiful home in Hancock Park, overlooking the historic golf course. Even the catering staff thinks it's a charity lunch. As a result, the press never got to sell one issue on our backs. I always roll my eyes when celebrities wail about their privacy being invaded by the media. If you are willing to make certain choices and live in a particular way, you can live a mostly normal life. But many stars would go insane without the attention, so they won't do what needs to be done to stay out of the spotlight.

On the big day, I'm fixing my tie, late for the ceremony, when the phone rings. It's Lorne Michaels. "Rob, I need you to come to dinner tonight with the studio to talk about the 'Wayne's World' movie," he says. Both he and Mike Myers had not forgotten my good show for them and want a "real movie actor" in what would be both Mike's and Dana Carvey's first film.

"Geez, Lorne. I can't make it," I say.

"Rob, it's a *very* important dinner."

"Um, Lorne, I'm walking out the door to get married."

"Then I guess even dessert is out of the question?" says Lorne, dryly.

I rush to Hancock Park. The wedding goes without a hitch. Sheryl and I say our vows in front of our semistunned friends and family, including Steve Tisch, Garry Marshall, and Emilio. Sheryl is breathtaking in her gown, and I feel like, together, we will blaze a new trail of love, hope, and possibility. I'm not sure that everyone else is down with this program, and that's okay by me. Hollywood has always had its share of bullshit marriages and, like my sobriety, only time will tell if ours will last. But as we have our first dance to John Barry's gorgeous *Out of Africa* theme, I'm hoping that Sheryl and I can beat the odds.

## CHAPTER 18

Never look a grizzly bear in the face, don't stare at the sun, and never, ever, look Dana Carvey in the eyes during a comedy sketch. There are a number of world-class comedy killers in Hollywood, but Carvey is without question the top assassin. Even during his tenure at *SNL*, when he was surrounded by what was probably the show's best cast ever, his superiority was acknowledged with a nickname: the Lady. Dana will do anything and everything to make you laugh, like they said about the Terminator: "You can't stop him! That's all he does!"

Now I'm doing a scene from *Wayne's World* on stage 14 at Paramount. I try to manipulate Garth (played by Dana) into turning on Wayne as he works in a basement on a mechanical hand. With each take, Dana tries a new way to get me to laugh. His eyes are demented.

I'm fairly well known for my ability to stand in the fire and not break character, but Carvey is rising to the challenge. My palms stream rivulets of sweat, my heart is pounding, but I'm not letting this maniac in his blonde wig take me down. I'm a rock. By take fifteen, Carvey has worked his way through ad-libs, faces, and baby noises. Now, from nowhere, he produces a cartoonlike mallet and smashes the robot hand to bits. It's hilarious.

My chest heaves like when you want to weep but bite your tongue not to. I stare at him, still stone-faced. It feels like an eternity before the director calls "cut." Then, I die laughing. Carvey winks.

Sheryl and I cut short our Cabo San Lucas honeymoon when my *Wayne's World* deal closed. Shooting was to begin right away. Now over a year into sobriety, I have gone through tremendous changes. The two most marked have brought me to this movie. I've learned to only concern myself with my end of any transaction. I do the best job I can and then let the results be what they will. I am out of the people-pleasing business. So I don't handicap the potential of a movie about two guys in bad wigs who have never acted, based on a three-minute comedy sketch directed by a punk rocker who's never made a hit film. It feels right somehow, so I say yes, and that's that.

But I've also learned to confront people when I'm being taken advantage of, to enforce boundaries, when in the past I either had none or let people encroach upon them while I stuck my head in the sand. This will prove great for growth and maturity, and not so great in show business, which thrives on actors being distracted, checked out, and fearful.

So when Paramount wants to pay me less than half the fee I've worked over a decade to establish, I say no, and head to Cabo with my wife. But just before we walk out the door, Sheryl (who has a fantastic business mind) says, "Tell them you'll take half your fee up front and half as a back-end payment, like the producers."

It's a brilliant compromise. And Paramount says yes. This will be the only back-end deal that will ever pay in my thirty-plus-year career.

*Wayne's World* also brings me closer to a group of people who will be friends, confidants, mentors, and collaborators for the next decade: Lorne Michaels, Mike Myers, and their manager, the legend Bernie Brillstein, whom I sign with as well.

"I remember the first time I saw you, Bernie," I tell him at our first meeting. "I was fourteen years old and you were with John Belushi at *The Tonight Show*."

"I remember when I first saw you, kid! You were with Fawn Hall at Jack Lemmon's AFI award. I thought, that kid is *so* cool. What balls!" says Bernie, who not only will help me navigate the next fifteen years of my career, but will become a second father as well.

*Wayne's World* is a hit. Mike Myers's vision is universally accepted into the rare category of smash comedy and timeless classic. Even today, it brings me a new crop of young fans every year. Thanks, Lorne. Thanks, Mike.

❖

One of my great thrills was having a big movie in the theaters and my Broadway debut simultaneously. Living with Sheryl in a penthouse at the Regency, being driven past the lines for *Wayne's World* to the stage door for *A Little Hotel on the Side* at the Belasco Theatre, I was living an actor's ultimate dream. I didn't become an actor to get famous. I didn't become an actor to get rich. I was too young and unsophisticated to really understand that these things were even an option; I just wanted to do what I loved. And now I was doing it at the highest levels in the two areas I most valued.

I also felt a sense of peace and a satisfaction from my marriage and early steps in recovery. I went to meetings with other alcoholics daily, and so each day my old ways and perspectives changed. I took fewer chances in my personal life and more in my work. I found fulfillment in new areas. I was no longer the It guy of the '80's or the sole star of studio movies, but I didn't care. I left that to others who kept track of such things and who never knew that particular club had been toxic for me anyway.

I worked with collaborators who challenged me and who weren't interested in "Rob Lowe," but wanted the right actor for the right role, people like Sir Richard Eyre of the National The-atre and Dame Maggie Smith. Working with them and Natasha Richardson on a filmed revival of Tennessee Williams's *Suddenly, Last Summer* satisfied me at a professional level I hadn't approached before. It wasn't about "looks," it wasn't about "heat," and we weren't chasing an audience. It was, instead, about story and lan-guage and performance. And I was happy to be with artists whose careers were made purely on talent.

(Side note for young actors: Say yes to *any* opportunity to grow and/or do good work. You never know where it will lead or who may be paying attention. When I asked the great Richard Eyre what inspired him to choose me to play opposite Maggie Smith, he said, "I saw you in *Wayne's World*." Go figure!)

While shooting *Suddenly, Last Summer* in London, I take Sheryl to see Pavarotti in *Tosca* at the Royal Opera House in Covent Garden. On the way to the men's room, I run into Sting, who gives me shit about dating the hot blonde dancer from his "We'll Be Together" video a few years back.

"I've hung up my spurs. I'm married now," I tell him as we stand in our tuxedos, waiting to pee.

"Well, bring the wife and come for the weekend with us!" he says.

Presobriety, I would've been too shy to accept, or written this invitation off as small talk. But now, I take people for their word and have almost silenced that inner voice that kept me from extending myself and making new friendships.

"Let's do it this weekend!" I say.

Sting and his wife, Trudie, live in a breathtaking manor house in the Wiltshire countryside. Built hundreds of years ago, it makes for a romantic weekend getaway. We walk to Stonehenge, which is practically in the backyard. Pavarotti drops by, and he and Sting record a duet of "Panis Angelicus" for a new album. The recording studio, in the converted chapel of the ancient home, is filled with two of the most heavenly voices of the twentieth century. In fact, as Luciano hits the high notes of the aria, both Sting and I weep in spite of ourselves. The next day, Sheryl and I are wowed again as Sting records "If I Ever Lose My Faith in You," his voice strong and high and clear as a bell.

After a glorious dinner in front of a fireplace more than five hundred years old, Sheryl and I retire to our room. The night was an occasion to remember, and as it turned out, we always would. Nine months later, our first son, Matthew Edward Lowe, was born.

I will never forget the first time I laid eyes on him, my shock at his blond hair and how he looked me directly and intently in the eye in the delivery room at Cedars-Sinai. I had suspected I would enjoy fatherhood, but holding this blue-eyed bundle and presenting him to his brave mother, I was filled with a passion that has not abated with time. I wanted meaning in my relationships? I wanted substance to go along with my natural exuberance for life? Well, here it was. All nine and a half pounds of him. He of the arresting stare. He of the blond and (for now) hilariously cone-shaped head. My boy. My Matthew.

I drove my new family home so carefully that you'd have thought I was carrying nitroglycerine. I mean, we could've walked faster! As so many couples in so many places throughout the ages have done before us, Sheryl and I began the magical journey of raising our child. And I couldn't help but think of my father and my mother. I felt a gratitude to them and a new kinship. I could see now that they were just as I was: doing the best they could, full of apprehension and full of love, with no directions to follow. And yet, I also swore allegiance to the common refrain: "I won't be like my parents were with me."

⁜

Stephen King's *The Stand* was one of my earliest favorite books. Part of the fun of a successful career are moments when you can think things like, What if you had told me when I was thirteen and reading *The Stand* that I would one day star in the miniseries?

Holding Matthew, I watched the series as it aired over four nights on ABC. I hadn't done network television since *Thursday's Child*, over a decade ago, so there was plenty of media attention focused on this classic and oft-tried adaptation. *The Stand* surpassed all expectations, delivering historic ratings. I was glad that so many people saw my work as the deaf-mute, Nick Andros, and I loved getting to know Gary Sinise and the great Mr. King, who is as nice and influential as he is prolific. But it was on location for my next movie, *Frank and Jesse*, that a totally new frontier opened for me: writing. The movie was a Western about the adventures of the outlaw Jesse James and his brother, Frank (played by my great pal Bill Paxton). I was producing with my old friend from *Oxford Blues*, Cassian Elwes, as well as starring. But the script was a mess, and with it I began what was to be a series of uncredited rewrites. There is no excuse for pedestrian dialogue, particularly when there is a great history of Western vernacular. Night after night, Bill and I would watch Ken Burns's *The Civil War* and pluck out odd 1860s colloquialisms to use the next day. With the director, Bob Boris's, blessing, I was also able to stage a few scenes. The sequence where Jesse James kills a bank clerk is pretty cool, and it got me thinking about one day directing myself.

Returning home from location in Arkansas, back in the L.A.

traffic, I had an epiphany. I needed to get my family away from the crowds and the chaos (which was great when I was single), to a place where they could be out of the media spotlight. I didn't want Matthew to grow up in a "company town," where all roads led to the entertainment industry.

Sheryl and I had always loved Santa Barbara, with its old-school elegance and diverse crowd. Yes, the people were decidedly more square, and *much* older than my circle in L.A., but I was ready to move away from anything too hip or too current. (I will now use a phrase I hate because I can't come up with one that says it better: I had "been there, done that.") We found a wooded acre with a cozy house and said good-bye to L.A., where I had lived since 1976. I had not one friend in Santa Barbara when I moved there. Again, I followed my heart and stayed out of the results. We've lived there ever since.

⚜

Sherry Lansing, the president of Paramount, has a private jet waiting for me at Santa Barbara airport. As was becoming standard, my deal to do *Tommy Boy* had gone south and only at the last minute had Bernie Brillstein gotten it on track. So now, with shooting twelve hours away, I board the Gulfstream IV for a comfy red-eye to location in Toronto.

The movie itself was Lorne's idea. "I want to do a movie about you and Chris Farley as brothers," he said one day on the tennis court.

"That's a funny visual," I replied, thrilled that Lorne was building a potential movie around me.

As with *Wayne's World*, he wanted help anchoring the film, since his comedy leads, Chris Farley and David Spade, had never made a movie. And while it's a little bizarre to be the wise movie veteran at thirty, I don't mind being the guy they call in such circumstances. And once again, I'm able to contribute beyond acting. In my first meeting to discuss the script, I tell the writers about the midwestern tradition of "cowtipping" and it becomes one of the movie's big sequences.

Chris Farley is one of those people whose presence causes you to remember where you were when you first laid eyes on him. Not yet famous, he was standing by the Porta-Potties at Lorne's wedding, squished into a loud, ill-fitting seersucker suit. Now, a few years later, he is the new It guy on *Saturday Night Live*, the latest heavy-set, giant personality à la his idol John Belushi.

"He is my hero," Farley says again and again. "I want to be just like him."

And by the time Chris's brilliant and short career is over, he will have gotten his wish.

But now I'm sitting with him and David Spade at Barbarian's Steak House after a long day on the set. Not surprisingly, Chris is a guy of huge appetites. The man has a shot of espresso before every close-up. Not before every scene, but every *take*. And so I shouldn't be taken aback by his order at our dinner. But as Spade and I stare in disbelief, Farley eats two giant porterhouse steaks. On the table are those old-school, iced individual squares of butter. Chris places an entire square on top of *each bite of both his steaks*.

Finally, I can take no more.

"Chris! What the hell!" I say, as he places another cube on top of another mouthful.

He giggles like a baby. "It needs a hat!"

*Tommy Boy* is a hit and remains a favorite among teenage boys, who approach me to this day. It's a movie with smarts and heart as well, and like *Wayne's World* is as good or better than a lot of comedies of that genre made today. It also contains what might be my most-quoted line in movies: "Did you eat paint chips as a kid?"

Chris and I remain close until his death. As he struggles with his demons, I work to help him find his way. Like me, Chris has a distinct public image and knows that it is merely a fraction of who he is as a human being, much less as an actor. And like me, he wants to move beyond this obvious and lazy pigeonholing. The "Fat Guy" and the "Pretty Boy," as it turns out, have a lot in common.

Unfortunately for Chris, he is unable to develop the muscle needed to say no to those who want him to remain the Funny Fat Goof. And, even though the concept of the movie makes him feel debased, he takes the Fat Goof role in *Beverly Hills Ninja* for a fortune, and is never the same. Within a year, he will go like his idol, dead from a drug overdose at the age of thirty-three. For me, it is a stark lesson that if you can't get honest with yourself, if you can't look yourself in the mirror, no matter how much money they pay you, or how much you are lauded, you are literally putting your life at risk.

❖

I think most self-employed parents lose a bit of their drive when they have a newborn in the house. With the birth of my second son, Johnowen (Sheryl wanted Owen, I wanted John), I was way too fulfilled and happy as a young dad to keep the career accelerator pushed to the floor. In Santa Barbara, out of the rat race, Johnowen was the piece of the puzzle that completed the life I had always wanted but never imagined. Turns out I wasn't going to be the Warren Beatty character from *Shampoo*, the cool, happening lady-killer at the center of the world (albeit a lonely one). I was instead just like most American men. In love with my wife, living in a normal town, and blessed beyond imagining with two precious, beautiful, and inspiring babies. The midwestern boy was back!

And after a string of workmanlike projects (some quite good, some quite bad), I was looking for a way to stop filming on remote locations and to build a different career where I wouldn't miss out on my kids growing up.

I began to branch out, and to do more writing. I wrote and directed a short forty-minute movie for Showtime called *Desert's Edge*. A harrowing black comedy, it was well received by critics and put me on the list of young writer-directors. I now spent my days talking to studios about directing instead of acting. But as my pal, mentor, and fellow actor-turned-director Jodie Foster wisely told me, "By the time material gets to a new director, all of the big directors with great taste have had their shot at it, all that's left is crap. You'll have to write your own material." I took her advice and got to work. But like the mafia for Michael Corleone in the awful *Godfather III*, the life of the actor kept "pulling me back in."

One afternoon Mike Myers hits a drive down the fairway. I shank mine to the rough. As we drive around looking for my errant shot, I'm making him laugh with a unique imitation I've been doing for years. Mike gets out his cell phone and calls his muse, his wife, Robin.

"Listen to this! Rob, do that impersonation for Robin," he asks.

I take the phone and do my Robert Wagner voice.

"Hullo, how ya doin'," I say, doing my best *Hart to Hart*.

I hear Robin laugh on the other end of the line, always a good sign.

"How funny is that!" says Mike. "He sounds just like RJ!"

We find my ball, finish our round, and I think nothing more about it. Two months later Mike calls.

"I'm sending you a secret script. I want your opinion. It's called *Austin Powers: The Spy Who Shagged Me*."

Sitting at my favorite Italian restaurant, I read it. It's vintage Mike. A totally fresh concept, with inspired characters (most of whom Mike will play) and odd but hilarious jokes. And on page

14, I read the following screen direction: "Young Number Two (as played by Rob Lowe) enters Dr. Evil's lair."

Mike has taken my golf-course joke, made it a character, and, in case anyone had other ideas, wrote my name into the script!

"You maniac!" I tell him later. "You want me to do my little impression as a character?"

"Yes. Just like you did Arsenio Hall on *Saturday Night Live*. You will *nail* this."

The shoot is a blast. Mike insists that music be played between takes. Whereas Coppola preferred opera and Elvis, Mike leans toward '70s dance music like "Car Wash"; to this day the opening hand claps remind me of the shoot.

With *Austin Powers*, Mike Myers is a true auteur at the height of his powers (no pun intended). Watching him play Fat Bastard, Dr. Evil, and Austin Powers and craft on-the-spot lyrics to his Dr. Evil rap version of "Just the Two of Us" is possibly the most fun and unquestionably the most hilarious time I've ever had on a set. He's making magic and everyone knows it. And I get my turn when I open my mouth as young Robert Wagner, and the crew assumes the real Robert Wagner is actually standing off the set and I'm lip-synching to him!

Mike can also be a great collaborator, and one day as we are shooting in the hollowed-out volcano lair, I have an idea. "Mike, how about if I get pissed at you and try and stand up to Dr. Evil. Maybe you end up bouncing the big globe off my head and taunt me like Robert Duvall in *The Great Santini*." He loves the idea and we shoot it immediately, ad-libbing the dialogue. It stays in the final film and is one of my favorite scenes.

*The Spy Who Shagged Me* is a monster success. By far the biggest movie I've ever been a part of, it cements my foothold in comedy.

To celebrate, Mike and Robin join Sheryl and me at the

Canyon Ranch resort. When we visit the Myerses in their room, Mike asks Sheryl if she thinks the room is up to par.

"No. I don't like it."

"Why not?" asks Mike.

"Too much foot traffic outside," says my wife, who knows about these things.

" 'Foot traffic'! I love you, Sheryl," says Mike, howling. "You sound like Lovey Howell from *Gilligan's Island*!"

So, the rest of the trip that's what he called her: Lovey. And the name stuck. I call her that to this day.

One night, all sugared up on low-cal chocolate pudding, Mike gives me some advice.

"Rob, you have great stories. You've seen so much and can write, you *have* to do a book."

"I never thought of that. I don't know," I say.

"You can and must. I'm never wrong about these things."

❖

Meanwhile, I've been following another mentor's advice: As Jodie Foster suggested, I have just finished writing my first screenplay, *Union Pacific*. After my agents send it out, I get a call from Bill Paxton. Bill has done many movies for his longtime friend James Cameron, and he has an urgent message for me.

"I gave Jim Cameron your script. He read it and wants to talk to you about it!"

"Holy shit!" I say. Bill tells me that James will call me in ten minutes.

*Union Pacific* is a road adventure in the vein of *Deliverance*. Two brothers, looking for the Last Great American Adventure, ride the rails like the heroes of Kerouac. But they get in way over their heads in the underground network of modern-day train hopping and come up against a vicious killer preying on the dis-enfranchised who populate this strange world. As a railroad special agent closes in, our heroes must confront the killer as they are all trapped on a runaway train.

The script has attracted some fans and I have been talking to a few of them about setting it up for me to direct, including Paula Wagner at Tom Cruise's company and Lawrence Bender, the producer of *Pulp Fiction*. But James Cameron, having just made *Titanic*, is in a whole other league. He truly is "the king of the world."

I pick the phone up on the first ring.

"Rob, it's Jim Cameron."

Cameron is generous with his praise, and when I hang up, I feel like I could retire and be artistically fulfilled forever. "Look, I read a lot," Jim says to me. This *is* special, you are really onto something. Let me know what you do with it."

After days of thought, I come up with a plan, because when you get cold-called by James Cameron, you have won the lottery and you had better cash that ticket. Jim is an auteur; he is unlikely to direct someone else's material. And he rarely produces movies he doesn't direct. So what am I left with, other than an amazing and generous show of support for my script, from the business's most powerful man?

Then I remember another larger-than-life director, John Huston, who delivered a stunning acting turn in *Chinatown*. I wonder if Jim would ever want to act? *Union Pacific* has a prominent villain part, much like Huston's (any other script similarities end there), and so, gathering my nerve, I call Cameron back.

"Hey, Jim. Would you ever consider starring in a movie?" I point out that, like Huston, he is now an icon and if he wanted, he could parlay that into yet another artistic experience, as both Sydney Pollack and François Truffaut did at certain points in their careers.

Having started his career in the art department (with Bill Paxton) with famed low-budget producer Roger Corman, Jim has worked at and mastered every possible job on a movie crew. Except for one.

"I'd like to know more about acting," he says, and my heart leaps. "Can we do a screen test?"

I bring a skeleton crew to Lightstorm, Jim's production offices. We set up in the large screening room. We will do two scenes and see how we feel about moving forward. As I work on the lighting setup, I wonder if anyone would guess that Cameron would take this kind of time to support a fledgling young director.

Like any actor worth anything, Jim comes prepared. He knows his lines and asks good questions. We work for about an hour or so. He has a tremendous presence (as all leaders do) and, above all, is just so *game*. I would love to work with him in any capacity, regardless of who's directing who.

"I'll look at the footage and then come show it to you," I say, thanking him.

"Oh no, no, no, no. I believe an actor should sublimate himself before his director. I'll come to you."

A few days later, in Santa Barbara, we watch the screen test and talk. I tell him he was really good.

"I don't know," says Jim. "But I want to know more about what actors go through. Maybe I should give this a try."

We agree that I will move forward with setting the movie up and, when that happens, we will decide.

"This could be really cool," he says on his way out. "My next movie after *Titanic*'s gonna be four actors in a hotel room for the entire picture."

I spend weeks talking to producers, financiers, and my producing partner on the movie, Gale Anne Hurd. It's always one step forward, two steps back. There's not enough action for the studios (it's not expensive enough), and the indie crowd feels it has too *much* action (too expensive). *Union Pacific* will die of promise, the most dreaded thing you can be in Hollywood today: a middle-range-budgeted script with real action but also with real characters.

I thought I was going to direct a movie with James Cameron. He thought he was going to make *his* next movie about four people on one set, for a tiny budget. Instead, he wouldn't make another movie as a director until *Avatar*. I also felt my acting career had stalled. I was rarely offered anything that energized me, although I worked constantly. And in spite of my setback on *Union Pacific*, there was clearly some traction for me as a writer-director. I began to mentally transition away from the life I had always known and worked so hard to achieve. I began to develop material, take pitch meetings, and otherwise begin down my new path as a filmmaker. But, as they say in sobriety, if you want to make God laugh, tell him your plans.

It's one of my agents, Tiffany Kuzon, on the phone.

"I'm sending you a script for a TV pilot. I don't know if it will get on the air, it's been on the shelf for a year already. I don't know if you want to do a TV series, I don't even know if you want to act anymore."

"C'mon. I'll *always* want to act." I chuckle. "I just need it to be of some quality."

"Well . . . this script's pretty damn good," says Tiffany.

"What's it called?"

*"The West Wing."*

CHAPTER 19

W ritten by Aaron Sorkin. Well, that's a good sign. I'm sitting down to read this would-be TV pilot script and I remember Sorkin's name from the movie *Malice*, a thriller I read a few years ago. I loved its big, snappy speeches (Google "Alec Baldwin, I am God" and you'll get a delicious taste) and had lobbied for a role to no avail.

Believe it or not, it never occurred to me that *The West Wing* might be about the White House. My agent gave me no backstory on the script, only that it was good. I halfway feared *The West Wing* might be a spin-off of the then popular *Pensacola: Wings of Gold*. I'm telling you, I was completely unprepared for what I was about to read. I didn't even know which character I should be considering.

Through no fault of my own, I've had a career where I play

guys you meet on page one. And on the first page of *The West Wing*, here comes a character named Sam Seaborn. Good name. Nice alliteration and romantic-sounding. He's standing at a bar slinging rapid-fire political-insider talk. From my years on the inside of campaigns I recognize at once the authenticity of his voice and the world that surrounds him. Oh, now Sam's flirting with a girl in a charming, self-deprecating way. I get the idea that Sam is more comfortable with public policy than private interaction with the fairer sex. Nice dynamic. I'm liking this Mr. Seaborn more and more. And now at the end of the teaser (the intro before the credits), Mr. Sorkin closes the deal. Sam's date asks who his boss, POTUS, is.

"President of the United States," he replies, dashing off to solve a White House crisis. My chest thumps, I feel my skin tingle, and I know that, God help me, I'm in love.

I've read hundreds of scripts. I've read a number that I would have killed to have been a part of, but I've read only one or two over the course of twenty-plus years that made me absolutely certain of this: I know this character at first blush and on the deepest of levels. He feels written for me. Everything I've done as an actor and as a person has prepared me for this part. The miles on the road campaigning, serving a candidate pursuing the calling of that elusive, magical oval office. My interest in policy, in public change, in service. My deep love of the majesty of our flawed democracy. Like Sam, I feel these things in my bones. When Sam Seaborn speaks, it's as if it's me talking, but elevated by the massive intellect and wit of Aaron Sorkin. Sam Seaborn, I realize, is my idealized self.

By the time I get to Sam's showstopping speech to the grade-school teacher, I can't wait to slip into this material.

*(As Sam tries to impress his boss's daughter's class, he appeals to the teacher after a less-than-stellar White House tour.)*

SAM

Ms. O'Brien . . . please believe me when I tell you that I am a nice guy having a bad day. I just found out that the *Times* is publishing a poll that says that a considerable portion of Americans feel that the White House has lost energy and focus: a perception that's not likely to be altered by the video footage of the president riding his bicycle into a tree. As we speak, the Coast Guard are fishing Cubans out of the Atlantic Ocean while the governor of Florida wants to blockade the Port of Miami. A good friend of mine's about to get fired for going on television and making sense and it turns out that I accidentally slept with a prostitute last night. Now would you please, in the name of compassion, tell me which one of those kids is my boss's daughter?

MALORY

That would be me.

SAM

You.

MALORY

Yes.

SAM

Leo's daughter's fourth-grade class.

MALORY

Yes.

SAM

Well, this is bad on so many levels.

Sorkin's writing is music and I can hear its melody clearly.

I call my agents. "What do we need to do to get this part?" The news isn't good.

"They don't want a star. They don't want any 'names' in the cast," my agent informs me. "But they are intrigued that you are intrigued. If you are willing to come read for them, they will give you a meeting."

I have auditioned throughout my career, but fairly infrequently because usually roles are offered to those with a body of work. And truthfully, that's the way it should be. It's an acknowledgment of an actor's length of service. If you want to know if I'm funny enough, you can watch *Austin Powers*, *Tommy Boy*, *Wayne's World*, or *SNL*. Interested in my dramatic chops? Look at *Bad Influence*, *Square Dance*, *The Stand*, or *The Hotel New Hampshire*. Can I pull off romantic banter? There's *About Last Night* and *St. Elmo's Fire*. If you don't like what you see, no problem, and if you do, then let's make a movie! Readings should be for newcomers who've never done the kind of work you're asking them to do. But I actually love the challenge and if I want this role, I've got to play it their way. It's their show after all; they can cast it any way they want.

Sheryl accompanies me for the long drive from Santa Barbara. If I do get this part, this drive (about eighty-eight miles one way) and the upheaval it would cause is just one of a few challenges we would face as a family. One-hour television drama is universally accepted to have the most grueling schedule in all of show business. And that's if everything runs like a Swiss watch. If the show becomes successful, I potentially would be looking at four hours in the car and at least twelve hours a day on set, five days a week, twenty-two weeks a year. But first, I've got to do this reading.

"Good luck, baby," says Sheryl, giving me a kiss. "Knock 'em dead."

It has been arranged that I will only have to read once. I won't have to run the ugly gauntlet of casting readings, showrunner readings, studio readings, and network readings. When I walk into the office on the Warner Bros. Studios lot, it's jam-packed with representatives of all the various gatekeepers. But I know there are only two who matter. John Wells is the man responsible for one of the finest, most successful and well-run franchises in TV history, *ER*. He is a writer himself and a tough negotiator of some renown. He will be the man whose prestige and power at the network will shepherd this brilliant but commercially risky project to fruition.

"Hey, Rob, thanks for comin' in," says John. For all his juice and power, he is down-to-earth and affable.

"Do you know Aaron Sorkin?" he asks.

Now the *real* gatekeeper. In TV the writer is God. Even lazy, cliché-favoring scribes are deities if they are running a television show. And now I'm shaking hands with the boyish, preppy-looking Zeus of *The West Wing*.

"Ah, hey there, Rob. Great to see ya," says Sorkin, in his unique cadence, which I will eventually and shamelessly emulate as Sam Seaborn whenever I can't hear "the music." The other twelve or so people huddle in the background as Sorkin sits in a chair in front of them and next to me. It's then I realize that Aaron will be reading with me. This is highly unusual; in fact, I've never encountered it before. He doesn't want to hear his melody played back to him from the audience, he wants to be onstage and play it with you. Fantastic! I'll be reading with someone who cares as much as I do.

The scene is Sam's big speech about his "bad day." I know this meeting is not much more than a curiosity-fulfillment exercise for everyone in the room. I know they want New Yorky, theater, character actors who have never "popped." And I am a lot of things and can be a lot of things, but I can never be those things. But I can be this character.

I intuitively know that there is no margin for error with the words. I either have to know them cold or read them off the script in order to make no mistakes. (This will prove to be an understatement when, during production, we will have a supervisor whose sole job is to make sure we say *exactly* what is written. "Rob, sorry, you said 'I'm.' It's supposed to be 'I am.'") I hold the scene in my hand as I begin. It's long, and one slip in front of Sorkin and it will be over for sure.

Sorkin and I play the scene and it sings. But the big speech is coming up fast now and like with another audition so many years ago, in front of Francis Ford Coppola, I know I've gotta stick it. I toss the script on the ground with some force and turn on Sorkin, giving him both barrels of his precise, rhythmic ammunition. And I'm reminded: This is what I live for. Beautiful fastballs right down the middle of the plate, just where I like them. Sure, they're coming in hot and one after another, and probably not everyone can hit 'em right, but I've put in the work and fouled off so many bad pitches that now, seeing these great ones, I'm parking them in the top level of the stadium.

"Well, that's bad on so many levels," I finish, and the room laughs, loud and as one. Sorkin is beaming. He looks across the room to John Wells: "See! I *told* you it was funny!"

Halfway back to Santa Barbara, my agent calls. "Congratulations. You got the part!"

My elation is short-lived. The offer is so low that there is simply no way I can take myself off the market for the length of the five-year contract. In comparison to my previous television deals, the offer to do *The West Wing* would've been a pay cut of 65 percent. But I understand. They were honest and up front from the beginning. They did not want anyone famous. And they certainly didn't want to pay for it.

"I don't care about my previous deals. I'll cut my price by half. I have to play this role," I tell my agents and my manager, Bernie Brillstein.

"Sometimes you have to sacrifice for a great part," I remind them.

"I hear ya, kid," says Bernie, "and I agree. But I won't let you work for this." Bernie and my agents try to negotiate a compromise, to no avail. I'm profoundly disappointed; it looks like someone else will be playing Sam Seaborn.

✜

My mother has divorced Steve (husband number three) and moved to Santa Barbara to be near her grandsons, whom she adores. She is teaching them to read and play the piano, and is otherwise spoiling them with a support and love that makes me love her all the more. And for some reason, with Steve out of her life, she is no longer incapacitated by her many mysterious illnesses. And so, with her late-in-life rebirth, I get the mother I have always wanted. My father, now divorced again as well, has a bittersweet reunion with his first love and mother to his oldest sons at Christmas as they both bunk at our house for the holidays. Among the many magnificent gifts Matthew and Johnowen have given me, this is the most unexpected. I have no memory of the early Christmases when my mother and father were together. And in the mysterious way life has of coming full circle, I am moved beyond measure to see them together again at last, enjoying their grandsons.

The holidays pass and I know I won't be getting the one thing I'd like to start the New Year. Now the role of Sam Seaborn is being read by a wide range of actors. I hear their names through the Hollywood grapevine and some are pretty good indeed. But, I also keep hearing that Sorkin's mind was made up weeks ago, after our meeting. I send back-channel messages to him as he does to me: "Can't we find a way to do this?"

Bernie and I talk every day about anything and everything. Having run a studio, hired and fired many of the town's top executives, and generally just being *in play* for so many years, he always knows the inside story.

"NBC wants a star to help sell the show," he says to me one morning. "We may be in business."

And sure enough, within days the studio has a new offer.

"Kid, it's still a fifty percent pay cut. I can get you more than double on another show if you want it," Bernie informs me. "If you want this show, it's a sacrifice."

I have literally been dreaming about this project at night. In all my career, that has never happened. For a kid who followed his dreams to a town that's built on the promise of them, I decided to listen to mine.

"Make the deal. I have to do this show."

I am fitted for my wardrobe by the lovely Lyn Paolo only one day before shooting. I sign my contract on the floor of her changing room. I'm over the moon. Bernie is less so.

"Political shows never work. It's a great script but I just don't know."

"It'll be great," I promise.

"Well, look at it this way. *If* it works, then they'll have to make you whole."

After choosing Sam's battery of navy and black suits, crisp white shirts, and reading glasses, I head over to stage 18 and take a peek at the newly completed set. It's awe-inspiring. Giant, luxurious, and detailed down to the stationery *inside* the desk drawers; my old pal from *The Hotel New Hampshire*, Jon Hutman, has created a set for the ages.

Although shooting will begin the next morning on location at the Biltmore Hotel in downtown L.A., I still haven't met the other actors. I also know that one important role has yet to be cast, that of President Josiah Bartlet.

"We're not gonna see much of the president in the life of the series," Aaron tells me. "The stories are going to be about his staff." And indeed, Bartlet doesn't make an appearance until the very end of the pilot, which is usually the dramatic template for any future storytelling.

"He'll be like the neighbor from *Home Improvement*," says one of the producers, referring to the character on that hit show who is constantly talked about but rarely seen. I had heard they were hoping to cast Sidney Poitier as Bartlet.

"Yeah, he'd be amazing," Sorkin tells me when I bring it up. "Also thinking about Martin Sheen. He actually called me, he's so excited!" says Aaron, clearly enamored.

Martin as Bartlet! Our families have been intertwined for so many years that I can't even express to Aaron the levels of history and subtext this would bring to the Sam-Bartlet relationship. So I just say this: "Martin Fucking Sheen is the greatest."

❖

*The West Wing* pilot may be the best one ever made. From the first frame to the last it is letter perfect, a freakish combination of the right actors playing the right parts, and a script with a witty, intelligent rhythm that had never been seen on television. *The Sopranos*, another Hall of Fame show that would become our good-natured blood rival, took a few episodes to find its sea legs. Not *The West Wing*. Right out of the gate, it blew your doors off.

When air-time advertising buyers are shown a ten-minute clip at the important network "up-fronts," they greet it with a standing ovation. Sitting backstage, the cast look at one another. "What is going *on* here?!"

Scott Sassa, the president of NBC, comes over and congratulates us. "I've been coming to these up-fronts for a lot of years. I've never seen this."

Sassa, who always believed in the script, has seen enough to give the show a prime spot on the fall schedule. "You'll be on Wednesday nights at nine p.m., right before *Law and Order*."

Sorkin is elated. He takes me aside: "I thought you should know that you tested higher in our audience research than George Clooney in *ER*," he confides. I could never have imagined that this type of feedback would not bode well for me in the future.

Later, at the cocktail reception, when all the local NBC affiliates go to individual areas to meet the stars of the shows, *The West Wing* section is bedlam. People are pushing and pulling for a moment with stars of a show that hasn't aired one episode.

"Holy shit," says my costar John Spencer, as a guy with ten stations in the Midwest pumps his hand like an old railroad sidecar. "We're gonna get killed! We gotta get out of here!" he says with a smile.

"Nah, man!" I say. "This is what it's really like at a presidential rally. We should all be looking at this as our research!"

I make my way over to Martin, also getting mobbed. Unlike all the other cast, both Martin and I have been in the spotlight for some time, so we have a little more perspective.

"None of this means a thing until we get the ratings," says Martin, looking at the rest of the cast happily taking pictures and signing autographs. I know he's right. We're big, we're state of the art, and we're coming to a town near you, but unless people watch, we could very well arrive like the *Hindenburg*.

The first person I ever knew to play the then new California State Lottery was Emilio and Charlie's dad. Martin bought enough rolls of tickets at the Mayfair Market on Point Dume to choke a donkey. He just loved the fun of it, the allure of that potential lightning strike that would cover you in massive, found money. He never did find that winning ticket when we were kids. But years later, with *The West Wing*, he finally did.

His contract to play Bartlet called for only a few episodes. But with his high-impact performance, the network wanted to see more of him. I think Aaron also discovered that being able to put words into the mouth of the president of the United States was more heady than merely writing for his staffers. But to integrate Bartlet more fully, they would have to make a new deal with Martin. And now, with millions committed to a show about to air that's been earmarked as a potential winner, Martin holds all the cards. As a veteran of many a negotiation where the studio holds all the cards and kills you, I was happy when Martin, "the neighbor from *Home Improvement*," got a gigantic raise, earning six figures for every episode. He's a great actor, been around much longer than I have, and I love him like a father. And besides, if we all get lucky and the show is a monster hit, everyone will be rewarded. In the meantime, I'm glad to be part of such a great team.

A few days before we begin shooting season one of *The West Wing*, I get a call from Bernie.

"Kid, I just got the strangest call. They want to take away your first billing in the main titles."

"But why? And, I mean, we have a deal, right?"

"Absolutely!" exclaims Bernie.

"What did you tell them?" I ask, shocked.

"What do you think I told them? I said, 'How 'bout, go fuck yourself'!" And I know he's not exaggerating. Bernie is one of the only people in Hollywood who is unafraid of fallout when defending a client.

"It's completely out of line and unfair. You were the one who got that show on the air in the first place. I don't understand it," he says.

We never did get to the bottom of this request. This lack of support would prove to be the first in a series of events that would eventually have me questioning my place on *The West Wing*. But I had to move beyond it. Actors work with emotion and passion and I could ill afford to have anything begin to dampen my love of this project.

"On my mark. One. Two. Three," the great composer W. G. "Snuffy" Walden counts off before a full orchestra on Warner Bros.'s giant dubbing stage.

There is a timpani rumble, a cymbal clash, and the strings explode into Snuffy's majestic and highly emotional *The West Wing* theme. I have snuck in to listen to this first take as the main title is recorded. The French horns play their heroic counterpoint and the violins swell. My eyes begin to eject water, like a cartoon character. I look at the technician at the mixing board. His arms are covered in gooseflesh.

I had a vision once before. A simple wooden sign on an island in Fiji pointed out to me a then almost laughable, but wondrous, future. Now, lost in *The West Wing* main title theme, I'm having another. And it, too, is visceral, crystal, detailed, and unlikely enough that I almost discount it. I see us—Aaron, the cast, all of us—in a huge auditorium. We are in black tie. This song is being played by another orchestra and now we are standing and people are applauding. We leave our seats and walk to a podium and walk to another, rising and walking, and now I know this is an awards show, and so is this one and that one and the next one. We rise and walk again and again, always with music, always in black tie. And I can see Aaron, and he's holding a statue. I see this as clearly as if watching filmed footage.

The music soars to its crescendo. John Spencer has dropped by as well and comes to me and asks, "Well, what do you think?"

"Johnny, I think this is walkin' music," I say.

"What do you mean?" he asks, but I don't dare share my vision. I just look at him and smile, putting my arm around him as the music fades out.

⟡

Somewhere in Manhattan, someone slips JFK Jr. a copy of the pilot. He loves it and makes plans for my *George* cover. Again, there is tremendous consternation at the idea of me representing the show in this capacity. But John Jr. is unmoved by the pressure to have me taken off his magazine's cover. "This show is exactly what I wanted *George* to be," he reportedly told his staff. And so when fate takes him just weeks later, everyone at *The West Wing* is proud to carry that vision, as long as we can. But to do so, we first have to face our own election. This vote is held every week by the A. C. Nielsen Company, and on September 22, 1999, it was our turn to face the nation. Most everyone thinks we have made what will prove to be a critically acclaimed but short-lived television show (a "six and out," as they say in industry-speak). Watching with the cast and crew at a big party thrown by Aaron Sorkin and John Wells, we are all hoping conventional wisdom is wrong. We will know the verdict before the next sunrise.

It's 5:00 a.m. and Scott Sassa is calling me at home. When network presidents call you, it's good news. When they call you at home, it's great news. When they wake you out of bed, it's fantastic news.

"Congratulations. The ratings were great."

America voted us into office and, as in a real administration, I would serve for a full four-year term. I couldn't wait to make my eighty-eight-mile drive on L.A.'s notoriously nightmarish freeways to get to work each morning, often rising at 4:30 a.m. I had never been part of a better ensemble. To watch Allison Janney receive her lines for the first time, sitting in the makeup chair, then grab a coffee, walk onto the set, and deliver a vintage C. J. Cregg press briefing was a thing of beauty all actors should have a chance to witness. To watch the late John Spencer say, "Thank you, Mr. President," was to see a man lay down a complex subtext of meaning and emotion far exceeding four simple words. I never tired of watching him work; he could do more with less than any other actor I've ever seen. And like the other cast members that populated *The West Wing*, John had that other rare but critical component for success on our show: He could always find the humor. My new cast mates were also pound for pound the most well-read and intelligent group of actors I've ever known. On *The West Wing* a typical coffee-break chat among the cast could cover the legacy of César Chávez, the history of the New York Yankees, the shortcomings of the Electoral College, and whether or not Nelson Rockefeller and JFK would be accepted by their respective parties in today's political climate.

And as I had suspected, working with Martin was replete with an emotional history and an intimate shorthand I'm not sure anyone else noticed. But the results certainly showed on-screen; Sam and Bartlet were like father and son.

As season one drew to a close, *The West Wing* was becoming a sensation. It was wish fulfillment for a nation looking for leaders and reviewers looking for quality. It was the right show at the right time.

❖

I'm walking through the set one afternoon to the area where I'm going to be shooting a scene. As I pass the Oval Office, a production assistant shoos me away nervously.

"Um. Sorry . . . you should go around the long way," he says, his eyes shifting from side to side. I can see that something is making him uncomfortable, and I can't imagine why he won't let me pass through. Then my eye catches strobe flashes coming from under the Oval Office door. And now I can hear the voice of what is obviously a photographer from inside the room.

"Great! Oooh! Looking good! You guys look fantastic," he exclaims.

As I pass by, I peek in. I see all my cast mates doing a photo shoot.

"What's everybody doing in there?" I ask.

The PA hesitates. It's clear he doesn't want to answer at first.

"Um. It's the cover of *Emmy° Magazine*. It's for all the Emmy Awards voters."

I watch for a moment or two, then move on to shoot my scene.

When the Emmy nominations arrive a few weeks later, every cast member from that photo shoot gets nominated.

*The West Wing* will win more Emmys than any other first-year show in history. And, during my four seasons on the show, it will win two Golden Globes, two Screen Actors Guild Awards, and four consecutive Emmys for Outstunding Dramatic Series, the only show ever to do so. The vision I had during the recording of the theme song would prove to be true on "so many levels," as Sam would say. I would be nominated for two Golden Globes for Best Performance by an Actor in a Television Series—Drama, an Emmy, and two SAG Awards, which I would win along with my other cast mates.

*The West Wing* won fans in all stations of life, but none more so than our real-life counterparts. The cast was invited to the White House numerous times. On our first visit, I'm standing near Wolf Blitzer of CNN as we clear security at the northeast gate of the White House.

"Hey, Sam Seaborn!" says Wolf, and even the Secret Service guys laugh.

After confirming that I have no felonies or arrest warrants and pose no threat to the government—and making me apologize for crimes against humanity perpetrated by some of my less-than-stellar performances—I am cleared to enter.

Along with a small delegation from the show, we have taken a break from shooting to receive a special West Wing tour. We enter through the door at the top of the driveway, just past "Pebble Beach," where the TV reporters do their live shots. It looks no different from the door I enter at Warner Bros. We pass through hallways that are much smaller and much less crowded than those on our show. And not one person in the building is walking and talking as fast as we do. (I'm told that when staffers catch themselves doing this today in the Obama administration, they high-five and say, "We just 'West Winged.'")

So I find myself standing with Aaron in an extraordinarily well-appointed office, as Sorkin is pitched potential new story lines.

"You know what you should do, lemme tell you what you should do, you oughtta write a story about how these young kids come up here to serve and then just get shit-boxed by the press when they don't expect it," says the forty-second president of the United States, leaning against the "Resolute" desk. "I mean some of 'em just have *no clue* about how tough it can get."

It is by now a terrific cliché to say that President Clinton is the most charismatic man you will ever meet, but it doesn't make it any less true. He is warm, funny, down-to-earth, interested in people of all stripes, and can speak chapter and verse on the minutiae of policy as well as any character Aaron Sorkin ever dreamed of. He could probably have been a television staff writer as well, had things played out differently.

I am awestruck to be in this sanctum and to be greeted as if my being there is the most natural thing in the world. Aaron and I try to focus on this surreal meeting in the Oval Office, but I'm having such an out-of-body experience that the president's voice is sounding like that of the teacher in the *Peanuts* cartoons.

I'm jolted back to reality when one of the marines in full dress motions for me.

"The national security advisor would like to see you in his office," he whispers, with import.

Before I know it, I'm hustled out of the Oval.

"Why don't you come by and watch my State of the Union here in the East Room," offers the president.

"Thank you, sir. That would be amazing," I answer as I'm shown the door.

Sandy Berger, the national security advisor, is standing in his giant corner office, waiting for me. And he doesn't look happy.

"Why is there no national security advisor on *The West Wing*?" growls Berger.

"Um. Well, sir, I don't really know. I'm sure at some point there will be one," I manage, hoping this guy can't have me audited.

"I'm just kiddin' ya," he says, breaking into a wide smile. "I *love* the show. We all watch it around here. Everyone says, 'I'm Leo, I'm C.J., I'm Sam,' and it pisses me off 'cause I'm nobody!" We talk for a while as if we are killing time on the golf course instead of eating up clock on a business day in the world's most important office complex.

Everyone I meet in the real-life West Wing is smart, warm, and there to make a difference, and this will prove to be true through the George W. Bush era and into the current administration. Republican or Democrat, it is my experience that with a few exceptions, the men and women who serve us in Washington work almost unbearably hard and have the best intentions. It's easy to knock the shit out of politicians from the sidelines. I do it myself sometimes, but overall, barring the crazy partisan commandos, when *The West Wing* made public service look cool, fun, and something to be held in esteem, we got it right.

Some of my most treasured memories of this era are of my boys chasing Socks, the White House cat, through the basement of the White House, dragging the briefcase with nuclear coordinates, or "football," as it's called, across the South Lawn as the naval guard watched, laughing (this was pre 9-11), or having President Clinton advising me father to father.

"It makes me sad that one day my kids will stop wanting to cuddle, one day those great hugs will be gone," I tell the president during one visit.

"If you raise 'em right, it'll never stop," he says, proudly showing me a photo on his desk. It's a recent photo of him and Chelsea snuggling on a couch. Again *The West Wing* got it right. Presidents are fathers, just like the rest of us.

Saying good-bye on that particular visit, the staff wants a picture. We all pose, crowded into Betty Currie's office, just off the Oval. It's me, Chief of Staff John Podesta, and the gang of young kids who make the place really run.

"Wait. Wait. Whatya doin'? Let me get in there!" comes the familiar southern drawl, as the most important man in the world tries to fight his way into the photo.

On my last visit to the Clinton White House, I'm standing on the South Lawn with Sheryl and the boys talking to the president before he hops onto Marine One. My youngest son, Johnowen, is holding his stuffed frog, Gwee Gwee, which he never lets out of his sight, under any circumstances. It has been his security blanket since he was an infant. But now, he takes it out of his mouth and hands his old, tattered frog to the president.

"Well, look at this!" says the president. "Is this for me?" he asks.

Johnowen nods shyly. "For you," he says in a small voice.

Sheryl and I look at each other in shock.

"Wow, Johnowen!" exclaims Matthew.

"Well, thank you, young man. I bet you didn't know, but I collect frogs. Have since I was a boy like you. 'Cause my daddy used to tell me: 'Son, a frog never knows how far it can jump until it's kicked,' " says the president. "I'll keep him nice and safe. You can come visit him at the Clinton Library someday."

He turns to board the sparkling marine chopper. He holds Gwee Gwee in one hand and salutes the marine guard with the other. The door closes and the rotors go up full throttle. At liftoff, the big helicopter does a slow turn, its tail turning toward those of us standing on the lawn. Sunlight glints across the fuselage illuminating the words: United States of America.

CHAPTER 20

On the last day of August 2001, I board my usual return flight from D.C. on American Airlines Flight 77 out of Dulles International. I've flown with this crew before and we chat, talking about D.C. gossip and our families. After a while I take my nap, and when it's time to land, I am awakened with a waiting coffee. Leaving the plane, I tell the gang I'll see them next time. But I won't.

Eleven days later, on September 11, American Airlines Flight 77 is flown into the Pentagon.

Like everyone, I grieve for the innocent victims of this hateful, cowardly mass murder. I try not to think of the horror the passengers and my friends on the crew must have endured. As I have many times in my life, I also marvel at the hand of fate. What if I had been shooting in D.C. eleven days later?

In late 2005, I receive a letter with the return address of the U.S. Attorney General's Office in the state of Maryland. Inside is a request for me to contact them at my earliest convenience to set up a face-to-face meeting concerning Zacarias Moussaoui, who is being held as "the twentieth hijacker" in the 9-11 attacks.

I wish it were a joke, but I know it's not. I call my longtime lawyer, Larry Stein.

"What the hell is this?" I ask.

"Let me get back to you. I'll call them right away," says Larry, his voice tight.

Within hours he has a horrifying update.

"You are on Moussaoui's list to be deposed," he informs me.

"Whaaaaat!"

"Yes," he says, incredulous himself.

"Were you on an American Airlines flight right before September eleventh?" Larry asks.

"Yes. On August thirty-first, why?"

"Rob. They were all with you. Your flight was the dry run."

I try to comprehend what my lawyer is telling me, but it's too unreal, like an episode of *The Twilight Zone*.

"The hijackers flew with me? I was sitting with them?" I say, shocked and sickened.

"Yeah. The Feds have the flight manifest."

We are both quiet for a moment, before he continues.

"Look, Moussaoui is crazy, he's spouting off and wants to depose you, no one knows why. The Feds want you so they can see what you know before you talk to this guy's public defender."

"Okay. Okay," I say, trying to make sense of this insanity. "Number one: If that fucking mass murderer wants to talk to me, he'll have to get a court order and then I'm not saying shit. And two: Tell the boys at Justice I'll be there for them any day, anytime."

But in the end it would all be moot, as Moussaoui fires his

lawyer and defends himself. Somewhere along the way his interest in me waned; I never heard another peep. And clearly the Feds needed no help; they put him away for life without parole.

I wouldn't have been able to provide much new information anyhow. I remember the flight clearly. Sitting in the smaller version of a first-class cabin, three of them would have been seated within feet of me, maybe even next to me. But I will never know, because here is the horrible truth: No one that day looked like a "terrorist." They looked like typical polo shirt–sporting, headphone-wearing, surprisingly young-looking men you might see anywhere. They looked like us.

On September 20, 2001, President Bush addressed a stunned nation before a packed joint session of Congress.

"The course of this conflict is not known, yet its outcome is certain. Freedom and fear, justice and cruelty have always been at war and we know that God is not neutral between them," said the president, in what is surely the most important and moving speech of his two terms.

A week later I receive a happier surprise in the mail. This time the return address says simply: The White House. Inside the large manila envelope is the embossed program given to those in attendance in the chamber that day at the Capitol. It contains the historic speech in its entirety. On the front cover, I discover it is signed to me from the president himself. And below his signature is this, from head White House speechwriter, Mike Gerson: "To Sam—could you do this?"

✤

With the massive critical and commercial success of *The West Wing*, it is clear that the show is big business. And so, my fellow cast members begin meeting in secret to plot an early renegotiation strategy. They don't include Martin because he got his monster deal before season one started, and they don't include me. I only find out because dear John Spencer can't face me, knowing that I'm the only actor uninvited and in the dark.

As is custom in that type of negotiation, there are threats of not showing up for work and counterthreats by the studio. The production pushes the beginning of the 2001 season back a day or two rather than take a chance the "West Wing 4," as they are now known in the press, would be no-shows. I watch this all from the sidelines with curiosity. Within days they all get the raises they asked for.

"Good for them!" says Bernie Brillstein. "Now you're the only one not taken care of. *Now* it's our turn."

This is why I love Bernie. He works on deals. I work on playing my character.

On the set, my cast mates are giddy. For most of them this is the apex of a long time working at their craft. They're great at it and now they've been rewarded. When they see me coming they keep it on the down low, but when they don't know I'm watching, I see the high fives. I congratulate them and focus on the upcoming season, which promises to be grueling.

In the middle of season two, Aaron writes my favorite episode of *The West Wing.* "Someone's Going to Emergency, Someone's Going to Jail" will end up being the only script in which my character has the main story line. It will earn me my only Emmy nomination for Outstanding Lead Actor in a Drama Series. I urge Aaron to write more for Sam based on the reaction to this episode. "I'm only as good as you make me. But give Sam Seaborn some meat, and I will get into the end zone for us every time," I say. But Aaron has many other actors to write for and has even added more, like the outstanding Mary-Louise Parker and Marlee Matlin. I hope that maybe they could work for, or be love interests of Sam (who never had a gal in all my four years), but they go to the character of Josh Lyman instead. I do end up shooting one scene with Mary-Louise Parker on my very last episode, a fun look at what might have been.

✤

"Hello, I'm Brian Williams," says the handsome MSNBC anchor as he stands in the Roosevelt Room set. "I brought my wife and kids to listen to the read-through of the script today. We are obsessed with the show!"

"Great to meet you. I watch you, too!" I say, shaking his hand. (I never got tired of discovering the diverse assortment of *Wing*-nuts. You never knew who they'd be or where you'd find them.)

The Williams family takes a seat in the corner of the set while the cast gathers around the large Roosevelt Room table as we always do to read each episode aloud. Aaron sits at the head like the nickname I've given him: "the maestro." I sit by my buddy Dulé Hill, whose on-set tap-dance solos during moments of boredom keep both of us from losing our minds. We begin the read-through.

Like many of our scripts, there is a main story that has the dramatic weight and a lesser story with more humor. This story concerns the beloved secretary to the president, Mrs. Landingham, played by Kathryn Joosten, getting a new car. It's sweet and very funny. The room is laughing, and I can see that Brian Williams and his family are as well.

At the end of the script is a scene where Dulé, who plays Charlie Young, answers the phone in Mrs. Landingham's office. She has just left in her new car. It's Leo on the line. He says there's been an accident on Eighteenth and Potomac. It's Mrs. Landingham. Charlie asks if she's okay.

John Spencer, who plays Leo, hesitates. Seeing this, I look down at his next line in the script. In shock, I turn to John, who now has tears streaming down his face. He won't say his line. He turns to the head of the table, to Aaron.

"Is this *real?*" he asks.

Sorkin nods.

John stares at him a moment longer. Then he looks down and, in a shaky voice, answers: "Charlie. Mrs. Landingham was killed."

We never see the scripts until we read them aloud, so the shock in the room is utter and complete. The Williams family, seconds ago laughing and enjoying this so much, are ashen. None of us saw this coming.

Later, Kathryn Joosten tells me that she had been told this story line was a possibility (she would go on to many other roles, including in the massive hit *Desperate Housewives*).

"Ah, Rob, it happens," she tells me. "It's been great, but it's always better to leave too early than stay too late."

Bernie Brillstein is getting nowhere with my bosses on *The West Wing*. For three straight seasons, the show has been the biggest thing on the network, an acclaim magnet not seen in the history of television. It's been almost a year since the rest of the cast received their well-earned reward for their contributions. And now Martin is renegotiating for the second time. It is reported that he may make nearly a quarter of a million dollars an episode. Bernie asks that I receive the same raise as my costars. We don't ask for "Martin money"—he's the president after all. I am refused.

Bernie can do no more. "John Wells says you are being paid exactly what you should be. There will be no raise for you. I'm sorry, kid," he says.

Finally I begin to see what is, as opposed to what I would like to see. It is clear to me now that I have had an unrealistic expectation that I would participate financially in the show's success. I know I am at a crossroads, with only two options: stay put or move forward. And if I am to move forward, it will require me to make a very difficult choice.

I'm contemplating this at the Four Seasons Hotel in Georgetown, where I've traveled to location and to shoot a *TV Guide* cover with Martin in front of the White House.

Sheryl has made the trip with me—she has been my rock and sounding board as I try to work my way to a path forward.

Kathy Kelly Brown is the head of publicity on *The West Wing*. She's smart, funny, and good at her job. Now she's knocking at my door. I open it, dressed for the *TV Guide* shoot. Seeing me, her face falls. She looks at her feet.

"What's wrong?" I ask.

She looks at me standing in my Sam Seaborn crisp white shirt and blue tie.

"I can't believe they didn't tell you," she says quietly. "Martin shot the cover an hour ago. With John Spencer instead of you."

Back in Los Angeles I have a meeting with Aaron about my future on the show. He's always been straight with me and I with him. I tell him: "I know that Sam Seaborn is the part of a lifetime. I love this part unlike anything I've ever encountered. But I think it's bullshit that I'm the only actor on the show who hasn't been given even a penny raise. But I want to stay if we can grow this part creatively. If there is no financial future, let's make a creative future."

But Aaron has many plates in the air, and he is clearly caught in the middle. (In fact, he will leave *The West Wing* in its fourth season as well.) When our meeting ends without any plan, I know it is time to move on.

I had been an alcoholic for an important portion of my life. During that time I had hidden from conflict, fearful of not being liked, worried about how I would be thought of. But I was sober now for almost fourteen years. I was not the little boy back in Ohio in the lumberyard who said what he felt and got emotionally sideswiped for his efforts. I was not the overwhelmed twenty-year-old "sensation" who found it so much less painful to just say yes than to say no, even when I knew I should. I was also not a boy, without any real advisors, making it up as best I could. I was none of those things. Not anymore.

So I came to the realization: Nothing in life is unfair. It's just life. To the extent that I had any inner turmoil, I had only myself to blame. I also thought of my two boys and what kind of example I hoped to be. I would always want them to take charge of their own futures and not be paralyzed by the comfort and certainty of the status quo or be cowed by the judgment of those on the outside looking in.

But how could I ask that of Matthew and Johnowen if I couldn't ask it of myself?

I left *The West Wing* after four seasons and some eighty-plus episodes. It was one of the highlights of my career and I have zero regrets. To fly down those White House hallways, hitting that brilliant rapid-fire dialogue with such unbelievably talented collaborators, was pure joy.

The passion of the show's fans continues to amaze and humble me, even today. I recently took Johnowen's class for a weekend tour of the real West Wing. The entire speechwriting staff came in on their day off to greet Sam Seaborn.

The level of love *The West Wing* inspires makes it a show for the ages. And I believe it will go down as maybe the best ever. I'm proud to have contributed to those record-setting first four years.

For me, the ongoing rewards of the series have been both professional and personal. By pushing through my comfort zone, I was able to train an emotional muscle that serves me well today. All of us on a daily basis have the opportunity to move forward or backward or stay put. Today, I know to move forward. And it's funny—initially I wanted to be on *The West Wing* because I knew it would challenge me as an actor. But its real gift was that, in the end, it challenged me as a man.

❖

Today, life's blessings continue to surprise me. And the stories that follow from this mysterious, glorious, maddening, saddening journey are enough to fill another book, maybe for another day. In the time I have worked on *Stories I Only Tell My Friends* I have shot three terrific television series in which I starred (*Brothers and Sisters*, *Parks and Recreation*, and *Californication*) all at the same time, sometimes two shows in one day. Moving from the real, human drama of *Brothers* to playing a true comic lead (not straight man) on *Parks* (after one fast fifteen-minute drive between sets) presented a thrilling contrast that few actors get to experience. I was blessed to be able to work in both comedy and drama surrounded by actors of such a high level of talent. In the middle of that hectic schedule I shot the controversial movie *I Melt with You*, playing one of the most rewarding roles of my career. It premiered at Sundance and will be released in 2011.

In a screening room on location in Australia in 2003, I watched *The Outsiders: The Novel*, a new edition of the movie that contained my long-lost scenes from almost twenty-five years before. On-screen I saw a boy more like my sons now than myself. In that beginning, unformed haze of my career, I thought maybe I had botched these scenes. Now I saw they were beautiful and heartbreaking; the emotional ending the author always intended. They say you can never go home again, but I'm not so sure. That day I caught a good glimpse of my former self, and I came very, very close.

Aaron Sorkin and I reunited in 2007 when I starred in the West End revival of his play *A Few Good Men*. I'm happy to say that the reception was everything we had hoped, as was our collaboration.

I continue to produce, for HBO, even for the E! channel. My best pal and mentor, Tom Barrack, and I have started an entertainment fund and, along with our other investors, purchased Miramax Studios from the Walt Disney Company for $640 million in December 2010.

In the middle of my life, I am in the middle of the thick of it. I am transitioning to new areas of passion and challenge; always driving forward, always pushing.

I finally took up surfing and fell in love with its inherent demands of fitness, balance, commitment, and risk-taking. When I paddled out for the first time at Point Dume, I was moved to share the experience with Matthew, who was now the same age I was when the local surf gang discouraged me from learning so many years ago.

The great Bernie Brillstein passed away in 2007, and was eulogized at one of the largest and most moving memorials ever held in Hollywood by the one who first introduced us back in 1978, Kermit the Frog.

My mother died of breast cancer, too young at sixty-four years old. In her honor, I work regularly for cancer charities; in her memory I have written this book. She wrote every day of her life. I hope this would have been up to her standards.

My father and my brothers are all well and ensconced in their lives; new wives, beautiful babies, and deep family reinvestment being the order of the day.

And in the most surprising fact of my life, one that at one point I thought I was incapable of feeling and unworthy of achieving: I am still in love with my wife. After almost twenty years of marriage, I look at her face and see her radiant light; I hold her and feel our hard-earned and sometimes difficult history passing between us, enveloping us in an aura of comfort, gratitude, and profound attraction. If you'd asked me when I was a young punk what would be the best thing that could come my way, I would've said, "A movie with Martin Scorsese." But God had other plans. He gave me Sheryl.

As I write this, Matthew and Johnowen are waiting for me at home. I am on a packed, delayed flight back from shooting a project I'm producing in D.C. I've only been gone a few nights, but we are so close, the three of us, that it feels like a lifetime. I want to get back to them; there is a Colts game to be watched and we will crunch together on our couch and laugh and snuggle under our comfy blanket, even though they are seventeen and fifteen years old. President Clinton appears to have been right. If you're lucky, those affectionate childhood bonds can grow even deeper with time.

And today, that is what I look forward to. Time. Time to grow as an artist, businessman, and now author. Time to love my wife and watch our young men grow to make us proud, as I have no doubt they will. Time to watch them crystallize into the strong, sensitive, witty, and engaging men they almost are. The future is theirs. It's all so close for them. It takes my breath away.

My plane is descending into Los Angeles, bringing me back again to the city I wanted so badly to conquer as a child, arriving with my mother in our old Volvo. Los Angeles looks huge from the air, particularly in the setting sun's magic hour. I can't even comprehend how many close-ups I've shot, standing in that incredible amber light. I see the Hollywood sign now and it, too, is bathed in an almost purple hue. I've looked at that emblem of so many people's dreams so many times that I often don't even notice it. But today I do and I realize: It still means something to me. And I'm glad.

## ACKNOWLEDGMENTS

Sheryl, Matthew and Johnowen: Thanks for your love and patience; you make life worth living.

My father, Chuck: For your inspiration and love; you are my hero.

My brothers, Chad, Micah, and Justin: I'm blessed to have you in my life. Thanks for putting up with me; I love you very much.

Brian, Jodi, Lucas, Jacob, and Darlene: For making my family complete and for your unwavering love.

Tom Barrack: For your friendship, generosity, and example. Together "we go!"

Bill Paxton: Thanks for the years of friendship and confidence.

Arnold Schwarzenegger: For being who you are. Friend. Father. Leader. Here's to many stogies to come.

Maria Shriver: For your beauty, brains, and friendship and for sharing your beloved father with the country in '72. It changed my life.

Aaron Sorkin: For your friendship. For Sam Seaborn.

Mike Myers: Thanks for the laughs, support, and the idea to write a book.

Kenny and Lyndie Gorelick, Scott Sassa, Brian Novack, Herb and Bui Simon, Beth and Tag Mendillo, Mark and Heather Melchior, Kevin Falls, Dallas Taylor, Dr. Mark Morrow, and Betty Wyman: for being my treasured friends and confidants.

Bob Timmons and Doug Fieger: I'm still going strong because of your wisdom. I miss you both.

Eva and Olaf Hermes and Laurel Barrack: You were the first to hear this book, and your thoughts and support helped make it happen.

Jennifer Dynof: Without you there is literally no manuscript. I am in debt for all you do for me, lowePROFILE, and the family.

Carol Andrade and Carmen Bautista: For your loyalty and love, and for treating our family as if we were your own.

Russell Strickland: For always having my back.

Marc Gurvitz, Adam Venit, Richard Weitz, Alan Nierob, Jon Liebman, Ari Emanuel, Jonathan West, Nicole Perez-Krueger, Esther Chang, Andrew Weitz, Sean Perry, Mari Cardoos, Craig Szabo, and Larry Stein: I am blessed to have your daily attention and guidance. Thank you.

Jennifer Ruldolph Walsh: For being there through the process with such tremendous encouragement.

Gillian Blake: My great editor and new friend. Thanks for your patience and for turning me into a writer.

Steve Rubin: For having faith in me and my stories and for making this all happen.

Everyone at Henry Holt and Company: For your confidence, vision, and hard work on such a tight deadline.

Jan Miller: For your faith in me and your added value in so many ways!

Richard Abate and Jonathan Karp: For your early confidence in me as a writer.

Nancy Josephson: Thank you for helping me put the pieces together.

Graydon Carter and Oprah Winfrey: For being early and enthusiastic supporters of this book. Thank you.

To all my friends and colleagues both current and throughout the years: some of you are mentioned in the narrative and some are not, but you *all* have inspired me.

To my fans and friends around the world: Without you it all stops. Thank you so deeply for the decades of support.

To all friends of Bill W's.

To all young actors everywhere.

## ABOUT THE AUTHOR

ROB LOWE is a film, television, and theater actor, a producer, and an entrepreneur. He also is involved in politics. He lives with his wife and two sons in California.